Nietzsche's *On the Genealogy of Morality*

Edinburgh Critical Guides to Nietzsche
Series editors: Keith Ansell-Pearson and Daniel Conway

Guides you through the writings of Friedrich Nietzsche (1844–1900), one of modernity's most independent, original and seminal minds

The Edinburgh Critical Guides to Nietzsche series brings Nietzsche's writings to life for students, teachers and scholars alike, with each text benefitting from its own dedicated book. Every guide features new research and reflects the most recent developments in Nietzsche scholarship. The authors unlock each work's intricate structure, explore its specific mode of presentation and explain its seminal importance. Whether you are working in contemporary philosophy, political theory, religious studies, psychology, psychoanalysis or literary theory, these guides will help you to fully appreciate Nietzsche's enduring significance for contemporary thought.

Books in the series
Nietzsche's *The Birth of Tragedy from the Spirit of Music*, Tracy B. Strong and Babette Babich
Nietzsche's *Philosophy in the Tragic Age of the Greeks*, Sean Kirkland
Nietzsche's *Unfashionable Observations*, Jeffrey Church
Nietzsche's *Human, All Too Human*, Ruth Abbey
Nietzsche's *Dawn*, Katrina Mitcheson
Nietzsche's *Gay Science*, Robert Miner
Nietzsche's *Thus Spoke Zarathustra*, Charles Bambach
Nietzsche's *Beyond Good and Evil*, Daniel Conway
Nietzsche's *On the Genealogy of Morality*, Robert Guay
Nietzsche's *The Case of Wagner and Nietzsche Contra Wagner*, Ryan Harvey and Aaron Ridley
Nietzsche's *Twilight of the Idols*, Vanessa Lemm
Nietzsche's *The Anti-Christ*, Paul Bishop
Nietzsche's *Ecce Homo*, Matthew Meyer
Nietzsche's *Late Notebooks*, Alan Schrift

Visit our website at edinburghuniversitypress.com/series-edinburgh-critical-guides-to-nietzsche to find out more

Nietzsche's *On the Genealogy of Morality*

A Critical Introduction and Guide

Robert Guay

EDINBURGH
University Press

Edinburgh University Press is one of the leading university presses in the UK. We publish academic books and journals in our selected subject areas across the humanities and social sciences, combining cutting-edge scholarship with high editorial and production values to produce academic works of lasting importance. For more information visit our website: edinburghuniversitypress.com

© Robert Guay, 2022

Edinburgh University Press Ltd
The Tun – Holyrood Road
12(2f) Jackson's Entry
Edinburgh EH8 8PJ

Typeset in 11/13 Bembo by
IDSUK (DataConnection) Ltd

A CIP record for this book is available from the British Library

ISBN 978 1 4744 3077 7 (hardback)
ISBN 978 1 4744 3079 1 (webready PDF)
ISBN 978 1 4744 3078 4 (paperback)
ISBN 978 1 4744 3080 7 (epub)

The right of Robert Guay to be identified as the author of this work has been asserted in accordance with the Copyright, Designs and Patents Act 1988, and the Copyright and Related Rights Regulations 2003 (SI No. 2498).

Contents

Acknowledgements	vii
Chronology	viii
Abbreviations	xi
Introduction	1
1. The Preface	11
Approaching the *Genealogy*	11
Knowing ourselves	11
A memoir of the genealogist	16
The descent of our moral prejudices	19
The critique of morality: the value of values	24
The Dionysian drama of the soul	27
2. The First Treatise: 'Good and Evil', 'Good and Bad'	29
Introduction	29
The basic narrative	35
Philosophical arguments	54
Methodological and rhetorical issues	71
3. The Second Treatise: 'Guilt', 'Bad Conscience' and Related Matters	83
Introduction	83
The basic narrative	94
Philosophical arguments	113
Methodological and rhetorical issues	123

4. The Third Treatise: What Do Ascetic Ideals Mean?	137
Introduction	137
The basic narrative	146
Philosophical arguments	178
Methodological and rhetorical issues	190
5. Conclusion	199
Glossary of Key Terms	206
Guide to Further Reading on *On the Genealogy of Morality*	209
Bibliography	212
Index	220

Acknowledgements

In writing about Nietzsche, one can accumulate a surprising number of debts. Unsurprisingly, the passing of years has overwhelmed my capacity to reckon them. So here I can only undertake a small fragment of the process; I hope my creditors will extend me some time to continue working on this project that I will surely never complete. I am grateful to previous commentators on the *Genealogy*, Dan Conway, Larry Hatab and David Owen, for both their intellectual example and their personal support. Two anonymous readers, as well as Dan Conway and Keith Ansell-Pearson, gave me valuable comments. Hans Gindlesberger and Keiko Bickmore provided additional support. I owe much to Robert Pippin, and have for some time. I would get nothing done, however, without my colleagues in Nietzsche in the Northeast (NiNE), my students – of whom John Gudenzi, Jeff Hastings and Seulki Kim read early drafts of this book – and especially my family. They have variously encouraged me, distracted me, reminded me what philosophy is for, and enabled me to write. There are others I could have mentioned, too; I hope to catch up with you soon.

Chronology

1844	Friedrich Wilhelm Nietzsche is born on 15 October in Röcken, Saxony.
1849	Nietzsche's father Ludwig, a Protestant minister, dies of 'softening of the brain'.
1850	Nietzsche's younger brother, Joseph, dies, and the family moves to Naumburg.
1858–64	He attends the elite boarding school Schulpforta on a full scholarship that he received as the orphan of a minister.
1864	Enrols at the University of Bonn to study theology, although he no longer plans to become a minister. He joins a fraternity, but resigns soon after.
1865	Follows the philologist Professor Albrecht Ritschl to the University of Leipzig. He buys a copy of Schopenhauer's *World as Will and Representation* in his landlord's shop.
1865	Refuses to take Communion during his Easter visit home to Naumburg.
1866	Publishes an essay on Theognis in a philological journal edited by Ritschl.
1867	Enlists in an artillery regiment after managing to pass a physical exam.
1868	Injures himself while riding. Reads Kuno Fischer's book on Kant. Meets Richard Wagner in a café in Leipzig, through the mediation of Mrs Ritschl. After his 24th birthday becomes emancipated from his guardian.

1869	Appointed Extraordinary Professor of Classical Philology in Basel on Ritschl's recommendation. Renounces Prussian citizenship. Begins frequent visits to Wagner in nearby Tribschen.
1870	Volunteers as a medical orderly in the Franco-Prussian War, but after two months becomes ill with dysentery and diphtheria.
1872	Publishes his first, controversial book, *The Birth of Tragedy out of the Spirit of Music*. Accompanies Wagner to Bayreuth for the laying of the foundation stone for the new opera house.
1873	Meets Paul Rée in Basel.
1873–75	Publishes *Unfashionable Observations*. Relationship with Wagner begins to sour.
1876	Begins working with Peter Gast, who takes dictation for an essay on Wagner. Visits the Bayreuth Festival and sees Wagner for the last time in Sorrento.
1878	Publishes the first part of *Human, All Too Human*.
1879	Publishes the two additions to *Human, All Too Human*. Resigns from Basel with a small pension. Begins a long period of wandering, mostly through Italy and Switzerland, staying in off-season boarding houses.
1881	Publishes *Daybreak*.
1882	His friendship with Paul Rée ends. Publishes the first edition of *The Gay Science*. In April travels to Rome, meets Lou Salomé, and proposes marriage to her. She declines and the relationship ends badly.
1883–84	Publishes *Thus Spoke Zarathustra*.
1884	Breaks with his sister Elisabeth over her fiancé's anti-Semitism.
1886	Publishes *Beyond Good and Evil*. Plans new editions of previous works, for which he writes five new prefaces, among other material.
1887	Writes *On the Genealogy of Morality* in July and August. It is published in November in an edition of 600 copies. He pays for the printing himself.
1888	Publishes *The Case of Wagner*. Writes *The Anti-Christ, Ecce Homo, Nietzsche Contra Wagner* and *Twilight of the Idols*.

1889	Suffers a breakdown and collapses in Turin, after writing megalomaniacal postcards to many friends and celebrities. He is retrieved by his friend Franz Overbeck, who takes him to Basel. Nietzsche's mother then takes him to an asylum in Jena.
1890	Nietzsche is moved to his mother's apartment in Jena, and then to Naumburg. His sister Elisabeth returns to Germany from Paraguay. She later takes control of her brother's literary estate.
1894	Elisabeth founds the Nietzsche Archive, which houses Nietzsche and his papers.
1896	Elisabeth moves Nietzsche and the Archive to Weimar.
1900	Dies in Weimar on 25 August.

Abbreviations

AC	*The Anti-Christ*, Nietzsche 2005
BGE	*Beyond Good and Evil*, Nietzsche 2014
BT	*The Birth of Tragedy*, Nietzsche 1967
D	*Daybreak*, Nietzsche 1997
EH	*Ecce Homo*, Nietzsche 2005
GM	*On the Genealogy of Morality*, Nietzsche 2014
GS	*The Gay Science*, Nietzsche 2001
HAH	*Human, All Too Human*, Nietzsche 1986
TSZ	*Thus Spoke Zarathustra*, Nietzsche 1978
UM	*Untimely Meditations*, Nietzsche 1983

Introduction

This is a philosophical commentary on Friedrich Nietzsche's *On the Genealogy of Morality*. My primary aim in this text is to offer analyses of Nietzsche's arguments. This is an unusual challenge in the case of *On the Genealogy of Morality*. For most works of philosophy, it is relatively easy to identify what conclusion the arguments aim to establish; usually one can even discern what premises are intended to support that conclusion, although at times it takes some charitable reconstruction. With Nietzsche's *Genealogy*, however, it is far from obvious what conclusion he is aiming at, or even what field of philosophy he is working in, let alone what arguments support his conclusion. Yet in this commentary I try to show that close attention to the details of the arguments can suffice to clarify Nietzsche's conclusions. Nietzsche, I want to show, makes a series of historical arguments, not as didactic support for some separate philosophical theories, but as themselves constituting his response to philosophical concerns.

Nietzsche did not intend *On the Genealogy of Morality* to be his masterpiece or the definitive statement of his views.[1] It has nevertheless become a common point of entry into his thought, as it offers relatively straightforward, sustained explanatory narratives; his other works can, by contrast, seem fragmentary and disjointed, or forbidding in other ways. The narratives present different strands of the historical emergence of morality by looking

---

[1] Nietzsche saw the *Genealogy* as a popularisation of his ideas. He was interested in generating some book sales, in anticipation of writing a masterpiece, through a short, polemical supplement to his previous book, *Beyond Good and Evil*. See Schaberg 1995: 150–1.

at some of its main conceptual elements and characteristic psychological features. 'The genealogy of morality' is thus most famously a pair of genealogies: that of the good/evil dichotomy in the First Treatise, and that of bad conscience and the moralised sense of 'guilt' in the Second Treatise. The narratives of the first two Treatises overlap at various points and then ultimately converge in the Third Treatise's discussion of the 'meaning' of the 'ascetic ideal'. Overall, the *Genealogy* starts from the awareness that morality has not always existed in its present form – in terms of either its basic ideas or the characteristics of moral agents – and tells conjectural stories of how it all came about.

The narrative form arguably makes Nietzsche's claims more accessible. But, however we judge Nietzsche's success as a storyteller, it renders the philosophical difficulties more acute: how are we supposed to understand the stories and what is Nietzsche trying to accomplish through them? Nietzsche aggravates the difficulties here. The presentation of the narratives is subverted even before it begins: Nietzsche classifies the book not as a study or an inquiry but as a 'polemic'. Voices interrupt the narrative to insist that much is left unsaid; the narratives are framed by, of all things, reflections on the scientific conscience; and Nietzsche declares the entire enterprise to be a contribution to the '*critique* of moral values'. This last point is the most important one. The stories are not merely intended to relate how morality came to be, but somehow to furnish a critique of it. Are the stories intended to persuade us to lose our allegiance to morality, reorder our conceptual framework and our psychological dispositions, convince us that our own moral beliefs are epistemically unfounded, establish the truth of some new set of values, or serve the ends of critique in some other way?

What I try to show in this commentary is that the historical narratives *are* the critiques, and not just illustrations of or support for extra-narrative claims. The narratives contribute elements to an account of the meaning of morality.[2] In them Nietzsche treats

---

[2] On the idea of the *Genealogy* offering a 'contribution', and the complexities involved in what that amounts to, see Ansell-Pearson 1991: 112–14. See also the discussion of Nietzsche's description of the *Genealogy* as 'decisive preliminary studies' in Owen 2007: 68.

morality as a wide-ranging set of practices, organised around ideals, that both reflect and shape our psychological functioning. Understanding the meaning of morality, then, is a matter of identifying what roles the practices of morality play in our lives, what ends they serve, and what they reveal about us. The narratives, insofar as they succeed in reconstructing what morality means for us, thus allow Nietzsche to make a number of critical claims. First, moral ideals have become *pervasive*. Morality functions as a 'prejudice' that affects all of our views about how the world (including human beings) works, even where it is ill-suited to do so. Second, morality, according to Nietzsche, has become *empty*. Our practices have become so accreted with conflicting historical meanings that our participation in them does not mean anything in particular any more; this has, furthermore, left our practices susceptible to being subverted for detrimental ends. Third, morality has become *pointless*. Nietzsche considers the practices of morality, as all practices, to be purposive in character, but argues that they no longer fulfil their purposes and have become unsustainable. Fourth, morality has become *destructive*: its pursuit damages us in various ways. There are other critical claims, too, that turn on contentions in the narratives about what morality means for us. These narrative claims are meant to inform reassessments of our practices, without appeal to further philosophical theories.

In this way, *On the Genealogy of Morality* is not primarily about morality or its emergence. It is a series of stories about who we are and what we want. These stories are filtered through elements of morality because of the central, authoritative role of morality in our lives. This role does not operate merely in terms of moral belief or conformity; morality, in the *Genealogy*, does not take the form of specific values or imperatives, and Nietzsche leaves its effectiveness in social control undiscussed. Morality, rather, has affected our capacity for self-understanding through the language we use and the psychological cultivation (or 'breeding') that it engenders. Human beings have used the shifting terms of morality to construct an understanding of who we are, and this has influenced our labour on ourselves. Through a moral self-understanding, we have transformed ourselves from creatures that relied on unconscious instinct to creatures that reliably hold ourselves accountable, that have concerns more powerful than self-preservation, and that need meanings and purposes in order to carry out our lives. According to Nietzsche, the categories of morality are defective, however. Our moral self-understanding leads us to misdescribe ourselves and our activities, misshape our practices of accountability, and inflict psychological damage on ourselves through internalised self-hostility.

Nietzsche's starting point in the *Genealogy* is that, as familiar as the language of morality is to us, we have no idea what we are doing when we pursue moral values. Indeed, although this ignorance is especially profound in the case of moral values, our activities are generally mysterious to us because we fail to understand ourselves as historical beings. We participate in ongoing practices that did not originate with us and that remain perpetually incomplete; and our activities involve taking up meanings and purposes that were already there but are subject to transformation by our participation in them. These activities are difficult to understand, not because we lack access to facts about them that are available from a suitably detached standpoint, but because understanding them requires reconstructing an unstable participant standpoint. It requires knowledge of the past, but also the possibility of carrying the activities forward into the future. In Nietzsche's account, we make sense of who we are by making sense of activities, and we do that by considering ourselves as participants in practices that we are always reconceiving and restructuring. The particular claim of the *Genealogy* is that there is no way to carry forward our moral self-understanding, and so we need a standpoint from which we can better make sense of ourselves and our direction for the future.

My main focus in this commentary is to present Nietzsche's narratives and the claims that they contain about morality and its implications for human self-understanding. This focus does lead me to neglect other interpretations of the text. There are many, many interpretations of Nietzsche's work, and it would certainly be a worthwhile project to write a commentary that dedicated itself to presenting conflicts of interpretations about this text. I have provided references to a few influential readings and rich veins of discussion. But I have avoided assessing many interpretations here because I believe that attention to the many theoretical claims that the *Genealogy* is taken to support would have distracted from understanding its main lines of thought. I have also tried to avoid citing Nietzsche's other works, except where I thought it was necessary to provide context for ideas in the *Genealogy*. It is tempting to construct a composite 'Nietzsche', with a unified and systematic position on a range of issues, and attribute views to him that are only partially reflected in any particular text; Nietzsche sometimes suggests such a project himself. That would indeed be a worthwhile project, but it is not the one that I am engaged in here. I have also avoided a focus on Nietzsche's quasi-technical terms, such as 'will to power' and 'revaluation of values'; I think that these terms are largely incidental to the case that he presents here. My focus is on the case that Nietzsche presents in the *Genealogy*.

After this Introduction, I dedicate a chapter each to Nietzsche's Preface and to the three Treatises that make up the *Genealogy*. The chapters about the Treatises are divided into four sections. The first section offers a brief summary of the Treatise and an overview of its philosophical agenda through an in-depth analysis of the opening aphorisms, the second explicates the main narrative, the third discusses some of the general philosophical issues raised in the Treatise, and the fourth discusses methodological and rhetorical issues. My conclusion summarises some of what I take to be the implications of Nietzsche's narrative arguments.

Nietzsche's philosophical conclusions often take an unusual form. In a work nominally about morality, one might expect a definition of morality, some arguments that articulate and criticise existing moral theories, and some further arguments that aim to establish a novel normative position. None of this appears in the text, however. Morality is depicted as a complicated set of historically contingent practices for which no coherent definition can be given. Nietzsche, for the most part, avoids directly addressing the arguments for specific positions, and he does not propose any alternative normative theory. Instead, he often takes philosophical theorising as an occasion for psychological reflection. That is, Nietzsche does not devote attention to specific thinkers and their arguments, but to types of philosophical approach or commitment; he does not engage with philosophical debates on their own terms so much as comment on what those debates reveal about the participants. He is interested less in the arguments than in what sort of person would make a certain argument, and what their motivations in doing so could be. From the beginning of the First Treatise, Nietzsche calls attention to philosophical positions not in order to address them directly, but rather to provoke reflection on what would be a suitable form of inquiry for us to adopt, and what psychic ends would be served in doing so.

So when I explicate the narratives, I try to avoid presenting them simply as vehicles for advancing traditional philosophical theories. Nietzsche does not specify positions in metaethics, value theory, or epistemology in *On the Genealogy of Morality*. In this commentary, I generally devote little space to what Nietzsche does not discuss, but there are two topics that are worth making an exception for here. There are two enterprises in particular that Nietzsche is not engaged in: a causal theory of moral belief and a prescriptive ethics.

Attributing a causal theory to Nietzsche seems like a reasonable way to assimilate his narrative to a familiar form of philosophical discourse. Nietzsche's narrative recounts changes, after all – from a pre-moral condition to a moral one, or from one set of values being dominant to another one being dominant, for example – and a causal account would be a way of explaining these changes. Such an account would explain the outcome by specifying a causal law or mechanism that, given suitable background conditions, would be sufficient to produce the change. If the relevant law or mechanism is a psychological one, the relevant outcome would be characterised as an individual's belief, disposition or behaviour of some kind. Philosophical accounts are typically speculative: they appeal less to empirical facts about individuals than to plausible inferences about what would most likely produce the relevant result, and thus they try to present their claims in very general terms. But as with any causal account, the aim is to identify the law or organisational structure that produces change by showing how such a law or mechanism can explain particular cases. And these accounts are arguably all the stronger for having a more general form and less restrictive specifications of necessary background conditions; in that way, perhaps, one can identify the structures at the root of human nature. These accounts, furthermore, can be accorded epistemological or metaphysical significance. One can argue that showing how beliefs are in fact formed shows something about the status of those beliefs and their objects. Nietzsche is not, however, offering a causal account of any kind. Nietzsche's accounts, rather, aim to reconstruct the conditions of meaningfulness for the emergence of morality. His approach, that is, is not to ask why morality happened and explain it by appeal to causal law or mechanism, but to grant that morality emerged, and then identify the semantic conditions for such a change to occur and what further new semantic possibilities are made available by such a change. Nietzsche's interest is in understanding how the conceptual world of morality could have arisen at all, where this is a question of the conditions in which moral judgements could have been meaningful, rather than what brought about changes in individuals' beliefs. In Nietzsche's stories, moral ideas take their sense in the context of whole lives, with characteristic forms of social and economic organisation, ethnic affiliations, background beliefs about human agency and so on. Having a moral vocabulary in place itself makes new shifts in sense possible, but so do changes in social arrangements and personal dissatisfactions; there is no single source of change, and change comes primarily in the form of novel possibilities for expression rather than in alterations of belief. The stories of the emergence of morality are ones about what is possible to say and think in human communities, not about how individuals are affected by causal processes.

For a mundane illustration of the kind of account that I am attributing to Nietzsche, consider the concept of a 'disc jockey'. We could ask what caused someone to form a belief about disc jockeys, and identify the relevant causal mechanisms and background conditions that would suffice to produce such beliefs. But a more genealogical inquiry would reconstruct the conditions under which the concept of 'disc jockey' made sense. Some of the conditions would be technological, some would be about the presence of a commercial mass culture, and some would pertain to circumstances under which 'jockey' was a role suitable for metaphorical extension. This account would serve to reconstruct what 'disc jockey' meant by identifying its conditions of meaningfulness.

Although it does in some sense explain how the role came about, there is no causal explanation; at most one could insist on some generality such as 'in those conditions, *something* had to fill that role' without picking out any specific vector of causal influence. Furthermore, with the account of emergence in place, one could move in the other direction, and fill in one's understanding of the sort of society that could support the role of a disc jockey. One could also look to the future, to see how the notion and name of a disc jockey, once established, could be appropriated and transformed into DJ, turntabilist, VJ, shock jock and so on. Nietzsche's genealogies, I am claiming, are like such an attempt to reconstruct the possibilities of sense by examining the historical transformation of practices. But Nietzsche is claiming that in the case of morality, the possibilities offered by conceptual innovation concern the whole range of what it means to be human.

One might also be tempted to attribute a prescriptive ethics of some kind to Nietzsche, although specific prescriptions or any clear basis for such an ethics is impossible to find. To some extent this temptation derives from the expectation that a critique of morality must conclude in a substantive alternative, with a suitably general and systematic account of what one ought to do, or what values one ought to recognise, to satisfy the demands of ethics; one should seek out Nietzsche's prescriptions, then, even if they are not readily found. Nietzsche does also praise certain cultural exemplars, especially from the archaic world, and decry the slavish or herd-like tendencies of others. All this could be taken to reveal Nietzsche's favoured ethical position or the grounds for his prescriptions, and then Nietzsche could be seen as endorsing primitive brutality, the production of superior individuals, or anti-morality for its own sake. Nietzsche's praise and denunciations are indeed important to note, but they are often like praising ancient Rome for its legal system, the Incas for their temples, or Kareem Abdul-Jabbar for being a good basketball player. They are acknowledgements of value or disvalue, that is, but they fall far short of claims of universal value that demand our emulation and present us with compelling imperatives. Those next steps are indeed what Nietzsche wishes to move away from. There are potential sources of value that offer no reasons *for us* to take them as important.

Nietzsche locates values in historically remote cultures to give us examples of how *others* managed to find reasons and sometimes entire ways of life compelling, not to instruct us on what we are obliged to do. We need our own reasons, the ones that appeal to us. To think that we need to adopt what others found compelling would preserve the old form of morality, with its compulsory, exogenous claims on us, but with topsy-turvy content.

There are two reasons internal to the narratives for why we should not take Nietzsche's enterprise as that of delivering a prescriptive ethics. First, his assessments are invariably ambiguous. The proud, happy warriors of the ancient world are shallow, foolish and dull; the priests who seethe with resentment and lust after power are also responsible for human spiritual depth and creativity. In Nietzsche's worlds, there are no unequivocal values; everything good is embedded in a context filled with shortcomings, pain and missed opportunities. The other reason that we should not take Nietzsche to be delivering a prescriptive ethics is that he insists that no such project is possible for us now. The narrative moves through culturally remote ways of life that are unavailable to us, and then arrives at a historical crisis in which nothing seems especially worthwhile or compelling. We lack even the ability to imagine what new values, beyond the failed legacy of morality, would be; different social relations and different forms of psychological responsiveness would be needed to begin reimagining new values. The problem that Nietzsche depicts is not that we lack the enthusiasm to affirm some values that are available to us. Attempts at value inversion and legislation have been tried and have turned out to be empty and repetitive. The problem that he depicts is that there are no available options that we could endorse and sustain in a life that we lead.

The critique that Nietzsche makes in the *Genealogy* is not that conceptualising things in terms of 'morality' is sound but that we should choose the opposite of morality. His point, rather, is that morality – as a way of thinking about practical requirements and of holding ourselves accountable for them – has failed. He is not concerned with replacing morality with a new set of imperatives, or even with arguing that the claims of morality do not correspond to anything real; he is claiming that we have to reject that way of organising the sense of our activities and ourselves. The story of morality, according to Nietzsche, is one of tying an imagination of who we are to our ideals and an imagination of ideals to what is compulsory; of identifying what is most important with what is within individuals' power of will; of interpreting our whole lives in terms of blame and punishment; of thinking of practical deliberation in terms of definitive but inaccessible answers; and so on. This is all defective as a way of understanding who we are and what we ought to do, and the remedy for it is not to make adjustments to our normative criteria, but to imagine some other way of thinking about ourselves. Morality has produced failures in self-knowledge that can only be remedied by an as-yet-uninvented standpoint from which practical self-direction becomes possible.

In what follows, I refer to the main divisions of *On the Genealogy of Morality* as 'Treatises' and the smaller sections as 'aphorisms'. Citations are given parenthetically, with the Treatises indicated using Roman numerals, or the abbreviation 'P' for Preface, and the aphorisms indicated using Arabic numerals: so, for example, '(II: 12)' indicates aphorism 12 in the Second Treatise. The translation I have used is the one by Adrian Del Caro (Friedrich Nietzsche, *Beyond Good and Evil/On the Genealogy of Morality* [Stanford: Stanford University Press, 2014]). In very rare cases I have made alterations to the translation; these occasions are identified and explained in the notes. Nietzsche made frequent use of emphasis and ellipsis, and when they appear in quotations they are original unless otherwise noted. Ellipses that I have added are indicated with square brackets.

1
The Preface

Approaching the *Genealogy*

In subsequent chapters, I will offer separate discussions of the explanatory narratives, the philosophical strategies and the methodological and rhetorical features of each of Nietzsche's three 'Treatises'. In the Preface, however, these elements are so thoroughly entangled that it would be challenging to divide up the discussions in this way. Nietzsche prepares us for reading the *Genealogy* with a mixture of personal confessions, philosophical hopes and modest, indirect attempts at persuasion. So, although I will try to analyse Nietzsche's presentation of his philosophical commitments separately from his autobiographical stories, these will inevitably be blended.

This chapter will proceed with a long examination of the Preface's magisterial first aphorism, which, with its attention to self-knowledge, stunningly manages to encompass nearly the entire argument of the book without discussing genealogy or morality at all. Then I will review Nietzsche's preliminary reflections on morality, the proper way to conduct inquiries about it, and the context and purpose of doing so. Nietzsche presents these reflections as a corrective to an ongoing failure to take up deep questions about morality. Addressing this failure, and assessing moral values, will furthermore require coming to terms with our shared status as knowers and our existential needs.

Knowing ourselves

Nietzsche begins the Preface invitingly and at the same time ironically: 'We are unknown to ourselves, we knowing ones: and this for a good reason. We have never sought ourselves' (P: 1). This is inviting in that Nietzsche is using the first-person plural to invent a group in which we are all offered membership: the readership and the object of inquiry share a common identity with the speaker. Nietzsche, then, is calling here for us to inquire from a perspective that is itself part of the investigation. This beginning is at the same time ironic, however, in that our shared identity is based on a thoroughgoing, internal failure. We have failed to accomplish something central to who we are, as if we were athletes who did not compete or prophets whom no one could hear. This failure, furthermore, is not just a contingent fact, that we happen not to have come across something important for discovery. Nietzsche is suggesting, rather, that we are experiencing a failure that we have not even managed to acknowledge to ourselves, even though it concerns an area where we should be successful. Our forms of inquiry have been somehow so misguided that we have not managed to think about ourselves at all. And this is what the Preface, and the whole book, is about: a deep, unacknowledged failure in self-knowledge, and how to address it.

Nietzsche, of course, continues the aphorism with a suggestion about whom he takes us to be, the nature of the self-knowledge we lack, and the kind of failure we have produced. He first expands on his idea of who we are as 'knowing ones' by, perhaps surprisingly, quoting the Bible: 'Someone rightly said: "wherever your treasure is, there your heart is also"; *our* treasure is where the beehives of our knowledge are' (P: 1). Nietzsche is referring to the Sermon on the Mount, in which Jesus enjoins against laying up one's 'treasures' on earth, where they are susceptible to physical decay and loss. Jesus' injunction is to devote one's care to spiritual rather than material things, and he declares that there is a transformative effect in turning one's 'heart' in this way. Nietzsche is thus claiming about us that our interest in knowing is not merely instrumental – to build a better mousetrap, as it were – and not even for its own sake, but something more like a matter of heart. 'As winged animals and honey-gatherers of the spirit' (P: 1), knowledge is important for us in a way that nothing material could be.

Nietzsche is using the Gospel according to Matthew to claim that who we are is a function of our passionate commitments, and for us, as inheritors of a cultural legacy, what moves us is a 'fundamental will of knowledge commanding from the depth' (P: 2). Modern culture, for Nietzsche, is characterised by a pervasive interest in truth: in the transparency we demand in our intimate and public relationships, in our scepticism towards myth and manipulation, and in the expectations we place on spheres such as art and religion. (Even if our post-truth commercial and political culture has gone astray, this is upsetting for us precisely because we can see how it is a deviation from our expected norm.) Above all, our passionate interest in truth is manifest in the enterprise of modern science. We have rigorous forms of inquiry to examine the natural world, liberate ourselves from superstition, and gain new abilities of prediction and explanation; these have transformed our way of life so much that our own knowingness has displaced other features of our shared identity. Even when technology allows us to be absorbed in other things, what we, as a cultural imperative, devote our industrious, bee-like activity to is the production of knowledge. But despite all our knowledge, according to Nietzsche, we remain ignorant of ourselves.

So how could we be defined by knowing and yet unknown to ourselves? Nietzsche offers a simple first explanation: we have never sought ourselves. But there are many disciplines devoted to understanding who or what we are: biology, psychology, anthropology and history, for example. Inquiry into human beings has not been lacking, but all this must, for Nietzsche, fail to count as contributions to knowledge about *ourselves*. Nietzsche could be saying that our inquiries have always been biased: they have been compromised by moralistic, theological or anthropocentric prejudices of some kind. Nietzsche could accordingly be calling for more rigorously scientific forms of inquiry. Another possibility is that Nietzsche is claiming that what we have never sought is knowledge of features of ourselves that are unavailable to conscious experience. We might have instincts and desires, for example, that comprise much of what we are, that we have never reckoned with. Our familiar forms of inquiry might be inadequate for uncovering the parts of ourselves hidden in the psyche, to which we lack transparent access.

These explanations – that our inquiries have been misformed and that we need to look for something to which we lack privileged, conscious access – tell part of Nietzsche's story. But Nietzsche offers his main explanation in the first aphorism in terms of an experience of *time*:[1]

> Whatever else life involves, the so-called 'experiences' – who of us even has enough seriousness for them? Or enough time? In such matters, I fear, we were never really 'focused on the matter': we just do not have our hearts there – and not even our ears! On the contrary, like someone divinely distracted and immersed in himself, who has just had his ears rung by the full force of the bell's twelve strokes of noon, suddenly wakes up and asks himself, 'what was that tolling anyway?' so we, too, sometimes rub our ears *afterward* and ask, quite amazed, quite disconcerted, 'what did we really experience here?' and moreover: 'who *are* we really?' and then we count, afterward as stated, all the trembling twelve bell strokes of our experience, of our life, our *being* – oh! And then we lose count . . . (P: 1)

Here the passing of time stands in for the experiences of one's life, and thus knowing what time it is stands in for self-knowledge; Nietzsche indicates that it is impossible to succeed. If one tries to account for the time by waiting until after the bells have finished striking, then there is nothing to do but rummage through memory, not entirely confident if one is recalling or reconstructing, wishing to verify at just the moment when this is impossible. So one might think that the epistemic ideal would have been to wait in advance for the bells to ring and then count them one by one, that the problem was a lack of attentiveness. But that would not work either. The events still pass: one can pay attention as they transpire, but our experience does not come in discrete units and the past will always be gone, leaving behind no complete assurance about what happened. But more importantly, the problem with

---

[1] For a discussion of Nietzsche's views of the modern experience of time, see Pippin 1991: ch. 4; see also the discussion of the 'problem of time' in Ansell-Pearson 1991: 4.

self-knowledge here is that what one wants is the after-the-fact perspective: self-knowledge is not the tabulations of a focused and attentive bell-counter, but a personal understanding of historical events and historical experiences from the perspective of one who has lived through them. We need both the immediacy and fullness of experience, and also the necessarily retrospective understanding of how and why momentous events are significant.[2] So there is no perspective from which self-knowledge is possible: 'We simply remain strangers to ourselves by necessity, we do not understand ourselves, we *have to* mistake ourselves, for us the proposition "each is furthest from himself" applies for all eternity – for ourselves we are not "knowing ones"' (P: 1).

We are not merely ignorant or neglectful of ourselves; we necessarily mistake ourselves because of a failure to grasp ourselves as historical beings. However 'knowing' we may be, the forms of knowledge we have developed fail to treat us as participants in a way of life rather than as things that have been completed and whose traces can somehow be retrieved. We need to understand ourselves from the standpoint of participants with ongoing desires, in an ongoing cultural process. Self-knowledge has a temporal form because understanding ourselves is not a matter of having an adequate theoretical grasp on a stable thing, but of having a suitable orientation towards ourselves as beings in time. This is how the first aphorism articulates the argument of the whole book. Nietzsche's genealogies will primarily be what he elsewhere calls 'no-saying': they are meant to disabuse us of some faulty ways of thinking. But the genealogy of morality, even if it can never be fully completed, supplies a view of ourselves that has been lacking, of ourselves as historical creatures, who are what we are because we have adopted ideals that obscure their own historical nature and thereby our own relationship to them and to our possible flourishing. Self-knowledge needs to be reconceived as a practical, hermeneutical activity, of making sense of ourselves, and genealogy should prepare us, at least, to find forms of commitment that help us express who we are and how to lead our lives.

---

[2] On the need for a retrospective understanding, see Arthur C. Danto's discussion of 'narrative sentences' (Danto 1985: 143–81).

A memoir of the genealogist

Nietzsche also uses the Preface to tell a story about himself, and how he arrived at the point of view of the author of the *Genealogy*. These are common enough tasks for a Preface: the author relating something about himself, and in the process of doing so telling the story of the work's development. Indeed, Nietzsche manages to tell mundane stories of childhood confusions, friendly rivalries and the long, arduous build-up to the successful writing of the book. The stories are so potted, however, that it makes them a little strange. Rather than conveying intimacy or stark realism, they fit comfortably into standard, coming-of-age narrative tropes: a loss of faith, sudden realisations and inspirations that get left behind. Although they contain some personal elements, Nietzsche relates them at a level of detail that makes them almost clichéd and universal, as if he wants his audience to identify with them rather than be informed by them. The autobiographical parts of the Preface thus function less to convey information than to anticipate and exhibit some philosophical points. There is little or no argumentation here, but instead an application of genealogy to his own case, in order to show the contingency of his own standpoint and its rootedness in a particular psychological constitution.

Nietzsche frequently interrupts his own story, but it begins with him as a child old enough to possess a solemn, contemplative regard for moral concerns. When he was thirteen years old, however, his moral concerns led him to the problem of evil: he wondered how to reconcile the existence of evil with an omnipotent, benevolent God, or as he put it, '*what* is the real *origin* of our good and evil' (P: 3). Nietzsche decided then that God is the '*father* of evil' (P: 3), and even if that solution did not last long for him, it nevertheless marked an important turning point. Childhood wonder gradually but irresistibly turned into sustained inquiry, moral reflection into interrogating morality, and practical concerns about leading a life into a philosophical career. In this movement, furthermore, Nietzsche not only acquired the intellectual skills to investigate his question, but his understanding of the question itself changed. Instead of a theological question about God's creation, it became a series of 'entirely new' (P: 7) historical and psychological questions about 'our' good and evil: that is, what we mean by the terms and what our experience of them is. The next milestone that Nietzsche mentions is that he started publishing about the origin of morality after reading a book by a friend of his from his student days, Paul Rée. By this point, Nietzsche had been a professor of classical philology for nearly a decade, and was in fact approaching retirement due to his declining health. Nietzsche spent the next decade wandering around Europe, and he insisted that genealogy was the product of these wanderings. Although he did not label the work 'genealogy' at the time, the work of that period represents Nietzsche's efforts to develop psychological accounts of morality. The other great influence that Nietzsche mentions is Arthur Schopenhauer. As with Rée, the influence pushed him in a contrary direction from its source, but it raised the question of the '*value* of morality' (P: 5) for Nietzsche. On the Genealogy of Morality, then, is the culmination of these influences.[3] Nietzsche even insisted that his works must be read together to be well understood, and suggested that the present work is distinguished primarily by its attention to the '*grey*' of historical record rather than sky-blue speculation.

Nietzsche merged the personal with the philosophical most emphatically after discussing some of his early thoughts about morality. He wrote,

> But *that* I still hold on to them today, that in the meantime they themselves have held ever more firmly to each other, indeed have grown into and through each other, strengthens in me the joyful assurance that from the start they might have originated in me not in isolation, not arbitrarily and sporadically, but from a common root, from a *fundamental will* of knowledge commanding from the depths, speaking ever more precisely, demanding ever more precision. For this alone is how it should be with a philosopher. We have no right to be *isolated* about anything: we may neither

---

[3] Nietzsche, on the title page of some editions of *On the Genealogy of Morality*, refers to the work as a 'clarification and supplement' of his previous book, *Beyond Good and Evil*.

make isolated errors or hit the truth in isolated instances. On the contrary, our values, our Yeses and Nos and Ifs and Whethers grow out of our thoughts with the necessity of a tree bearing its fruit – all related and connected to each other and testifying to one will, one health, one soil, one sun. (P: 2)

Nietzsche is offering an academic message about how to read his work: think of everything, from the early book *Human, All Too Human* on, as pieces of a larger project. Nietzsche framed this advice as part of a deeper point, however. Ideas are not arbitrarily entertained, one by one, independent from the person thinking them, and they may not even be meaningful enough individually to be candidates for truth or falsity. There are close connections, rather, from one idea to another, and to the person who holds them. These connections are furthermore organic in character: they possess a unity that gives the ideas a direction of growth, and they stem from a 'common root' that feeds both basic values and abstruse thoughts. Nietzsche seems to be using his story to offer a version of what has been called 'practical holism', 'the view that while understanding "involves explicit beliefs and hypotheses, these can only be meaningful in specific contexts against a background of shared practices"' (Stern 2003: 187, quoting Dreyfus: 1980: 7). Ideas make sense only within a broader context in which they play a role in how activities are carried out. For Nietzsche, furthermore, the philosopher has a special burden to become aware of this context and bring coherence to himself, his thoughts and his life.

Where the Preface is about himself, then, Nietzsche is making initial presentations of philosophical positions that will re-emerge later in the work. Above all, Nietzsche characterised philosophy as a deeply personal enterprise.[4] Making arguments or offering theories reveals something about a philosopher's affects and interests; even where the philosophy seems abstract and formal, it shows what sort of a person they are and what they care about. Nietzsche

---

[4] Nietzsche develops this idea at greatest length in BGE §6.

is telling us in particular that genealogy is not just impersonal theorising that he happens to be offering. He is, rather, a late participant in the processes that he is accounting for: the story turns back on itself, to account for its own standpoint. This account will aim to show, then, that the origin of morality is only available as a domain of inquiry in a particular cultural moment, where such concerns fit within a broader interest in historical explanation and have come to seem pressing. And the genealogist's cognitive grasp on the topic depends not merely on the accumulation of data, but on a 'vista opening up' (P: 7) through affective engagement – having something at stake in one's feelings and motivations.

The descent of our moral prejudices

At the beginning of the second aphorism, Nietzsche identifies 'the subject of my polemic' as 'the *descent* of our moral prejudices' (P: 2). This is a dense claim that raises four important points for the rest of the book. First, Nietzsche refers to the book (as he does on the title page) as a 'polemic': it is an intensely motivated, aggressive piece of writing that takes sides and has a target. One typically finds a polemic amid a religious or political controversy, rather than in scholarly investigations. Nietzsche does not specify immediately what the sides in his polemic are, but he is indicating what kind of writing he is engaged in. It is not neutral, objective inquiry; however well it marshals facts and makes arguments, it is meant to carry out an attack of some kind. A second point to note here is that Nietzsche refers to the 'descent' (*Herkunft*) of our moral prejudices. There are many similar words, such as 'origin' and 'emergence', that Nietzsche sometimes uses interchangeably with 'descent'. But 'descent' seems to indicate a long, equivocal process of development, as opposed to a single point of origin or a sudden innovation. Third, Nietzsche refers to the subject matter as the descent of *our* moral prejudices. The scope of this 'our' is not clear, but Nietzsche is suggesting that the influence of morality is not limited to the moralisers who proclaim explicitly moral values. Morality's influence is widely shared; it extends even to Nietzsche himself, and perhaps everyone else, too. Fourth, Nietzsche specifically addresses our moral *prejudices*. This suggests that morality functions as something prior to judgement for us. That is, our moral prejudices confer on us, before any conscious reflection, complicated, theoretically inflected commitments that shape how we think and feel about other things. Nietzsche is implying, furthermore, that morality itself functions as a prejudice. Morality can come to seem inevitable for us, as representing the whole range of non-instrumental practical values. But Nietzsche will want to claim that it is a very particular, historically specific kind of valuing that contributes to distorting all of our views.

What are these prejudices? As with some other kinds of prejudice, they do not take the form of well-formed beliefs or explicit rules for action, and this makes it difficult to specify exactly what 'morality' is. Nietzsche nevertheless provides three broad suggestions in the Preface as to what is distinctive about morality. The first is that morality is distinguished by its emphasis on the dichotomy between 'good' and 'evil'. Discussing how this took place is the topic of the First Treatise, but Nietzsche is claiming that the idea of 'evil' represents a conceptual innovation around which manifold other concerns can be given sense, or at least appear to be given sense. Morality involves incorporating this innovation in some form, whether or not the word 'evil' is in active use. Second, morality places special importance on 'the value of the "unegoistic"' (P: 5). Whether considering what perspective to take on the world, or deciding what actions to undertake, morality promotes the idea that one should be, in some way, 'selfless' by abstracting away all the contingent features of oneself, or even by valuing self-denial and sacrifice for their own sakes. Third, in morality 'the problem of the value of compassion' (P: 6) arises in a special way. The word 'compassion', like the German word that it renders, *Mitleid*, stems from roots that mean 'suffering-with'. Nietzsche notes that compassion has not been highly regarded in much of the history of philosophy (P: 5), but nevertheless insists that morality prioritises the suffering of others, and in particular calls upon us to share that experience of suffering. These features of morality help Nietzsche fix his topic. At the same time, however, he is not promising a theory of the nature of morality, let alone of its content. His approach involves taking issue with how we understand the domain of morality at all: it is important not to presume that 'morality' forms a unity or has a determinate meaning.

In discussing morality in this way, Nietzsche aggregates a number of themes from his earlier writings. In the Preface he even suggests that he has been engaged in one long, continuous project of uncovering the prejudices of morality. This retrospective claim of unity is not entirely sincere: it is one part wisdom in hindsight and one part sales pitch for his previous books, which had their own topics and approaches. In *Human, All Too Human*, Nietzsche offered explanations of human psychological capacities that diminished any special role for the unegoistic. *Daybreak* identified morality as comprising a series of prejudices, in particular about the nature of the self and agency. *The Gay Science* extends Nietzsche's account of the influence of morality to considerations about knowledge. *Beyond Good and Evil* is the closest work to the *Genealogy*: it presents a historical account of the emergence of a range of ideas and links them together, among other means, by reference to the good/evil dichotomy. The value commitments of morality are implicated in a broader set of cultural phenomena that need to be reinterpreted and revised. But the *Genealogy* does not present these ideas as theoretical results that Nietzsche has accumulated over time; the past works function more like a learning experience that has enabled him to arrive at his view of morality. The details of old positions are less important than this question: 'What, seen in the perspective of *life*, is the significance of morality?' (BT Attempt at a Self-Criticism §4). This question, from the second edition of *The Birth of Tragedy*, is very poor at relating the content of the book, but it does convey the outlook that Nietzsche brings to the *Genealogy*. Morality is deeply implicated in all our practices and our views of ourselves; it is too familiar to take proper notice of, and yet it needs to be investigated from a more general standpoint.

Nietzsche is claiming, on one hand, that there are prejudices that run so deeply in us that they can hardly be brought to articulation, and on the other hand, that notions such as evil, selflessness and compassion contribute to forming a comprehensive whole outside of which it has become nearly impossible to think. This presents Nietzsche with a challenge in finding the right way of thinking about those prejudices. *Genealogy* is his way of doing so.

Unfortunately, he does not say much about what genealogy is, apart from contrasting his approach with 'an inverse and perverse kind of genealogical hypothesis, its genuinely *English* kind' (P: 4). Nietzsche elaborates on the English genealogists again in the First Treatise, but their kind of genealogy seems to be one that offers a speculative account of basic features of human nature, such as representational capacities and principles of association, and explains how human beings under typical circumstances would then arrive at something like current moral beliefs. Among the many complaints that Nietzsche makes against them, two are that they take their own moral beliefs for granted, and that their explanations seek to show that it is advantageous for moral beliefs to be adopted and held. Nietzsche later delves into the mechanics of their approach, but the approach as a whole is what he finds fault with. They set their task as showing how an 'altruistic manner of evaluation' (P: 4) could be widely adopted when it is collectively but not individually beneficial; it looks for proximate pathways to particular beliefs. This is the inverse of Nietzsche's approach in that he looks to understand how the whole conceptual world of morality could have emerged at all, rather than how individuals would adopt morality in a context in which moral belief already made sense; for Nietzsche, the 'English' approach is perverse in thinking that usefulness or altruism could play any explanatory role in such a process.

Genealogy, for Nietzsche, takes on the task of how moral valuing is possible at all; it is such a strange and complex phenomenon that its historical conditions of possibility need to be identified. That is, prior to the task of explaining particular, morally characterised events, there needs to be a background understanding of how humanity made the category of the moral available at all. Nietzsche conveys this understanding not in terms of a single comprehensive account that arrives a particular conception of morality, but in terms of a series of discrete narratives that collectively fill out a context of conditions and ends. Genealogical investigation, Nietzsche writes, asks,

> under which conditions did humanity invent the value-judgments good and evil? *and what value do they have themselves?* Have they so far promoted or hindered the thriving

of human beings? Are they a sign of distress, impoverishment, degeneration of life? Or conversely, do they reveal the fullness, strength, and will to life, its courage, its confidence, its future? (P: 3)

Two main topics, one backward-looking and one more forward-looking, encompass an account of the descent of our moral prejudices. One topic is the invention of moral 'value-judgements'. The task is to identify the 'conditions' of this invention, rather than explain particular instances of judging. Identifying these conditions presumably contributes to addressing the second topic, identifying the harms and benefits that this invention has brought about for humanity as a whole, and what our future prospects are for living with these value judgements.

Nietzsche's genealogical treatment of the descent of our moral prejudices raises another point. Genealogy evinces a commitment to what might be called 'naturalism'.[5] Nietzsche was interested in understanding human activity without recourse to any supernatural powers: he treated human nature as continuous with animal nature, and wished to understand all of what he sometimes called 'higher' or 'ideal' phenomena in these terms. It could mean many things to treat human activity as 'natural', however: it could mean adopting a scientific approach, excluding distinctively human powers from a basic explanatory role, or seeing human beings as governed by the pursuit of survival or power rather than moral or rational considerations, for example. In the Preface, Nietzsche explains his approach in this way. He writes that over time, he gradually learned to detach 'theological prejudice' from his inquiries. He used to look for 'the origin of evil *behind* the world' (P: 3), as if evil were something that existed completely apart from human practices, which one needs metaphysics or theology in order to explain. But 'historical and philological schooling' (P: 3) taught him to see evil not as a fundamental feature of existence,

---

[5] Brian Leiter's book *Nietzsche on Morality* (Leiter 2002) is perhaps most responsible for calling attention to Nietzsche's commitment to naturalism. But there are many different advocates of and versions of naturalism. See also, for example, Schacht 2012; Cox 1999; Clark and Dudrick 2012; Patton 2004; and Emden 2014.

but as a category invented by human beings. At least in terms of his personal development, then, Nietzsche's naturalism includes history and language in its study of morality, and raises questions such as why morality was invented, what human ends are served by maintaining a category of the moral, and whether or not we are better off making sense of our lives in terms of such a category. This does not preclude adopting other forms of naturalism – perhaps with more of a focus on biology or psychology – at different points in time, however.

The critique of morality: the value of values

As Nietzsche already indicated in the third aphorism, the aim of genealogy is to reveal something about the *value* of morality. He reiterates this point in the fifth aphorism, contrasting his own concerns with his friend Rée's interest in the 'origin' of moral sentiments: 'At bottom something much more important was on my mind at that precise time than my own or anyone else's indulgence in hypotheses on the origin of morality . . . For me it was a matter of the *value* of morality . . .' (P: 5). The origin as such – or at least indulging in hypotheses about it – is not important. Nietzsche is thus avoiding the 'genetic fallacy': inferring something's worth or importance from its origin. He does not argue that morality is bad because it has a bad source, for example; he does not even think that its source is particularly revealing of what it is now. He is looking, rather, for the contextual knowledge that helps us to figure out how and why moral values are important to us. But how does that serve the end of evaluation?

Conducting a moral inquiry is difficult: it is not at all clear what is being investigated or how to investigate it, what if anything our deliberations are responsible to, or how to acknowledge our own biases as investigators. The history of philosophy offers a variety of ways to proceed, but Nietzsche proposes a novel approach, in the form of a critique couched in terms of the value of values:

> Let us pronounce it, this *new demand*: we need a *critique* of moral values, *the value of these values must itself first be questioned* and for this what is needed is knowledge of the

conditions and circumstances from which they grew and under which they developed and shifted (morality as consequence, as symptom, as mask, as tartuffery, as illness, as misunderstanding; but also morality as cause, as remedy, as stimulus, as obstacle, as poison). (P: 6)

The task that Nietzsche sets for himself is not to determine what moral values are true, and he does not aim to refute them or assess them on moral terms. He presents his critique, rather, as an evaluation of values: some kind of inquiry that looks at rival schemes or systems of valuing and determines what the worth of such evaluative systems are. And this worth is to be determined not along moral lines, but in terms of what best promotes human strength, health, fulfilment or, most simply, 'life'. Nietzsche's suggestion is, of course, that the future of humanity might be better served with values other than moral ones.

Nietzsche's approach, I take it, has this structure. Rather than weigh particular moral assessments, or even general moral principles or claims, Nietzsche proposes to take morality as a whole as a system or practice of valuing. Morality has come to be seen as our most fundamental interest in the practical – all of our most important, non-instrumental values – but really it is just one historically and culturally contingent system of evaluating ourselves. We can assess this system as a whole by asking what the value is of sustaining this system, by continuing to hold these values. Nietzsche proposes a meta-level evaluation of the value of morality, and provides at least two ways of thinking about how to conduct such an evaluation. There are not merely two alternative sets of possible outcomes here, but two different kinds of evaluation: morality might, under certain *conditions*, tend to produce or have already produced particular *effects*, and it might *signify* or *reveal* something. (Morality, according to Nietzsche, should be considered as 'cause' but also as 'symptom' and 'mask', among other things.) If genealogical investigation shows that morality indeed constitutes an interconnected structure of value (or 'value-judgements'), then presumably it can reveal what effects morality has produced and what this in turn reveals about humanity, and this furnishes the basis to make an assessment of morality as a whole.

We might, of course, worry about regress problems here, or at least that the meta-level analysis would be no sounder than the first-order assessment of moral judgements. But the attractiveness of this approach, presuming that it can be supported by genealogy, is that it does not depend on being able to identify independently authoritative criteria of evaluation: we do not seem to have to appeal to metaphysical standards of truth or correctness in order to assess the value of values. This responds nicely to Nietzsche's suggestion in aphorism 3 that morality is 'invented': it is a human creation so we can assess it as such, locating its merits or faults in its own worldly functioning rather than trying to discover whether it satisfies some criterion external to it. The evaluative considerations that Nietzsche invokes are perhaps ones that he takes to be internal to having a set of values at all, in which case we can take them as suitable for assessing what set of values to have or – if genealogy reveals that the values are harmful – to reject. There might be other reasons to criticise morality, ones that are not based on its harms, but one important form of critique for Nietzsche is examining what effects are promoted in the conditions of morality's invention and what this expresses or 'reveals' about us.

As a critique, Nietzsche's approach depends on taking some actually held values as its starting point, and furthermore depends on figuring out how those values might be harmful. This is puzzling because it seems to require us to take *morality* as inflicting harm on *humanity*. Nietzsche's doubts about morality and moral phenomena extend to whether or not they exist at all; it is not easy to see how morality could be causally effective, or what it would mean for it to be so. And Nietzsche characterises that which the damage is inflicted on as 'humankind' or 'the human type':

> Precisely here I saw the *great* danger of humankind, its most sublime enticement and seduction – where to? to nothingness? [. . .] the backward-looking weariness, the will turned *against* life, the ultimate sickness. (P: 5)

> What? if there were a symptom of regression in the 'good' too, likewise a danger, a seduction, a poison, a narcotic

through which perhaps the present lived *at the expense of the future?* [. . .] So that precisely morality would be to blame if the *highest powerfulness and magnificence of the human type*, in itself possible, were never attained? So that precisely morality were the danger of dangers? (P: 6)

Genealogy, Nietzsche suggests, will show that morality makes us sick, renders us indifferent to our future ends and hinders our future growth; because of morality, humanity has made less of itself than it otherwise would have. But how can humanity as a whole be affected? Of course, we might take this as shorthand for some aggregation of individuals and the ways in which they are affected; this would even help us connect moments in the genealogical narratives to the infliction of harm. But the whole story of genealogy has to be more than the effects on particular individuals in the historical past or in Nietzsche's almost typological, almost mythological storytelling. If we take 'humanity' to stand in for some set of individuals, then we have to make sure to explain how we bear some connection to those individuals, how those individuals are *us*, on pain of making the result of genealogy unimportant.

The Dionysian drama of the soul

Late in the Preface, Nietzsche writes that a familiar modern personality type can no longer take morality seriously, and that this is a mistake. One can become so worn down, cynical and distrustful of anything but the brute facts of science that morality, if not seriousness itself, comes to seem like a wasteful diversion. According to Nietzsche, however, 'there is nothing at all more *worthy* of being taken seriously' (P: 7) than the problems of morality. Morality used to be something that was very important to take seriously in an explicit, direct way: the state of one's soul depended on it. If that old imperative no longer seems compelling, it is tempting to dismiss it altogether. But morality still needs to be taken seriously, if now in a second-order way, for understanding how it has shaped who we are and how it continues to be important to us in ways that we fail to recognise. The reward of investigating the problems of morality this way, Nietzsche writes, is that 'someday we will perhaps be granted permission to take them *cheerfully*' (P: 7). By gaining in self-understanding, Nietzsche hopes, we can put ourselves in a position to look back at morality, as a formative but laughable stage in our past that no longer seems as traumatic as it once might have been.

Nietzsche has a very particular way of expressing this point: 'But on that day when we can say from the fullness of our hearts: "forward! our old morality also belongs *in the comedy!*" we will have discovered a new complication and possibility for the Dionysian drama of the "destiny of the soul"' (P: 7). Dionysus was the Greek god associated with wine, ecstasy and fertility, who was periodically rent limb from limb and then reborn; he was, significantly, patron of the Tragic Festival in Athens. Nietzsche is thus suggesting a number of things by situating the genealogy of morality within the Dionysian drama of the soul. Most generally, morality plays only a small but necessary part in a much larger drama about what we are; genealogy accounts for an aspect of our 'destiny' that we stand apart from even as it shapes 'the soul'. This might put the soul in the position of protagonist, but Nietzsche does stage his narratives as *dramas*, too. Instead of a recitation of the grey of historical actuality, they are filled with competing, sometimes unreliable voices, meaningful silences, curious reversals and moments of belated recognition. The overall drama, finally, is *tragic* in character.[6] Self-knowledge only comes about after costly, inevitable failures that stem from the very nature of the dramatic action. At the same time, Nietzsche holds out hope that genealogical knowledge can help transmute tragic doom into comic rebirth.

---

[6] For an extended discussion of this topic, see Hatab 2008.

2
The First Treatise: 'Good and Evil', 'Good and Bad'

Introduction

There is one clear task of the First Treatise. It aims to provide a narrative account of the transition from a set of values, in archaic times, that revolved around the distinction between 'good' and 'bad', to a set of values, in more recent times, that revolves around the distinction between 'good' and 'evil'. Nietzsche claims that this change has been underappreciated, in part because the same term, 'good', is used as one half of the opposed pair in each set of values. Part of the narrative, then, describes how insidious the change was: superficial continuities in the function of calling someone 'good' conceal that a new concept with the same name is being created. Nietzsche nevertheless claims that there is abundant evidence, primarily philological and historical, for this change. It was a radical change, too: the two senses of 'good' are not merely different from, but contrary to, one another. So Nietzsche needs to offer a narrative of a change that was imperceptibly subtle and at the same time revolutionary. This accordingly requires providing the conceptual clarifications for understanding the nature of the change, identifying the psychological underpinnings of the change, and establishing the outcome of the process: that the older set of values primarily resides in historical memory since it has been decisively supplanted by the newer set.

Despite the clarity of this one task, the First Treatise nevertheless leaves room for a number of auxiliary tasks, strange digressions and lines of philosophical argumentation. It even leaves room for doubts about its main task – not just whether it accomplishes what it is supposed to, but also whether the apparent main task conceals ulterior aims, whether the narrative genuinely possesses the epistemic standing it purports to have, and whether it is indeed asserted sincerely or is intended to accomplish some performative aim. In *Ecce Homo*, a book written about a year after the publication of *On the Genealogy of Morality*, Nietzsche discussed his previous works. There, in a section titled 'Why I Write Such Good Books', Nietzsche writes of the *Genealogy*: 'In each case, a beginning that *should* be deceptive: cool, scientific, even ironic, intentionally foreground, intentionally evasive' (Nietzsche 2005: 135–6). Nietzsche is suggesting that the beginning of each Treatise, at least, is deliberately unreliable in a number of ways. Of course, we can take Nietzsche's later declaration of unreliability as itself unreliable. It does, however, raise a number of interpretative questions that we can consider when reading the whole text; these questions cannot be answered at the outset. Nietzsche claims that he adopts a 'cool, scientific' tone that is in fact 'ironic': that is, his accounts pretend to a scientific objectivity that he does not intend them to possess. Furthermore, the presentation of the account might be 'intentionally foreground': it could be the superficial presentation of a deeper agenda. Even if all this is overstated, the simple explanatory task, of tracing out the history of a conceptual development in morality, is not the whole story of what is going on in the text. Nietzsche is telling us to consider the accounts not only on their own terms, but also in the context of what it means to make such a case, what the purpose of doing so might be, and who the narrator and the audience are.

The treatise begins, oddly enough, with a discussion of the 'English psychologists'. Nietzsche gives little indication of why this belongs here, except that they, in attempting a history of morality, are his closest rivals in his genealogical project. He surely has specific, if perhaps ill-described historical individuals in mind.[1] Yet he

---

[1] On the identity of the 'English psychologists', see especially Janaway 2007: 40–1, 74–89. Janaway makes a compelling case for Paul Rée as the primary referent of the 'English psychologists'. On the Darwinian influences on Nietzsche's characterisation, see Jensen 2013: 168–70. For the influence of David Hume, in particular, on Nietzsche's characterisation, see Thatcher 1989.

does not mention anyone by name in the opening aphorism. His interest does not lie in specific persons and their arguments, but rather in a type of philosophical approach or commitment; he does not *engage* in their investigations and debates, but instead offers meta-level commentary on their approach in general. (When he does later raise an objection to something internal to their position, he prefaces it with 'in the second place' [I: 2], as if it were secondary to his overall assessment; it is as if someone had some critical things to say about astrologers in general, but also wanted to mention that they had their dates or star positions wrong.) The identity of the English psychologists is thus defined not by names but by his characterisation of them as the ones 'seeking what is truly effective, guiding, decisive for our development [. . .] in the *vis inertiae* of habit or in forgetfulness or in a blind and random interlocking and mechanism of ideas or in some purely passive, automatic, reflexive, molecular and thorough stupid thing' (I: 1). English psychologists accordingly need not be either English or, in any typical sense, psychologists. They do offer causal explanations of human behaviour and thought, in particular with respect to our 'development'. In doing so they appeal to biological mechanisms or principles of association. Nietzsche is including a wide variety of approaches here, but they all offer explanations of how morality was adopted that appeal to non-intentional, non-reflective processes. Their types of explanation treat human beings like non-sapient creatures or things, for which instinct, habit, reflex or 'molecular' reactions are causally effective, but not reasons or ends.

One might expect Nietzsche to sympathise with them. They view morality as a human creation, and perhaps even view human nature as subject to historical change. They explain the origin of values not as supernatural, and not as the product of conscious deliberation, but as the product of natural drives and forces. But Nietzsche finds them boring and perverse. More precisely, their books are boring and they are interesting only as 'riddles in the flesh' (I: 1). So Nietzsche does not discuss their writings in this initial consideration; his thoughts on the kinds of explanations they offer is just a means to discussing what kinds of persons they are. Their habits and motivations, Nietzsche writes, also reveal who they are as persons: 'We always find them, whether willingly or unwillingly, at work on the same thing, namely on forcing the *partie honteuse* of our inner world into the foreground' (I: 1). They seem to be driven by a strange compulsion to undermine our self-image as moral beings by finding the 'shameful parts' of our psyches, exposing them as it were, and using them to explain our only apparently moral behaviour. That they do so in a boring way does not qualify the perverse zeal that they seem to take in 'looking for what is decisive in our development exactly where the intellectual pride of humanity least *wished* to find it' (I: 1). With an apparent eye to self-belittlement, they not only treat human beings as machines of a sort, but as machines whose mainsprings are distasteful or repellent.

If we take Nietzsche to be concerned with evaluating their approach to explaining the development of morality, then his objection to the English psychologists seems to take a form such as this. There are many different types of explanations or interpretations of the development of morality and of human moral behaviour. Different types are more or less successful at fulfilling different explanatory ends, but what is most distinctive about the English psychological approach, other than its boringness, is that it seems to express a strangely enervated, erotic self-disgust and self-humiliation. So, given that there are alternative approaches available that can serve our cognitive ends, and the English psychologists' approach seems to have expressive faults, why not take a different approach? Nietzsche's response to this question is complex and largely implicit here, but on his view the English psychologists' answer is that their approach is compulsory: it carves nature by the joints, or in some other way is necessary in its method of explaining the natural world. Their claim, that is, is that they are seekers of truth, and even if the truth is 'plain, harsh, ugly, repulsive' (I: 1), then they are still required to structure their inquiries in such a way in order to gain truth, or at least arrive at objective claims about reality. Nietzsche's suggestion is that this answer, although it seems to be so, is not really an epistemic claim at all.[2] The nature of the compulsory force is something else, and can be called into question while we still

---

[2] Nietzsche provides a more sustained discussion of some related issues in GS §344.

pursue understanding of ourselves and nature. Furthermore, the English psychologists' commitment to truth manifests the same expressive character as their first-order approach. Their answer is thus, one might say, existentially circular: it defends a particular expressive, personal commitment by calling upon the same expressive, personal commitment.

What Nietzsche is doing, then, is initiating his historical account not with data or methods, but rather with reflection on who carries out a historical account and what they hope to achieve in doing so. After declaring that the English psychologists' books are boring, Nietzsche asks, 'What do they really want?' (I: 1). For Nietzsche, this is the basic question of psychology, and that which informs his historical approach. At the beginning of the First Treatise he has shifted the subject from the nominal topic of explanation to what it means to adopt the right kind of inquiry and what psychic ends are served by doing so. Nietzsche's psychologising takes place *within* the historical accounts, too, but here his point is that the accounts are not to be assessed merely as adequate explanations of historical events. We should, rather, assess our genealogising on roughly practical grounds: we inquire because we are inquirers about ourselves, and this is a kind of activity that we should judge according to how it expresses or satisfies our ends. His dispute with the English psychologists is not about the details of their theories but about what sort of person to be; someone's theoretical outlook reveals or informs what one is.

Nietzsche uses the English psychologists not only to make such a general point, but also to offer some initial examples of his own practice of psychologising; he even takes the occasion to find them hypothetically praiseworthy. He runs through five sets of possibilities as to the nature of their motivations: they could be maliciously driven to belittle humanity, idealists made gloomy by their own disappointment, unconsciously motivated by hatred of Christianity, consumed by lust for the disconcerting and absurd, or all of the above. Any of these would make them psychologically interesting. After entertaining these possibilities, however, he reports the imaginary hearsay that 'they are simply old, cold, boring frogs that crawl and hop around on humans, into humans, as if they were so properly in their element there, namely in a swamp' (I: 1).

None of this is confidently asserted by Nietzsche, so its purpose is not to attribute characteristics to particular individuals. He raises speculative possibilities and reported hearsay, rather, for two main reasons. One is to raise the suspicion that certain forms of inquiry into human nature are swampish: they function to sully our understanding of ourselves rather than establish how we fit with the rest of nature. Second, he uses this opportunity to praise the English psychologists for qualities that he wishes they possessed because he possesses similar ones. He writes, 'if one is allowed to wish where one cannot know, then I wish from my heart that [. . .] these explorers and microscopists of the soul were at bottom courageous, magnanimous, and proud animals, who [. . .] have trained themselves to sacrifice all desirability to truth' (I: 1).[3] This is indirect praise of himself by praise of others: although 'sacrifice' is something he wishes to avoid, he is dependent for his own epistemic authority on a similar stance of carrying out inquiry until the very end, as painful and unpleasant as it may be. This serves as an introduction to the Treatises: Nietzsche acknowledging that, although he has a better method and better practical judgement than the English psychologists, his genealogical inquiries come from the same swamp as they do.

The rest of this chapter will proceed with the same format as the following two. First I will review the details of Nietzsche's slightly swampish, possibly ironic, psychologically and historically informed narrative. After putting the narrative in view, I will discuss some of the philosophical topics that Nietzsche raises within the narrative. In the case of the First Treatise, those topics are the cognitive standing and uses of narrative, the nature and evaluation of values, agency and social identity. Then the final section of the chapter will discuss some of the methodological issues with respect to understanding human activity and some of the rhetorical devices and tropes that Nietzsche makes use of, including one of his many digressions.

---

[3] The opening of this quotation is a parody of Kant's famous declaration of his need 'to deny knowledge to make room for faith' (Kant 1998: 117, B xxx; see also 677, A 805/B 833). Nietzsche would occasionally parody Kantian formulations. He never read the *Critique of Pure Reason*.

The basic narrative

The First Treatise has the most straightforward narrative of the three. Values do not begin either with considerations of self-interest or with the conflation of private interest with public utility, but with the spontaneous self-affirmation of ancient nobles. These nobles' sense of superiority allowed them to affirm themselves as 'good'; they classified those who were unlike them, derivatively, as 'bad'. The nobles created enmity, however, among those whom they harmed. This enmity could not be acted on – the 'bad' were powerless to seek reprisals – so it festered, generating a reactive feeling that Nietzsche names with the French word *ressentiment*. Eventually this *ressentiment* led the weak to exact 'imaginary revenge' on the nobles: since they could not act against the nobles, they invented a new scheme of values that they could use to praise themselves and condemn the nobles. Through this 'slave revolt in morality', they inverted the nobles' values, referring to themselves as 'good' and calling the nobles 'evil'. Although the older set of values persists in an attenuated way, the slave revolt has been so successful that the good/evil dichotomy has come to dominate evaluative thinking.

This brief sketch contains the major elements in Nietzsche's narrative of the descent of good and evil. Like most narratives, however, this one allows for considerably more fineness of grain; Nietzsche accordingly fills in his story with additional details, complications and, occasionally, arguments against his opponents. He indeed begins with a contrast between his own approach and that of the English psychologists. According to Nietzsche, they get the history of morality wrong right from the very beginning, with 'the descent of the concept and judgment "good"' (I: 2), and they do so because 'they all think in an *essentially* unhistorical manner' (I: 2). To understand this objection, and what Nietzsche takes to be the uncritical, default view that he is working against, it helps to consider his presentation of the English psychologists' view:

> 'Originally' – so they decreed – 'unegoistic acts were praised and called good on the part of those to whom they were done, therefore by those to whom they were *useful*;

later the origin of the praise was *forgotten* and the unegoistic acts were simply perceived as good because they always *habitually* praised as good – as if they were something good in themselves.' (I: 2)

Nietzsche has an objection that is internal to this explanation. According to this explanation, unegoistic actions are praised because they are immensely useful, but forgotten because they are habitually praised. Nietzsche finds this process to suffer from 'an inherent psychological absurdity' (I: 3): that the immense usefulness of unegoistic actions, which is sufficient to attract habitual praise, is somehow forgotten even while its usefulness persists and attention is repeatedly called to it. Even beyond the need for forgetfulness and attention at the same time, this, for Nietzsche, is a typical move of the English psychologists. Their explanations require reflective, rational judgements until the moment the important transition happens, and then that moment of change is shrouded in oblivion.

But this internal objection, about the implausibility of the main *explanans*, is relatively unimportant. Nietzsche makes that clear when he notes that even if, following Herbert Spencer, one were to revise this explanation, it would still be wrong. His main objection is independent of the internal one, and speaks to their general approach, regardless of their details. The problem with the English psychologists once again is that they 'all think in an *essentially* unhistorical manner' (I: 2) as a whole, and however their theories are revised, since they 'lack the *historical spirit* itself' (I: 2). Since Nietzsche refers to them as 'historians of morality' (I: 2), their shortcoming is not a failure to consider the past at all, but a failure of the 'manner' in which they consider it, extrapolating their present standpoint into the past. Nietzsche explains this by using the role of 'egoism' in their theories as his main example. They take the process by which morality arose to revolve around egoism: most persons, by default, view their situations in egoistic terms; occasionally they might choose to adopt an unegoistic course of action; others recognise their unegoistic actions and praise them for it; persons seek praise by performing unegoistic actions, and so on.

But Nietzsche claims to the contrary that this entire framework of language and thought is a modern imposition; it would not even have been available, let alone effective in directing behaviour at the origin of morality. He writes, 'it is only with a *decline* of aristocratic value-judgments that this whole opposition of "egoistic" and "unegoistic" imposes more and more on the human conscience' (I: 2). Because of the English psychologists' lack of historical sense, they take their own viewpoint as the whole range of semantic and psychological possibility; they then wish to explain why persons who are much like themselves adopt particular ideas. Nietzsche insists, however, that understanding the descent of morality involves understanding how it could emerge among persons who did not have it as an option in language or thereby in thought. The English psychologists work with a view of modern personality the terms of which would not have made sense millennia ago. The concepts of the 'unegoistic' and 'egoistic' are, according to Nietzsche, part of a complex of ideas that grew up around morality and thus would not have been available to participants in a pre-moral context. And for reasons that I discuss below, Nietzsche thinks it generally incoherent to account for actions on such terms at all, and all the more so to ascribe them, from our own perspective, to those who did not think in that way. Nietzsche also seems to think that there were biological and cultural conditions, and not just conceptual conditions 'on the human conscience', for thinking in certain ways, and that these, too, were profoundly different from what the English psychologists take for granted. But the basic problem with the English psychologists is that the concept of the 'unegoistic' and many of the other ideas surrounding morality were no more available than being bourgeois, a *flâneur*, Asian-American, bisexual or a samurai. A proper appreciation of the historicity of morality requires working with the conceptual possibilities of the distant past.

Nietzsche's properly historical account can therefore only appeal to what was already meaningful for those who did not have the linguistic resources to think about egoism or altruism, or a wide range of other ideas that came along with the development of morality. Nietzsche starts, then, with the pre-moral concept 'good', and seeks to base it in something that does not require further conceptual articulation in order to make sense of it. As he later warns, 'all the concepts of more ancient humankind were understood initially in a crude, clumsy, superficial, narrow, straightforward, and especially unsymbolic sense to an extent that today is scarcely conceivable to us' (I: 7). As a result, the narrative starts with the merest sentiment of self. According to Nietzsche,

> it was 'the good' themselves, that is, the noble, powerful, higher ranking and high-minded who perceived and determined themselves and their doings as good, that is, as ranking foremost, as opposed to all who were lowly, low-minded, base, and of the rabble. From this *pathos of distance* they first took for themselves the right to create values, to coin names for values. (I: 2)

The beginning of values was nothing well-considered or well-reasoned, but rather a 'pathos of distance'. Nietzsche uses the Greek word for transiently experienced feeling, *pathos*, to emphasise that it this neither an *ēthos*, a settled state of character, nor an act of judgement on the part of the nobles. These nobles merely feel themselves to be superior; they unreflectively experience themselves to be powerful, strong and healthy, and thus as standing apart from ordinary humanity. Although such nobles could hardly articulate any clear sense of this, they might consider themselves 'good' in much the same way that a good sword or a good horse is good: they are excellent examples of their kind. Such an ascription involves no reference to anyone else, and indeed, these nobles are so generally indifferent to non-nobles that the idea of the 'bad' is merely a 'by-product' (I: 11). 'Bad' merely marks off a lack or deficiency: those are called 'bad' who do not match up to the good, without a sense of blame or condemnation or even criticism.

Nietzsche's prehistory of morality is thus about how a mere feeling was transformed so as to extend and exert social authority. Through the creation of a concept and its deployment in judgements, the nobles shaped their social world in a way that confirmed their authority to themselves. What began as a transient feeling was memorialised in value judgements. By effecting change in language, furthermore, they change what is generally possible to say and think in their communities. Nietzsche expresses this in terms of a general authority to 'give names' to things:

> The pathos of nobility and distance, as I said, the lasting and dominating overall and basic feeling of a higher ruling order in relation to a lower order, to a 'below' – *that* is the origin of the opposition 'good' and 'bad'. (The master's right to give names goes so far as to allow us to conceive of the origin of language itself as an expression of power on the part of the rulers). (I: 2)

Language is itself, Nietzsche suggests, a domain in which power operates; through language, the 'masters' convert their contingent standing into a broader social power to establish their own viewpoint among others.[4] Language also allows for slippage in how particular things are thought of. With particular regard to goodness, Nietzsche insists, 'the political concept of superiority always resolves itself into a concept of the superiority of the soul' (I: 6). That is, the nobles manage to name themselves on the basis, in part, of their superior standing in their communities. These names that designate social standing, however, once established, can come to designate 'superiority of the soul'. The nobles conflate their feeling of being better situated with being internally or inherently better, and over time they tacitly convince others to adopt the same conflation.

Nietzsche expands this last point when he discusses the philological evidence for his view. He claims that the terms for 'good' in a wide range of languages 'all lead back to the same conceptual transformation' (I: 4). Nobles start with a concept that they use to designate a readily apparent characteristic of themselves and gradually extend its content. The concept comes to encompass other qualities that the nobles associate with themselves, and eventually comes to stand for a unified condition of excellence in which the original nuances are lost; the concept can stand for an inner

---

[4] For a contemporary discussion of related issues, see Fricker 2007.

condition if the outward characteristics are not reliably present. In the examples that Nietzsche gives, words meaning 'wealthy', 'blond', 'truthful', 'warlike' and 'godly' arrive at a general, diffuse sense of goodness, while words meaning 'plain', 'dark' and 'cowardly' arrive at a general sense of badness.

Nietzsche's discussion here – although brief and lacking scholarly references – is important for two reasons. One is that it shows that his primary evidence is philological: one understands the history of morality by looking at the historical use of words. The other reason is that it shows what might be called semantic compression.[5] A word such as 'good' (or the Greek *agathos*, for instance) serves functions of self-affirmation and self-identification for a noble elite. It also picks out a set of qualities that constitute an idealised self-image. Someone who exemplifies goodness, such as Achilles, is powerful, brave, beautiful, rich and bold in leadership; these qualities can seem to be inseparable from one another without any of them being explicitly affirmed.[6] In a relatively undifferentiated and conceptually unsophisticated society, all of these senses can be entangled and associated, while none of them are necessary, so that a word such as 'good' can mean very many things and nothing in particular. The same, of course, applies to the contrasting negative terms: they can pack a lot of content together without any conceptual clarity. Someone who is 'bad', such as Thersites in the *Iliad*, is represented as ugly, vain, lame, balding and impudent:

> one man, Thersites of the endless speech, still scolded, who knew within his head many words, but disorderly; vain, and without decency, to quarrel with the princes [. . .] This was the ugliest man who came beneath Ilion. He was bandy-legged and went lame of one foot, with shoulders stooped and drawn together over his chest, and above this

---

[5] Nietzsche gives as an example 'the aristocratic value equation (good = noble = powerful = beautiful = happy = beloved of God)' (I: 7), but does not a have a general name for the phenomenon. He does, however, later discuss how a 'synthesis of "meanings" [. . .] crystallizes into a kind of unity' (II: 13); I will discuss this in the next chapter.
[6] For a discussion of this in terms of the '*arete*-standard' of ancient Greece, see Adkins 1975: 30–6.

his skull went up to a point with the wool grown sparsely upon it. (Homer 1951: 81–2)

Those who use 'good' and 'bad' can thereby be thinking many things at once, without realising what associations they are making or noticing when conceptual change takes place. For Nietzsche, much of our ethical vocabulary can function in this way, richly but amorphously shaping the possibilities for how we think about ourselves.

There is a transitional stage before the revolution in morality.[7] In this transitional stage, the '*priestly* caste' (I: 6) becomes the highest caste. Rather than designating itself by its social rank or political power, this caste uses a designation 'reminiscent of its priestly function' (I: 6). 'For instance', Nietzsche writes, '"pure" and "impure" first appear opposite each other as class distinctions: and here too a "good" and a "bad" are later developed in a sense no longer based on class' (I: 6). With this development, a series of somewhat countervailing effects take place. 'Pure' and 'impure' originally marked off literal qualities: 'pure' designated those who bathed and avoided certain things, and 'impure' those who did not. 'Pure', however, since it designates the priests, is used to make a class distinction and can thereby become the basis of deep, symbolic, socially important distinctions. At the same time, 'good' and 'bad' start to become disconnected from class, because 'good' is associated with the priests, who are 'pure', but 'pure' can refer to others besides the priests. Through this metonymic chain, ascriptions of basic ethical value are potentially severed from class standing or anything literal. That is, one can be good by being pure, even without belonging to the highest caste, or even washing. New, more spiritual ways of being 'pure' can arise.

Here Nietzsche's narrative breaks down slightly. On one hand, not much has happened: pure priests have surpassed wealthy warriors in social status, and have appropriated some of their vocabulary. On the other hand, this minor change was momentous enough that Nietzsche interrupts his story with a series of extended

---

[7] This transitional stage has recently attracted some scholarly attention. See, for example, Anderson 2011; Snelson 2017; and Loeb 2018.

digressions. The change primarily affects the flexibility in the concept 'good'. 'Good' maintains its sense of social superiority but, as society is organised differently, conceptual space is created for senses of superiority that are not based on brute force and naïve self-affirmation. Nietzsche has nothing to say about how or why the priests came into power, but this silence itself suggests that ethical change can take place on account of contingent changes in the forms of social arrangement. Changes in political authority, in this story, are things that simply happen, without needing further explanation; they function as background variables. Yet they bring about a shift in the meaning of 'good', not because of individuals' decisions to revise their beliefs, but because language reflects the dynamics of the social order.

The new conceptual flexibility of 'good' introduces another important idea that anticipates later discussions. Nietzsche leaves it ambiguous which, if either, is causally primary between the conceptual flexibility of 'good' and the character of the priestly aristocracies. He identifies the priests' 'habits', their 'cures' and their 'metaphysics' (I: 6) as dangerous, but does not isolate any of these things as important factors. What is important about the priestly aristocracies is that 'precisely here the valuation opposites could soon become internalized and sharpened in a dangerous manner; and in fact through them chasms were ultimately ripped open between one human being and another, over which even an Achilles of free-spiritedness could not leap without shuddering' (I: 6). Nietzsche is claiming that a tremendous change took place when 'good' (or the terms used for other value-opposites) no longer refers to outwardly manifest qualities or concrete social relations. When value terms are literal and social, the range of possible disputes and range of intensity can only be so great: one can bathe or argue about who is cleaner only so much, and there are a limited number of social ranks, the higher of which are especially fragile. But when 'good' purportedly refers to valuable inner states, there can be infinite gradations to argue about; the only constraint is the invention of symbolic significance. Nietzsche initially seems to be horrified by the new creation of hierarchy and difference: it is 'dangerous' to treat human beings as if their inner worth varies from the sublimely great to the wretchedly abject. At the same time, however, Nietzsche embraces this danger:

> It was only on the soil of this *essentially dangerous* form of human existence, the priestly form, that human beings became *an interesting animal* at all, that only here the human soul acquired *depth* in a higher sense and became *evil* – and these are in fact the two basic forms to date of the superiority of human beings over other creatures! (I: 6)

On account of the priests, we human beings became interesting and thus attained our superiority to the rest of nature. This transformation, furthermore, was not incidental to the invention of evil, but precisely because of it. 'Evil' is this condition of a potentially infinite range of difference.

This assessment of the priests represents a breakdown in Nietzsche's narrative. On the verge of relating the one main event in the First Treatise, the slave revolt in morality, Nietzsche breaks away from the history of morality for a long aside on the priests and our 'depth'. He delays the presentation of the slave revolt quite a bit further, too. Aphorisms 7, 8 and 9 not only digress from the overall narrative of the descent of morality, they are told *in other voices* than the main narrator's.[8] Nietzsche marks off these voices with a dash at the beginning of each aphorism. One of them is the voice of a 'freethinker' (I: 9). The others seem to be Nietzsche's own, but distinct from that of the narrator who presents the historical facts in the proper order; these voices pose questions in the second person, anticipate later stages in the narrative and claims in other parts of the book, and make a number of evaluative claims. Nietzsche also declares that he has 'much . . . to be silent about' (I: 9), as if he is at that point refraining from saying something that it is important to convey.

Since these aphorisms depart from the main narrative, I will mostly pass them by for now, and bring them up again when

---

[8] See the view attributed to Foucault by Gary Gutting: 'Nietzsche, he said, showed us the importance of always asking of a text "Who is speaking?"' (Gutting 2005: 12, referring to Foucault 1973: 305).

discussing the issues that they raise. There are a few points that are worth mentioning now, however. First, these digressions are valuable because they comment on the main narrative and what its implications are supposed to be. They also, however, undermine the main narrative, by establishing a point of view outside of it and suggesting that it is withholding important points. Second, Nietzsche's declared attitude towards the process of descent is insistently *ambiguous*. On the one hand, he declares the priests to be 'the most evil enemies' (I: 7), who are vengeful and filled with poisonous hatred, and whose remedies make everyone more ill. On the other hand, 'human history would be a far too stupid matter without the spirit it has acquired on the part of the impotent' (I: 7). Nietzsche's view of the legacy of morality is mixed, despite anything that he might write about particular moments in the process or its outcome. Third, Nietzsche introduces some of the terminology, such as 'slave revolt in morality' and 'revaluation of all values', that he is about to place into the narrative. His point in doing so is to claim that moral values, despite their surface appearance, represent a 'grand politics of revenge' (I: 8). He credits 'Jewish hatred' (I: 8) with bringing about the slave revolt in morality, but finds the purest manifestation of this hatred, the most tremendous and uncanny form of spiritual revenge, in Christianity. Fourth, Nietzsche claims that we no longer notice the effects of the slave revolt in morality because it has been victorious: we have internalised its values to such an extent that they appear throughout our various commitments and we have come to take them for granted.

The fundamental shift in values comes with the 'slave revolt in morality'. Nietzsche abruptly and efficiently takes up recounting its story:

> The slave revolt in morality begins when *ressentiment* itself becomes creative and gives birth to values: the *ressentiment* of those beings who are denied genuine reaction, that of the deed, who make up for it only through imaginary revenge. Whereas all noble morality grows out of a triumphant Yes-saying to oneself, slave morality from the start says 'No' to an 'outside', to a 'different', to a 'non-self': and *this* No is

its creative deed. This reversal of the value-positing gaze – this *necessary* direction to the outside instead of back onto oneself – belongs to the very essence of *ressentiment*. (I: 10)

In Nietzsche's story, those who are not esteemed 'good' by the nobles suffer at their hands, or at any rate resent their own relative misery. They experience '*ressentiment*' – Nietzsche uses the French word for 'resentment' here. According to Clark and Swensen, 'this French term has stronger associations with revenge than the corresponding English term' (Nietzsche 1998: 135), and in Nietzsche's usage, the term is connected with the experience of hostility, injury and impotence. When the 'bad' are unable to pursue compensation or retaliation for the harms that they suffer, their characteristic feelings of anger and resentment develop into *ressentiment*. This sentiment consumes the psychic lives of those who suffer or fear suffering. Their lives come to revolve around feelings of malice towards the nobles, and dominate their sense of what is important. In just this way the very powerlessness of the weak allows them a means of resistance to the value judgements of the nobles. Their inability to act compels them to seek and exact 'imaginary revenge'. This is not to say that they imagine themselves to have exacted revenge when they could not. Rather, where they could not exact revenge in deed, they exacted a novel sort of revenge. This revenge operated primarily on an 'ideal' or 'spiritual' level rather than a factual one. The noble and the person of *ressentiment* would agree for the most part on who was who and what transpires. But those filled with *ressentiment* retaliate by imagining that precisely the characteristics by which the nobles identified themselves were the undesirable ones, and that they themselves were the virtuous ones: they look at the same facts 'only recolored, only reinterpreted, only reseen through the poisonous eye of *ressentiment*' (I: 11). Thus *ressentiment* 'becomes creative', and, through 'a reversal of the value-positing gaze' (I: 10), produces the 'good/evil' dichotomy of values.

The basis of this story is simple: the weak, unable to harm the nobles directly, exact revenge against them by creating new values. But Nietzsche's story is not a simple one of explaining how one set of values was replaced by another; indeed, he has little if anything to say about how the replacement was effected. Nietzsche's story, rather, is directed to understanding the creation of the new categorical possibility of evil. He offers an account of this new categorical possibility in three primary ways: as *vengeful*, as *reactive* and as an *inversion*. Nietzsche claims that the creation of the good/evil dichotomy is a matter of 'the *most spiritual revenge*' (I: 7). This kind of revenge was not consciously planned, and could not have been: it takes a lot of heedlessness and confusion to switch basic terms of assessment. This lack of calculation or planning is, however, what makes it so insidious. A more literal revenge would be a mere striking back to inflict harm in exchange for harm. The ancient Greek word sometimes translated as revenge, *apotinesthai*, simply means to exact repayment, for example; it presumes an equivalency that can be satisfied. The new spiritual revenge, by contrast, requires a sustained intensity of malice. It is not about repaying harm in kind or recovering damages; it seeks, instead, to permanently recolour the social world so that the nobles are harmed in their very being. Vengeance from the 'cauldron of unsatiated hate' (I: 11) reclassifies what it is to be noble as odious: it affects what someone is rather than what they happen to have. This vengeance, furthermore, extends past the terms 'evil' and colours other ideals. Nietzsche's main example is that of 'love' (I: 8). Love, Nietzsche claims, has a new 'sublime' (I: 8) form accompanying the invention of evil that manifests vengeance by providing a means of finding fault with anyone. No one can live up to a sublime ideal of love, so all ordinary human relationships seem defective by comparison. 'Love' can thus not only serve as a means of showing that others are unworthy, but also of excusing one's own misbehaviour: if failure is the inevitable result of trying to live up to an impossible ideal, then failure is to be expected.

Nietzsche's historical argument that the good/evil dichotomy manifests vengefulness takes two forms, metaphysical and textual. The metaphysical one appears in Nietzsche's parable of lambs and birds of prey. He does not himself make a metaphysical argument, but rather argues that the imputation of good and evil, in order to make sense, involves constructing a metaphysical scaffolding for support, and that the purpose of this scaffolding is to find new ways of blaming others. He writes,

No wonder that the repressed, secretly glowing affects of revenge and hatred exploit this belief for themselves and basically even uphold no belief more ardently than the one that says *the strong is free* to be weak, and the bird of prey to be a lamb: – this way after all they gain the right to make the bird of pretty *accountable* for being a bird of prey . . . (I: 13)

I will return to the lambs and birds below, in the discussion of agency. But here it is worth noting Nietzsche's point that a special kind of blame is created, one in which the blamed are *accountable* for what they are.[9] One feature of Nietzsche's discussion is that the birds of prey are blamed for their malice when they simply cause harm, as a function of their natural condition. The kind of blame here is novel in two respects: those blamed are not merely deficient, but *choose* malice when they could have chosen otherwise, and because of that they are blameworthy for *what they are*. Supporting this picture of blame involves revisions in the ideas of choice, effect, essence, merit and so on. Above all, Nietzsche insists, it involves a metaphysics of free will attributed to a subject independent of external causal influence. Attributing this power involves 'counterfeiting and self-deception' (I: 13), and as such is motivated by the wish for vengeance rather than being responsive to how things are.

Nietzsche's textual argument for the role of vengeance is less of an argument than a pile of evidence in Latin. Nietzsche quotes St Thomas Aquinas and, at great length, the Church Father Tertullian.[10] The implicit argument is plain, however: in the formation of the ideas of good and evil, we can see that the praise of goodness is inseparable from the desire for vengeance against the evil because that is precisely what the delightful reward for the blessed consists in. Nietzsche quotes Aquinas as claiming, 'The blessed in the kingdom of heaven will see the punishments of

---

[9] Compare Bernard Williams on 'everyday blame' and the 'blame system' (Williams 1985: 192–4).
[10] Nietzsche associates both of them with positions on the controversy over the relative authority of faith and reason. He refers to the phrase typically attributed to Tertullian, *credo quia absurdum*, in *Daybreak* Preface §4 and §417 (Nietzsche 1997: 4, 176).

the damned *in order that their bliss be more delightful to them*' (I: 15). Tertullian, after telling of his joy at the sight of monarchs, poets, actors and charioteers undergoing various tortures, asks, 'What quæstor or priest in his munificience will bestow on you the favor of seeing and *exulting in such things as these?*' (I: 15). We see that the institution of the good/evil dichotomy is rooted in vengeance because its imaginary revenge is rooted in imagined revenge.

Also central to Nietzsche's account of the slave revolt in morality is that its values are *reactive*.[11] This is, of course, in contrast to the nobles' values. The nobles simply affirm their own sense of self-worth; the primary value is 'good', and the articulation of 'bad' is an afterthought, standing for the absence of 'good' qualities. The story of how this came about is, furthermore, important not for its own sake, but for what it reveals about nobles' values. What matters here is not the meaning of a single term, but the whole evaluative orientation that comes out of a particular descent. Nietzsche describes the nobles as spontaneous, carefree, joyful, contemptuous but forbearing, impatient and naïve, for example. As one might expect, they are unreflective and self-centred, and Nietzsche describes them as largely unconcerned with how they relate to others or even their own completed deeds: 'Not being able to take seriously for any length of time one's enemies, one's accidents, even one's *misdeeds* – that is the sign of strong, full natures in whom there is an excess of plastic, reconstructive, healing, and even forgetting-inducing power' (I: 10). They cannot, at any rate, sustain any concern for anything that does not reflect directly on themselves. The 'slave morality', by contrast, 'always needs an opposing and external world' (I: 10). The negative term, 'evil', is primary. The 'slaves' denigrate their enemies and use 'evil' to stand in for the bad qualities that they attribute to them. They make sense of themselves as 'good' only derivatively, as lacking an evil nature. Their concept formation is thus driven by hostility and grievance.

Once again, the story of descent is meant to show something about the nature of these values. According to Nietzsche, the

---

[11] This is a central idea in one prominent interpretation of Nietzsche, that of Gilles Deleuze (see Deleuze 1983).

use of the good/evil dichotomy fundamentally involves a lack of self-understanding on the part of the slaves. Understanding themselves as 'good' is *dishonest* because it depends on falsely demonising their enemies, and conceptualising themselves, just as falsely, as the opposite. The nobles had their own failures of self-understanding, but the slaves' failure involves 'falsification' (I: 10) of who they and their enemies are. Since their evaluations are '*necessarily* directed outside', furthermore, there is no real self-scrutiny; only confidence that they are unlike their enemies. The slave morality also involves an inability to affirm anything. 'No is its creative deed' (I: 10): invidious comparison is its only basis of satisfaction. Without finding enemies of some kind, then, there is no way to conceptualise what is valuable, and as long as there are enemies then anything valuable is under threat. Contentment with how things are, or the unqualified desirability of ends, are things that are not just empirically unlikely in slave morality, but have no real conceptual space.

Nietzsche does not provide any historical evidence, beyond his etymological claims, for the reactive nature of slave morality. He does dramatise it, however, with his allegory of the 'workshop' where '*ideals are fabricated*' (I: 14). The story is told as 'Mr. Nosey and Daredevil' relating what he sees, hears and smells to someone, presumably Nietzsche, who had invited him to descend into the workshop. Mr Nosey witnesses a variety of faults, such as weakness and cowardice, being 'lied into' (I: 14) ideals, and recoils in disgust at the process. The story as a whole seems to be Nietzsche's bombastic way of illustrating how defects, with much effort, can be reinterpreted as virtues, but he also makes some subsidiary points. First, 'slave morality' is not exhausted by the good/evil dichotomy. Manufactured along with the new moral notion of goodness, rather, is a host of virtues such as kindness, obedience and patience that fill out that sense of goodness. Second, these moral ideals must be 'fabricated' out of existing materials; the formation of these values is a reaction to flaws and failings that cannot be corrected. For example, 'patience' and 'forgiveness' are not entirely original inventions, but appropriations of what had been 'cowardice'. Third, the process of fabrication is inevitably dishonest. It does not genuinely transform weaknesses into merits.

Nietzsche even seems to suggest that ideals, as such, are modes of self-deception: they elaborate ways in which faulty materials can seem valuable. Fourth, 'vengeance and hatred' (I: 14) motivate the process of fabrication, and there is something psychologically troubling about shaping all of one's values in that way.

The slave revolt in morality also involves *inversion*. This is perhaps a further specification of reactiveness. The weak invert the nobles' value judgements by calling 'the nobles, the powerful, the masterful' (I: 11) 'evil', and calling themselves by contrast 'good'. The 'good' of the noble morality are thus precisely those who are 'evil' in the slave morality: they are careless of others and prone to fits of violence. And the new 'goodness' comprises meekness and humility rather than overflowing strength. It takes a number of contrivances to carry out this inversion. Nietzsche refers to slave morality as 'anti-nature' (I: 16): persons need to be given reasons to deem it important to oppose their own instincts and believe in ideals. These artifices of belief, as anti-natural, bear a cost in physiological health.

This inversion is not so simple, however, as making the good bad and the bad good. It functions that way extensionally, but in the process of inversion underlying values and social relations are altered. In particular, the nature of opposition and conflict changes fundamentally. For the nobles, 'enemies' were simply those who had ends that conflicted with one's own: they wanted the same scarce good, or stood on the opposite side of a battle. The nobles did not imagine their enemies as despicable or wicked; in fact, they sought out worthy opponents, thinking that only genuine competition reflected well upon them. For those who 'know nothing but *evil enemies*' (I: 11), however, all social conflict involves engaging with repugnant persons who *deserve* not only to lose, but to be eliminated from the pursuit of their ends. There could not be stable terms of social cooperation with such persons; the most that they could hope for in social life is mitigating the destructive effects of distrust.

In general, the process of inversion depends on the fundamental lack of clarity in the central term 'good'. The inversion takes place with one term but not both preserved in the new dichotomy. Although no one could confuse 'bad' and 'evil', 'good' must be sufficiently confusing in both of its forms that the revolt can revolve around it. And indeed, goodness is consistently inexplicable, albeit for different reasons. Noble goodness is inexplicable because it is primitive. Even if it is associated with particular self-ascriptive terms, it is not reducible to any of them. It is a term of self-assertion, based on a mere pathos. Moral goodness is inexplicable because it is senseless. It depends on building an elaborate architecture of metaphysical commitment (innate evil, free will), reactive attitudes and social organisation that almost but does not quite manage to support it as meaningful. This continued emptiness makes it a suitable endpoint for inversion.

Only the conclusion, where Nietzsche relates how the contest between noble and slave values has ended, remains of the First Treatise's main narrative. One of Nietzsche's digressions is also worth briefly discussing. Nietzsche writes of the 'blond beast roaming lustily after prey and victory' (I: 11), and further refers to the 'blond Teutonic beast' (I: 11) and 'the descendants of all [. . .] pre-Aryan population' (I: 11). This might give the impression that Nietzsche is glorifying brutal violence, and moreover doing so in a racialised manner, whereby Teutonic blonds are somehow entitled or justified in acting violently, or at least can be extolled and exempted from criticism because of their natural superiority. Nietzsche, no doubt, intended to shock in this passage: part of his interest here is to trace the descent of morality back to something outrageous, so as to disrupt settled attitudes to morality by provoking a counter-reaction. But this is precisely one reason why Nietzsche is not celebrating violence and predation here. He is not trying to provoke outrage at himself, personally, for advocating primitive violence. His aim, rather, is to replace a progressivist narrative of the moral development of culture with one according to which valuable cultural possibilities have been lost in exchange for an attenuated ability to 'say Yes to life' (I: 11). The passage as a whole is difficult to read because it is curiously ironic: Nietzsche switches from trying to articulate the point of view of the 'noble races' (I: 11), to 'supposing' (I: 11) a modern point of view, to returning to his own voice. The story here, however, is that the movement from a recognisably valuable 'highest culture' (I: 11), such as Periclean Athens, that finds its 'ground' (I: 11) in the blond beasts, to modern culture is not a steady advance from primitiveness to civilisation, but in some ways a 'regression' (I: 11). Our esteemed cultural antecedents are not lesser versions of ourselves, but stark alternatives whose vitality was inseparable from the presence of violence. The 'blond beast', furthermore, is an epithet for a lion rather than a racial description.[12] The blond beasts include Arabs and Japanese, and, at least in the case of the Teutons, have no 'blood relationships' (I: 11) to modern peoples.

The sole remaining element of the main narrative is the outcome of the competition between the 'noble' values, structured around the good/bad dichotomy, and the 'slave' values, structured around the good/evil dichotomy. After some equivocation, Nietzsche claims that slave morality has triumphed, and indeed triumphed so decisively that we now identify it as morality itself – as inevitably structuring our sense of selves, our social relations and our culture in general. We have forgotten any sense of a recognisable alternative, and dispute only small differences of what remains.

Nietzsche announces the outcome of the 'millennia-long struggle' by claiming, first, that *ressentiment* values have 'long been preponderant' and then that aristocratic or noble values, as represented by ancient Rome, have 'succumbed beyond all doubt' (I: 16). He offers a contemporaneous and personal, and a future-oriented and social, qualification of this outcome, however. About the present he writes,

> even now there is no shortage of places where the struggle continues undecided. One could even say that in the meantime it has been carried ever higher and therefore has become ever deeper, ever more spiritual: so that today perhaps no mark of the *'higher nature'*, of the more spiritual nature is more decisive than being split in this sense and still a real battleground for those opposites. (I: 16)

---

[12] On 'blond beasts' as lions, see, for example, Kaufmann 1974: 225. For a more general treatment of the figure of the 'blond beast', see Conway 2006.

This, at least, seems conclusive in a way: any remaining struggle is going to be 'more spiritual' and take place internally, as it were. But Nietzsche also claims that the victory of slave values has been resisted at particular moments, such as the Renaissance and the rise of Napoleon. He then asks rhetorically whether there *must* not be more intense periods of resistance in the future: 'Should there not someday have to be an even more terrible flaring up of the old fire, one much longer in the making?' (I: 17).

So on the one hand the conflict of values seems decisively settled, and on the other hand it is bound to flare up again. Nietzsche does not explain his equivocation. He does, however, raise the issue of what the stakes for *us* of such a conflict are, in terms of *nihilism*, and in doing so he implicitly offers an account of why the conflict still seems unresolved. 'Nihilism', from the Latin word for 'nothing', appears throughout the book, but Nietzsche does not offer a clear or consistent definition of it. In the First Treatise he writes, 'the sight of human beings now makes us weary – what is nihilism today if not *that*? . . . We are weary of *human beings* . . .' (I: 12). The meaning of 'nihilism' can be clarified when it appears late in the work. But the background idea, as Nietzsche articulates it here, is that the triumph of the slave revolt has led to a morality that is centred around attending to and remedying grievances and ameliorating suffering. As valuable as this has been, it has left us without the means to make sense of what about our lives is ultimately valuable, worthy of admiration or respect, or to be believed in or hoped for. This is the 'nothing' of nihilism: Nietzsche asks 'In faith in what? In love of what? In hope of what?' (I: 15) and suggests that we do not know what would even count as an adequate answer. Without some aspiration to make life seem worthwhile, 'we suffer from human beings' (I: 11): suffering, however much it is moderated, comes to seem pointless and thus intolerable. So as decisively as *ressentiment* values have won, the conflict is permanent because there remains a need for some redeeming or inspiring hope, and perhaps a human instinct for seeking one. Nietzsche gives no indication of what this might amount to, except that it would take place, as the title of his previous book indicated, 'Beyond Good and Evil' (I: 17).

Philosophical arguments

The First Treatise focuses on questions of value, and yet it seems to bypass a familiar set of philosophical questions. One might expect straightforward claims that something is especially valuable, that some values ought to be promoted, or that values have a particular meta-ethical or motivational standing. Nietzsche's narrative of the conceptual emergence of 'good' and 'evil' certainly speaks to these matters, but at the same time it seems to crowd out philosophical arguments and even conclusions; claims of the form 'one ought to live in this way' or 'this is the highest value' do not appear. Despite the absence of the familiar moves of ethical theory, Nietzsche does manage to incorporate philosophical argumentation into his discussion, however. After some brief remarks on Nietzsche's use of narrative, I will review his arguments in the First Treatise on the nature and assessment of values, agency and social identity.

Nietzsche embeds smaller narratives into the First Treatise's main narrative, and appends still more to the beginning and end of the Treatise, but there are no philosophical reflections on narrative as such. The Second and Third Treatises, with their digressions on historical method and meaning, more closely approximate reflection on narration in general. By initiating a 'genealogy', however, Nietzsche provokes questions about the form of his account. His inquiry results in an imagined story about morality's past. We can ask, then, why Nietzsche's account takes the form of a story, what ends are served in doing so, and how the story could achieve them. The story is not a mere diversion: it should convey something about the present status of morality and bear implications for our own ethical judgements. Nietzsche could have tried to explain this in terms of a 'genealogical method'. That is, he could have offered a procedure, justified this procedure as being epistemically privileged in some way, and legitimated his results in terms of following the procedure. But Nietzsche does not declare a method, does not attempt to legitimate a procedure, and does not indicate that the story exemplifies a method.

There is no methodology, but we can reconstruct the nature of Nietzsche's approach by reflecting on his aims. The text has a declared purpose: to criticise morality by providing a genealogy of its constitutive concepts and other elements. So what good does it do to tell stories about morality? There are many ways in which the stories could contribute to the overall aim. For example, stories of how moral concepts emerged and developed might show us that they emerged as a way of constructing an imaginary opposite to lived conditions, and this might shake our confidence that the concepts genuinely apply to anything. The stories might, by reference to long-forgotten purposes, show that morality has outlived its original usefulness and fails to contribute anything newly helpful or productive. The stories might function diagnostically, by showing how the adoption of moral discourse lies at the source of apparently unconnected ailments. Or telling stories might work like spreading malicious rumours, to make us like morality less whether or not we believe all the details. To varying extents, Nietzsche intends his stories to function in all of these ways.

Some of these tasks could be carried out without narrative, however, or by simply reporting the end of the story. Some of these tasks could even be carried out without regard to the accuracy of the telling. But Nietzsche's suggestion was that genealogy itself does the work of criticism. Insofar as we grasp the story of conceptual emergence and development, we understand morality better, and insofar as we understand morality better, we are more critical of it, or at least in a better position to question its standing. To be sure, Nietzsche's narratives also have heuristic and persuasive functions. But at least part of what Nietzsche wants to say is that the stories convey a distinctive form of understanding that enables criticism. The narratives can only function in this way, however, if morality itself is treated as distinctively historical; Nietzsche's use of narrative indicates something about what he takes the object of his inquiry to be. The narrative form is suitable if morality is not merely something that occurs in time, but something with a past, which may or may not have a future. For some things, such as persons, the Crown of Charlemagne, great rooms and nearly any other product of human culture, saying what it is requires more than specifying its qualities at particular moments. For such things, explicating what they are involves identifying the relationships that they sustain through time, the roles that they play, and what they mean to participants in shifting human practices. Genealogy treats morality as similarly historical, and thus to be revealed through the narratives about it. Furthermore, for these narratives to be critical, they must show something internally or inherently defective about it.

My suggestion, then, is that Nietzsche uses narrative to serve philosophical ends in two noteworthy respects. First, narrative serves cognitive ends by bringing together disparate phenomena to be understood as constituting morality. As Louis Mink has written, 'narrative is the form in which we make comprehensible the many successive interrelationships that are comprised by a career' (Mink 1987: 185–6). In this way, recounting the history of morality enables us to understand it by following the course of its 'career' rather than looking for a single, underlying unity. We can use narrative to grasp the fit by which a succession of changes belong together amid shifting contexts and purposes. Second, narrative conveys something about what Nietzsche is taking morality to be. He avoids treating morality as a theory about a particular, coherent, determinate value. In Nietzsche's telling, there is not a value of moral goodness that could be subject to analysis and explication. There is a range of practices that centre around a vocabulary that remains superficially somewhat stable while everything around it changes. These practices involve different ways of esteeming things, connected to different outlooks, relationships and attitudes. They may include normative theorising, too, but the use of genealogy puts the focus on how moral notions shape what people think, feel and do in their lives as wholes.

The narrative, in any case, contributes to the *assessment of values*; genealogical inquiry is meant to support a normative project. One thing to note about this project is that it does not involve any deep question of what value 'is'. Within the narratives, what is important is how people talk: what words, such as 'good' and 'evil', are available, what they are used to mean, how the 'value-judgments' (I: 3) that incorporate them shape what people think about themselves. The 'values' that Nietzsche discusses refer to particular vocabularies. The 'slave revolt' occurs when an old vocabulary is no longer adequate to the moral experience of a people and needs to be replaced. The revolt, that is, institutes a new way of talking, which in turn brings about a number of other psychological and social effects. So what Nietzsche represents in genealogy is not the occlusion or discovery of something independent from social practices that is somehow inherently valuable or compels our recognition of value. He is not trying to show us that, from a suitably neutral point of view, we can discern which of two alternatives is the better or more genuine value. Nietzsche represents, rather, alternatives between two modes of living, each of which has its own characteristic vocabulary to account for itself. Genealogy thus does not ask us to find the best value; rather, it calls us to compare how one vocabulary functioned within the context of a particular way of life with how another vocabulary functioned within the context of a different way of life. And this comparison does not lead to a judgement regarding which alternative is better, from some third standpoint. The comparison informs how we might arrive at the right vocabulary for our own potential future way of life.

Of course, it might seem as if Nietzsche is endorsing one set of values, and merely using the genealogies as a pretext for elaborating a conclusion that he has already drawn – the narratives would be a bit of propaganda for what he independently believes. In particular, Nietzsche is often taken to be championing the 'master morality' of the nobles in the process of relating the narrative. He claims that the priests brought on 'disease' (I: 7) and that the slave revolt in morality was incited by the hatred and vengefulness of the 'rabble' (I: 8). Aristocratic values, by contrast, 'presuppose a powerful physicality' (I: 7) and betoken flourishing, joyfulness and spontaneity. The 'nobles' generally seem to attract complimentary terms, while pejorative terms accrue to the inventors of slave morality. Perhaps most distinctly, Nietzsche offers a series of rhetorical questions about a possible resurgence of noble values: 'would precisely *that* not be something to desire with all our might? Even to will? Even to promote?' (I: 17). To be sure, Nietzsche wants a corrective here: a renewed contest between master and slave morality and a reintegration of noble values into our own self-understandings. This falls short of endorsing the adoption of master morality, however. Not only is no such endorsement made, but Nietzsche suggests later in the book – in the context of nihilism, which I will discuss again in Chapter 4 – that no such endorsement is possible; there is no set of values that is psychologically or culturally available for us to adopt. Genealogy, far from promoting a foregone conclusion, is better suited to refusing any clear result.

Nietzsche's examination of historically remote cultures is meant to bring to light something about *our own* practices, rather than to furnish examples for us to emulate. One conceit underlying Nietzsche's approach is that we do not really understand how *we* esteem, in part because this is tied up with a conceptual framework that we use without understanding what we are doing. The enterprise of genealogy illuminates what we are doing, then, by treating both master and slave moralities as our strange axiological inheritance, rather than as options that we should currently choose between. This inheritance, transformed and yet still unsettled, continues to shape who we are and what we do. Nietzsche insists that, however preponderant slave morality has become, we retain a complex legacy of competing values:

> One could even say that [the struggle between opposing values] has been carried ever higher and therefore it has become ever deeper, ever more spiritual: so that today perhaps no mark of the '*higher nature*', of the more spiritual nature is more decisive than being split in this sense and still a real battleground for these opposites. (I: 16)

We confront these values in a 'deeper', 'more spiritual' form than that in which they appeared earlier in their descent – the values in the narratives are not quite the same as what we might encounter today – and genealogy helps us with this confrontation.

The simplest reason not to take Nietzsche as endorsing one set of values over another, however, is that he is steadfastly ambivalent towards both sets.[13] He associates 'good and bad' and 'good and evil' each with both positive and negative characteristics, and

---

[13] For an account of one important form of ambivalence, the suggestion that 'spiritual illness' introduces the conditions for its own cure, see Neuhouser 2014. A similar position can be found in Zamosc 2011.

does not propose a procedure to weigh their relative merit. There is one complication in making a comparison here: Nietzsche has little to say about the values *per se*, but rather discusses them with respect to their typical exemplars or characteristic individuals. One might, on the one hand, make judgements about the values of pleasure and health, for example, and on the other hand, make judgements about people who value pleasure and about people who value health; Nietzsche's considerations are more like the latter. Nietzsche might not even think that 'good' in either sense picks out determinate qualities that can be attributed to actual individuals; his characterisation of the values is of the lives in which they play a prominent role.

Nietzsche associates master morality, in any case, with bold, loyal and generous nobles, who are healthy and cheerful. But they are also shallow and unreflective, prone to bouts of senseless violence and, ultimately, boring. Slave morality, by contrast, engenders low-minded, envious, deceitful and fearful types. In short, moral values represent the 'ultimate sickness' (P: 5) and the 'danger of dangers' (P: 6) for peoples who were already psychologically and physiologically sickly. At the same time, however, Nietzsche insists that this is a productive sickness that makes novel human capacities and ends possible. So, as I mentioned above, Nietzsche claims that 'human history would be a far too stupid matter without the spirit it has acquired on the part of the impotent' (I: 7), and furthermore, 'it was only on the soil of this *essentially dangerous* form of human existence, the priestly form, that human beings became *an interesting animal* at all' (I: 6). Slave morality comes with costs in well-being, but it also contributes to making life more interesting and meaningful. To be sure, one could try to assess the trade-off between a healthy, vigorous stupidity and an enervating, melancholy depth, but Nietzsche does not even do that. He presents the possibilities of moral experience that lie in our past but that do not persist as possibilities for us.

This presentation nevertheless suggests one of the three main ways in which the genealogical narratives serve the assessment of values. For lack of a better term, we can call this first line of thought an argument about *styles* of valuing. When Nietzsche refers to 'good and evil' and 'good and bad' as 'values' (I: 16), he does not treat them as determinate magnitudes, as if they reduce morality to points along a continuum. Each 'value', rather, brings with it a whole range of related attitudes, considerations and privileged forms of interaction that systematically differ from the other practice of valuing. At least that is part of what Nietzsche aims to show: that 'good and evil' is not a single quality, but a style comprised by a range of interconnected practices. His first proposal for the assessment of values, then, is simply that, once genealogy depicts these styles more clearly, we can assess them in terms of how well they maintain their own values, or the values that we might otherwise be committed to trying to maintain. His argument is not that he can show, by some decisive feature, that one value is better or worse than another. The general form of his argument, rather, is that a better understanding of how various commitments are possible or impossible together in a way of life could give us reasons for rethinking our commitments.

One example of this line of thinking appears when he is discussing the noble human being's inability to take harms and misdeeds seriously. Nietzsche writes, 'Here alone real "love of one's enemies" is also possible – assuming that it is possible at all on earth' (I: 10). Nietzsche's reference, of course, is to the Gospel according to Matthew, where Jesus enjoins, 'Love your enemies, and pray for those who persecute you' (Matt. 5:44). Jesus' instruction is meant to be paradoxical, and Nietzsche's claim is that it is in fact impossible within slave morality. We need to reconstruct Nietzsche's thinking here, but his main argument seems to be that slave morality involves a style of personality and interpersonal regard that is inherently fearful and suspicious, so that the most philanthropic attitude that it could sustain would be a suspension of hostilities or, perhaps, an impersonal regard for general welfare. Slave morality, although good at regulating behaviour in predictable ways, emphasises the susceptibility to harm of private individuals. Even if it fosters a mode of living in which welfare is protected and there are no overt hostilities, Nietzsche contends, the regard for others as potentially hostile remains. Social life is filled with suppressed enmity that is governed by impersonal regard; there is not even conceptual space for loving one's enemies. Noble morality, by contrast, involves a social world

THE FIRST TREATISE

filled with contempt and indifference, but also views enemies as worthy and even admirable rather than as vicious and malevolent. Nietzsche's general argument is one about consistency, then. Insofar as we might place importance on 'loving one's enemies', then we should consider the values with which that coheres. Slave morality, as Nietzsche sees it, attempts to co-opt the value of noble morality but it cannot, and thus does not respect the commitments that it endorses.

The second main way in which the genealogical narrative serves the assessment of values regards *availability*. Genealogy can show, that is, that values depend on historical background conditions: particular values make sense in the context of a way of life in which they have a role, and fit with the prevalent social hierarchies and forms of organisation. Noble morality, for example, fits where there are nobles, and there are nobles where economic arrangements and other social relationships allow for it. If values do depend on background conditions, they might be unavailable to us as candidates for acceptance. One could imagine changing the background conditions to make attractive values available: we might change the world to make it hospitable to noble values so that we could meaningfully affirm them. It is hard to see, however, how Nietzsche's genealogy could be endorsing this. Genealogy's appeals to history show values as rooted in their contexts; they are not surveys of the best values of all time. But the imagined imperative to change the background conditions requires two positions akin to the latter enterprise. It requires not only acontextual claims about the best value, but also a demand that we should take a kind of demiurgic standpoint. The best value in the best possible world, even if there were such a thing, would not be compelling *for us*; we have no reason to take up someone else's values. The unavailability of values can thus at least furnish a negative criterion of assessment. We can reject the values that we cannot have, and seek out the values that are available to us in the contexts we might find ourselves in.

If we were to take genealogy as offering explanatory accounts of individuals' changes in belief, then no morality would ever in principle be more unavailable than another, since an individual can adopt almost any belief at a given moment in time. (Taking this perspective perhaps makes it difficult to see how individual nobles were persuaded or compelled to look at things from the point of view of the slave, and Nietzsche does not address this matter.) Nietzsche's genealogies, however, attempt to account for socially prevalent patterns of authority, and not just private beliefs: a morality or a 'manner of valuation' (I: 7) involves a common discourse that identifies particular ends as worthwhile, makes it possible to justify actions to others, and helps to impart understanding of the practical demands that arise in the course of one's life. A morality performs a function in Nietzsche's telling, that of enabling persons to gain a sense of purpose and make sense of their lives; it thus both reflects and organises the structure of a way of life. For Nietzsche, however, the moralities that he describes have distinctively failed.

Nietzsche is clearest about this when he claims that after thousands of years of competition, slave morality has achieved 'victory' (I: 8) over noble morality. We lack a social world in which noble morality might fit and the psychological dispositions to make it tenable; it can hardly make sense of lives in which people go to work, separate their private lives from their public identities, wait in line at the supermarket and expect strangers to respect their rights. (Hercules would have fared poorly in applying for a job or nearly any other aspect of modern life.) This defect, furthermore, is conclusive and irremediable: noble values (as represented by 'Rome') have 'succumbed beyond all doubt' (I: 16). The defeat was not a one-off event, but part of a historical process. The nobles, strong but stupid, could not bother with articulating and defending a basis for their standing, and however admirable that might have been, it was not conducive to their kind of authority perpetuating itself over a long period of time; social authority seems to need a publicly articulated rationale to survive. Inarticulate force was effective for some local tasks, and re-emerges in sporadic outbreaks, but cannot shape enduring social institutions, and this failure shows itself in the impossibility of bringing back premodern social relations.

In distancing himself from the slogan 'Beyond Good and Bad' (I: 17), however, Nietzsche also implies that that value – the good/bad dichotomy – is ultimately ineliminable: no way of life could function without any interest in being better or worse in that sense.

One passage even combines the 'subterranean' character of slave morality with the heroic purposiveness of noble morality, suggesting that the victory of slave morality is a preparation for something else: 'born as we are to a subterranean fighting existence [. . .] we experience again and again the golden hour of victory – and then we stand there, as we were born, ready for new, more, difficult, more distant things' (I: 12). Here Nietzsche offers a strangely optimistic recasting of the historical process, so that it makes a reappropriation of noble values newly available. Nietzsche's position is certainly complex, but in any case he uses genealogy to show that not every value is available at every moment, and that this can furnish a criterion for us in our assessment of values.

A different way – and the most prominent one in the First Treatise – in which the genealogical narratives serve the assessment of values is through the identification of *harms*. Most of Nietzsche's attention goes to the harms of slave morality, but surprisingly, this is not because he claims that slavishness is inherently bad or that its values are aesthetically corrupt. Nietzsche claims, rather, that an outcome of slave morality's triumph over noble morality is that 'we *suffer* from human beings' (I: 11): its victory has been costly for us all, in particular because what admiration for humanity that we were capable of has been replaced by self-aversion, or because we experience our own condition as a fundamentally unpleasant, painful one. Nietzsche elaborates the harms of morality, and of slave morality in particular, in many other ways, too. These discussions help to fill out the picture of the 'value of values' that I discussed in the previous chapter. In the Preface Nietzsche suggested that we evaluate (or 'critique') moral values by assessing the value of those values: 'we need a *critique* of moral values, *the value of these values must first be called in question* . . . morality as symptom, as mask . . . but also morality as cause, as remedy, as stimulant, as restraint, as poison' (P: 6). A primary way of understanding the 'value of moral values', then, is in terms of how they are implicated in harms. Morality itself functions 'as a cause' of psychological or physiological damage, or moral values 'represent' (I: 11) or signify something pathological about those who hold them. This gives us a way to assess values: in terms of the harms that they cause or represent.

In that case, we need to figure out what the harms are and how they are connected to morality; these are puzzling matters. They are puzzling because they seem to require us to take *morality* as inflicting harms on *humanity*. Nietzsche's doubts about morality and moral phenomena extend to whether or not they exist at all; it is thus not easy to see how morality could be causally effective, or what it would mean for it to be so. And Nietzsche often characterises that which the damage is inflicted on as 'humanity' – but how can humanity as a whole be affected?

There are a number of ways in which we could think about the connection between morality and possible harms, and to some extent Nietzsche endorses all of them. We could think about 'humanity' as a collection of individuals, each of whom are affected with respect to their actions, beliefs or feelings; the harms accrue to individuals who would otherwise be better off. Or morality could cause damage to culture as a whole, by preventing the creation of great exemplars or foreclosing important possibilities for human excellence. The long history of morality might, alternatively, have implanted instincts in human beings that conflict with the current conditions of our flourishing. It is worth noting, however, that Nietzsche does not explicate the harms of morality in quite these terms, and he does not offer an account of what actions to perform, how culture should be restructured, or how our instincts might be reshaped. He does, however, insist that the critique of morality culminates in a 'revaluation of values' (I: 7; I: 8): the only way to address whatever harm morality has caused is by reassessing all values, or by replacing morality with a new scheme of values. We can understand this as a way of capturing what it means for harms to be properly attributable to morality: if present harms do not require a change in morality to be remedied, then the harms do not belong to morality. Not all harms work this way, of course: if a building suffers damage from flooding, then the remedy is not to challenge water, and a wound is not healed by revaluing weapons. But the harms of morality are presumably, somehow, *ongoing*; if they were merely a past trauma, then they would not be of much concern to us in the present. Addressing them would thus require a challenge to morality, and not contravening moral rules and finding balms for morality's effects.

I cannot offer a more substantive defence of my proposal until Chapter 4, but here I can at least suggest what sort of harm requires a revaluation of values to address. The harms of morality do not come *primarily* from morality's effect on occurrent psychological states, prevailing cultural relations or the implanting of instincts, although it has a deleterious effect on all of those things. The primary way in which morality effects harm, rather, is by systematically depriving persons of the interpretative means to make sense of their activities, desires, feelings and selves. What morality does is create a hermeneutic situation in which individuals have no alternative but to understand themselves in moral terms; it thereby becomes impossible for anyone to articulate what they are and what they want so that they might lead their life in a satisfying way. Nietzsche's point is that there are social conditions for being able to meaningfully relate to one's own activities, emotions and drives, and so on, and morality destroys those conditions. When all of our possible self-descriptions are filtered through moral categories, persons become estranged from their own wants and needs. Because of morality we lack the discursive resources to make sense of ourselves, and this is not a momentary condition but an ongoing process in which morality thins out and empties our discourse of the specificity of cares and satisfactions, and we, pursuing misshapen ends or misrecognising our own emotions, intensify our own failures of self-understanding. And this constant misunderstanding could, in turn, be the basis of ill health, both psychological and physiological.

In the First Treatise Nietzsche also makes a series of arguments about the nature of *agency* and some associated topics. One argument, about the idea of egoism, comes up only in passing, although it anticipates some of his later discussions. While discussing the English psychologists, Nietzsche criticises the distinction between 'egoistic' and 'non-egoistic' acts. He writes, 'it is only with a *decline* of aristocratic value-judgments that this whole opposition of "egoistic" and "unegoistic" imposes more and more on the human conscience' (I: 2). The immediate criticism is that the prevalence of the distinction depends on value commitments that are themselves historically local. So Nietzsche's suggestion is that the distinction is bad because it is a limited way of looking at things, and one that reflects 'moral valuation' (I: 2).

Nietzsche's case against 'egoism' runs deeper than this, however. What he calls attention to is how the concept of egoism is 'imposed on the human conscience'. That is, 'egoism' functions in agents' reflective views of their actions, rather than the actions themselves. The distinction between egoistic and unegoistic appears to distinguish actions into two kinds: either generated out of one's conception of self-interest, or generated out of one's conception of others' interests. This, however, does not track anything independent about the workings of agency. It arises from an evaluative standpoint that treats our activity as divided between those actions to which we are selfishly driven and those we are burdened by others to perform; Nietzsche's implicit claim here is that this is a poor way of thinking about our motivations, our relations to others and our interests. We are not driven either by pure self-regard or by exclusive regard of others, and we could not make sense of our interests in such terms in any case. For reasons discussed below, Nietzsche also rejects characterising actions by their source and locating that source in rational calculation. So he is not praising egoism and denigrating altruism. He is saying that it is misguided to classify actions in this way. For Nietzsche, then, the distinction is thus worse than the famous categories of animals in Borges's imaginary Chinese encyclopedia ('those that belong to the Emperor, embalmed ones, those that are trained, suckling pigs, mermaids . . .') (Borges 1993: 103); those categories might be fanciful, overlapping and subjective, but they at least have clear extensions or intensions. The distinction is more like Bronson Alcott's division between 'aspiring vegetables' that reach towards the heavens and the base ones that are unworthy of being eaten (see, for example, Blanding 1971). Nothing properly fits in either category, and so the categories can only be used poorly.

The main discussion of agency in the First Treatise takes place in aphorism 13.[14] It starts with a parable, so it is worthwhile to

---

[14] My reading of this passage has been influenced by two important papers: Bernard Williams's 'Nietzsche's Minimalist Moral Psychology' (Williams 1995) and Robert Pippin's 'Lightning and Flash, Agent and Deed (*GM* I:6–17)' (Pippin 2006). Aaron Ridley's recent book, *The Deed is Everything*, would have been influential had I managed to read it before writing this (Ridley 2018: esp. 76–81).

review the parable before addressing the philosophical conclusions that Nietzsche draws from it:

> It does not seem strange that lambs bear a grudge against the great birds of prey: only this is no reason to hold it against the great birds of prey that they snatch themselves little lambs. And when the lambs say to each other 'these birds of prey are evil; and whoever is a bird of prey to the least possible extent, rather even its opposite, a lamb – does he not have to be good?' then there is nothing wrong with this construction of an ideal, even if the birds of prey were to look upon this a bit sarcastically and perhaps say to themselves: '*we* do not bear a grudge against them, these good lambs, in fact we love them: nothing is tastier than a tender lamb'. (I: 13)

The parable is not meant to justify or glorify predation, although it does undercut the lambs' point of view. Nietzsche's aim here, rather, is to give an account of the metaphysical interposition that underlies the invention of evil and the creation of a distinctively moral account of agency. The default account of the relevant action is that a bird of prey snatches a little lamb; if further explanation were added, it would simply be that that is the sort of thing that a bird of prey does – that is, snatching lambs fits into the character of what it does, given its abilities, dispositions and preferences. But the 'construction of an ideal' allows the lambs to re-characterise what happened, even though the birds of prey do not recognise this ideal and therefore speak a different language, as it were, in describing what happens. By inserting the effecting of will prior to the performance of the deed, the lambs make room for the possibility of evil. According to the lambs' re-characterisation, then, the birds of prey are faced with a choice; they choose to snatch the little lamb; their choice is rooted in their evil nature; and they are accountable because of the nature of their choice. At the same time the lambs recast their own weakness as a voluntary achievement.

In Nietzsche's analysis, the moral characterisation of action – in part influenced by the 'seduction of language' (I: 13) – places a subject before the effecting of the deed. The grammar of the subject–predicate form makes it seem necessary to do so. Typically, a *subject* acts, and if this can be taken to reflect something deep about the structure of agency, then an inside-out model of agency might seem intuitive. An action, then, is the externalisation of some bit of private mental content, as effected by a subject who has a capacity to take up different internal states but is, at some level, indifferent with respect to them. There are some specially motivating internal states, whether they be volitions, choices, passions or something else, and an agent is someone who brings these already determinate states out into the world by enacting them. Nietzsche's argument here, however, is that there is no content to the internal state except for that of the performance, and thus nothing to attribute efficacy to; as he claims, 'the doing is everything' (I: 13). The subject's effecting of the action is just added on as a doubling of the deed, whereby the same occurrence is posited once as an effect and again as a cause of the very same effect. This double-positing is a moral prejudice, however, and stems from vengeful motivations. It allows for a form of blame that treats persons as culpable for who they are. In the parable the lambs 'gain the right to make the bird of prey *accountable* for being a bird of prey' (I: 13).

Nietzsche uses the analogy of a lightning flash to illustrate his point about doubling. If we say, 'the lightning flashes', then it appears as if we are saying something about a subject, lightning, that it is performing a deed, namely flashing. But there is only the lightning – nothing, as Nietzsche says, that serves as a 'substratum' (I: 13) of the deed, nothing that is 'behind' (I: 13) the deed. And according to Nietzsche, just as 'ordinary people' separate lightning from its flashing, in the same way 'popular morality' separates strength from expressions of strength, 'as if behind the strong one there were an indifferent substratum *free to* express strength or not to' (I: 13). The idea of an 'indifferent elective subject' (I: 13) who stands behind the deeds, determines what they are independent of performing them, and possesses a freedom that can make them praiseworthy or culpable is a 'fiction' (I: 13) added on. The event that we identify is simply the deed. The addition of the indifferent subject purports to be essential to the performance of the deed, but it is superfluous; it represents a strategy for imputing moral blame to agents rather than agency itself.

Nietzsche nevertheless preserves the category of agency. He might have insisted that, without the neutral subject, nothing could count as a deed: descriptions of actions need to be re-characterised as mere movements, without aims or 'wills'. But, of course, in claiming that 'the doing is everything', Nietzsche insists on understanding events as *activity*; there may even be subjects, as long as they are not duplicative, moral ones. With the idea of a moral subject, one understands actions by locating the source in hidden depths, 'as if behind the strong one there were an indifferent substratum free to express strength or not to' (I: 13). Nietzsche's point, however, is that one only recognises a subject through the expressions; there is a 'strong one' only on account of the expressions of strength, in the above example. Expressions are outward and thus subject to public criteria of effectiveness and interpretation, so we can recognise activity as such in these terms. The subject, then, is what bears a public relationship to its public activity, rather than a source of private volitional content.

This feature of agency, that it involves instituting a public relationship to one's expressions, connects it to *politicised identity*. Nietzsche does not explicitly make this connection in the First Treatise, perhaps because he is primarily discussing an archaic world in which there are few possibilities for a public identity beyond 'good' and 'bad'. His characterisation of agency has nevertheless influenced some contemporary ways of thinking about identity. Judith Butler, for example, after quoting I: 13, writes, 'In an application that Nietzsche himself would not have anticipated or condoned, we might state [. . .] There is no gender identity behind the expressions of gender; that identity is performatively constituted by the very "expressions" that are said to be its results' (Butler 1990: 25). One might think, on the contrary, that gender identity is given by nature, as it were, and this identity defines the person. Gender, on this view, is what one is prior to any 'expressions', and how one thinks, feels and acts flows from that. Butler claims, however, that the performances are prior to the identity; the expressions are everything, as Nietzsche might have said. Gendered performances 'constitute' a sense of identity: that there are determinate kinds of gendered subjects, that everyone belongs to one of these kinds, that this belonging makes us what we are, and that our encounters with others are structured around these identities.

Butler elaborates on how gendered identity is manufactured through performance:

> Such acts, gestures, enactments, generally construed, are *performative* in the sense that the essence or identity that they otherwise purport to express are *fabrications* manufactured and sustained through corporeal signs and other means. That the gendered body is performative suggests that it has no ontological status apart from the various acts which constitute its reality. This also suggests its reality is fabricated as an interior essence. (Butler 1990: 136, emphasis original)

In Butler's telling of the process, the performance works by sustaining a belief in gender as an 'interior essence' that is ontologically separate from all activity. Activity gives content to 'corporeal signs' that are manifested publicly; this content is linked to identity when it is falsely seen as rooted in something hidden that stands behind the performance; the hidden essence, more than the behaviour, is taken to represent what the person is; and then ascriptions of this essence are imposed on the 'gendered body', creating expectations for particular kinds of performance. Nietzsche, as Butler notes, neglected gender in the *Genealogy*, and his story of the process placed greater emphasis on the metaphysical roots and practical consequences of establishing such a belief in an inner essence, but he nevertheless has a similar account.

What Nietzsche's and Butler's accounts have in common is attention to a transposition whereby agency is located in an inner essence rather than an outer activity, with the effect that regulating subjects is carried out by producing norms of behaviour. For both of them, this is a disorienting and dangerous process. In forming politicised identities, we establish a relationship to our deeds by acting on norms: we express who we are by trying to live up to the standards that define us. The standards do not, however, have any content apart from everyone's enactment of them, or any binding force apart from their recognition. The norms seem compelling because they seem to exist independently; indeed, we construct them so that they seem to stand apart from all 'expressions'. But, with respect to identity, we act on norms that we are instituting while we act them out, all the while trying to express something that purports to be already established. So on this picture, we make sense of who we are at the cost of chasing after empty ideals and deluding ourselves about their sanction, and at the same time producing new content with every performance. The regulatory work of politicised identity functions by making it seem as if there is an unrevisable standard we have to meet. But since identity is constituted out of performances, every new performance allows for a revised authorship of identity.

There is a good side and bad side, then, from the perspective of this view of politicised identity. If the norms that we try to live by are always indeterminate and shifting, then they are uninhabitable: we can never realise them in ourselves. This makes the norms of identity self-estranging, since we always fail by our own standards; self-deluding, since our performances never mean what we think they do; and self-hostile, since we internalise these failures as part of our identities. On the other hand, the performance of identity is inevitably productive. It perpetually creates new forms of identity that are not accountable to anything outside of our shared practices. Some of these new identities could be based on hopes, as yet unrealised aspirations for solidarity or dreams of unattainable ideals. Because politicised identity is about how we make sense of our shared practices rather than accountability to an inner essence, this can be a way to think of ourselves as aspiring to lives with others.

Methodological and rhetorical issues

There are two goals of this section. One is to begin a larger argument about Nietzsche's methodology in the *Genealogy*. Not only do the three Treatises of the *Genealogy* fill out an account of morality through their narratives, but they also – I want to show – successively develop an argument about method that moves from a naturalistic approach to a genealogical one. Here I present an outline of the overall argument and its first part, which correlates to the First Treatise. The other main goal of this section is to examine some of Nietzsche's rhetorical strategies through a close reading of an exemplary passage, aphorism 9. I will not offer a comprehensive analysis of its rhetorical features; I am not going to mention the paralepsis and all the other figures in that passage. I do intend, however, to show how closely its philosophical aims are interconnected with its rhetorical strategies, and indicate some of the ways in which it is representative of Nietzsche's rhetoric in the *Genealogy* as a whole.

My broader argument is that Nietzsche begins with a very basic commitment to naturalism, at least in a minimal sense of intending to offer a 'this-worldly' account of how morality emerged among human animals, and concludes with a genealogical understanding of how to make sense of meanings. This argument proceeds in three steps. First, Nietzsche's naturalistic account of morality commits him to providing a role for semantic content. In particular, Nietzsche offers psychological explanations to account for the 'conceptual transformations' that make moral judgements available. These psychological explanations not only account for semantic change, but they also depend on appeals to semantic content. Second, Nietzsche links psychological explanation to a historical account of concept use. Psychological explanations require situating the relevant phenomena in the context of social practices, and this leads to a historical account of semantic content. Third, Nietzsche makes a case that a historical account of the correct use of certain concepts should be responsive to an account of which concepts to employ at all. That is, we need assurance not only that we are applying our concepts correctly, but that we are using the right ones. Providing an account of morality, then, requires explaining the relevant semantic content from what might be called the 'inner' perspective, and this in turn requires a genealogical understanding of how to make sense of the meaning of human activity.

The steps of Nietzsche's methodological argument correlate with the three Treatises. In the First Treatise, Nietzsche aims to carry out an inquiry that is naturalistic at least in spirit. Although he might be committed to a more robust form of naturalism, with a privileged ontology or model of inquiry, the basic task that he sets for himself is to locate morality within the practices of biologically constrained creatures with no special powers of discernment. This differs not only from a supernatural account of the powers or sanctions, but also from the enterprise of moral theory, which aims to set out the privileged ground and content of morality. Since Nietzsche instead considers the 'descent' of morality, he needs to come to an understanding of how moral practices could have emerged from a condition without them. His account of this transition turns out to depend on appeals to semantic content. Not all human behaviours depend on the grasp of conceptual content, but the descent of morality would be incomprehensible without the roles that meanings play.

There is a simple case for understanding Nietzsche's project in this way. His accounts of 'the *descent* of our moral prejudices' (P: 2), or alternatively 'the origin of morality' (P: 5), are about the conceptual history of the basic vocabulary of morality. The big change that Nietzsche wishes to understand is that persons could conceive of themselves in moral terms: in particular, it became possible for persons to think of themselves and others as *evil*. So the accounts are not directed to explaining how individuals came to believe or do something at particular moments in time; they are not causal accounts that fill out a sequence of events by appeal to states of affairs and lawlike generalisations. Nietzsche, rather, accounts for the availability of the conceptual categories that allow us to think of ourselves – falsely, for him – as moral beings. The focus is how it became *possible* for something to think something, rather than what caused someone to believe something or otherwise affected them. In another work Nietzsche wrote, '*what things are called* is unspeakably more important than what they are' (GS §58), and here, then, he accounts for our capacity to call things 'evil' rather than evil itself or even thoughts about evil. The availability of conceptual resources is not a purely linguistic matter: the conceptual resources only become available (or 'grow', as Nietzsche sometimes likes to say) under certain 'material' conditions, and the availability of the resources does contribute to the explanation of some behaviours. But Nietzsche's attention is directed to the general availability of moral concepts, and perhaps why they were adopted and became prevalent, rather than the effective cause of particular events. And this gives semantic content a role in both what is to be explained and how it is explained.

The textual evidence that Nietzsche is pursuing a kind of conceptual history is straightforward. There are, for example, the titles of the first two Treatises: they announce their topics as the terms 'good and evil', 'good and bad', 'guilt', 'bad conscience' and so on, with quotation marks to indicate that he is referring to the terms rather than to the things. At various points, furthermore, he makes his interest in *'conceptual transformation'* (I: 4) more explicit; indeed, this seems to be the distinctive task of the First Treatise. For example, when criticising the English psychologists, he insists that their mistakes concern 'the descent of the concept and judgment "good"' (I: 2). Much of the First Treatise is carried out in terms of etymological claims, and he concludes by proposing an essay competition on the *'the history of the development of moral concepts'* (I: 17n). In the Second Treatise, he discusses what I have called the availability of moral concepts in terms of the emergence of the 'moral conceptual world' (II: 6). More generally, Nietzsche's accounts invoke figures and types rather than historical individuals, and the 'broadest and longest facts' (III: 11) rather than particular events, because he is interested in how and why moral concepts became available.

One could offer a counter-argument to my claim that giving a conceptual history depends on an ineliminable role for semantic content by insisting that a conceptual history is just a kind of causal history. Concepts, the counter-argument would go, are just representations in particular minds at particular moments in time, so conceptual history is just explaining how those representations got there. In that case, there is no separation between occurrent mental entities and conceptual contents, so there is no question of conceptual repertory on this picture – only whatever ideas someone happens to have at particular moments – and Nietzsche's explanatory project would thus simply turn out to be a causal one. I think there are independent reasons to reject such a picture of conceptual history, but in any case it is not

Nietzsche's.¹⁵ A distinctive aspect of Nietzsche's approach is that he takes as an issue how we understand the domain of morality at all. It is not obvious, even to Nietzsche, what 'morality' means or how it might form a unity, but it is a topic worthy of consideration. In the other picture of conceptual history, there is no such topic: there is *only* the diversity of particular representations in particular minds. On the causal picture, there would be nothing for Nietzsche to do but resort to the English psychologists' approach. That is, without the emergence of the 'moral conceptual world' as a distinct topic, the only available task would be the one that he criticises: taking contemporary views of morality as a starting point and speculating on the proximate pathways that led up to them.

There are also some bits of textual evidence that speak against taking Nietzsche's story of moral concepts as a causal account of particular representations. Nietzsche later refers to the terms of morality as 'paradoxical and paralogical concepts' (III: 16). This characterises them in normative terms, of how they seem to violate the demands of consistent belief and inference. That is to say, Nietzsche does not treat them merely as the result of a causal process, but in terms of the defective ways in which they fit into our making of judgements. Thus, in a passage I quoted earlier, Nietzsche refers to the 'matter of determining the descent of the concept and judgment "good"' (I: 2). Judgement would be superfluous here on the causal picture, as it would just be the same representation once again. But Nietzsche expresses interest in both the content of concepts and also in how those concepts are used to form and assert beliefs; to invoke judgement here is to insist that concepts are suited to such a role. Nietzsche often distinguishes between singular representations and the forms of authority that underwrite judgements; judgements have a warrant and a logical structure, so they are congruous with but distinct from concepts. So moral concepts are not merely things that happen to minds, because they need to be used in structuring judgements.

---

¹⁵ See, for example, Gardner 2009: 27: '*Sinn* . . . is treated generally by Nietzsche in a way that either does not imply, or that positively precludes, its hedonistic psychological reduction.' Sense or meaning, that is, cannot be explained in non-semantic terms.

Even if we did take the project of the First Treatise to be one of causal explanation, there is still an irreducible role for semantic content. There are surely causal processes taking place in the emergence of morality, since things change and states of affairs are replaced by others. The processes by which this happens in Nietzsche's narratives are typically psychological ones, however, and these, as Nietzsche describes them, require meaningful activity. Much of the story of morality turns on 'vengefulness' (I: 7; cf. I: 14), for example. But vengeance is semantically complex: it requires a source of past harm, a way to cause harm to that source, and an appropriate connection between the harm suffered and the harm inflicted. For vengefulness to proceed, it has to do so under that description; one cannot be vengeful entirely by accident, for example.[16] A distinguishing feature of Nietzsche's characterisation of vengeance and other psychological processes is thus that they are *expressive*. That is to say, they do not merely produce movement, but operate under a description. 'Strength', in a very general example, 'expresses itself as strength' (I: 13). This suggests that it is effective when it brings about its appropriate content; it can fail, but its activity is just the realisation of its particular expressiveness. And this is why meanings must fit into the project of the First Treatise and whatever form of naturalism it involves. The appeal to human psychology requires an understanding of its expressive character.

 I will resume the methodological argument in the next chapter, but now I turn to the rhetorical strategies of aphorism 9. Nietzsche begins this aphorism with a rhetorical question in the form of an interjection: ' – "But why are you still talking about *more noble* ideals?"' (I: 9). If the dash and the quotation marks go unnoticed, then the reader will not realise until the end of a long speech that this is not Nietzsche speaking. Only at the end of the aphorism does Nietzsche attribute it to a 'freethinker': 'This is the epilogue of a "freethinker" to my speech, an honest beast as he has richly demonstrated [. . .] he had listened to me up till

---

[16] See, for example, Griswold 2013: 87: 'How vengefulness is understood by both parties is therefore essential to its meaning and achievement [. . .] parties to the exchange must understand each other's state of mind in a suitable way.'

then and could not stand to hear me be silent' (I: 9). There is nothing here that fits well in a philosophical treatise, even if none of it is entirely out of place in the *Genealogy*. The most striking thing is the incorporation of another voice and other kinds of texts into the work. There is not only a 'freethinker' who speaks, but this freethinker is reacting to a speech that Nietzsche had made in the previous aphorism. That speech was given in the second-person plural, implying an audience apart from the reader; the freethinker, meanwhile, shifts oddly between 'you', 'I' and 'we'. All this gives the discussion a dramatic context, with a dispute among various personae rather than just the voicing of hypothetical objections. Nietzsche's characterisation of his interlocutor might be unreliable, however. 'Freethinker' appears in scare quotes, and the other terms of description seem sardonic: that he has demonstrated himself to be an 'honest beast' (I: 9), for example. The dispute, in Nietzsche's telling, also turns on an audible silence.

Nietzsche's presentation raises a number of puzzles: who is the freethinker, why can he not help but reply, why not talk about noble ideas, and many others that arise within the freethinker's speech. The most immediate puzzle, however, is why Nietzsche uses separate voices and a dramatic context at all. One thing this accomplishes is that it makes the relationship between the author and the text problematic. Normally we might expect, in a philosophical treatise, the words on the page to represent the author's views; the author is asserting them in some unproblematic way. But Nietzsche is calling this into question. The words are perhaps not properly his own, or they are his but he is not asserting them, or they are his fictive literary creation. He invokes dramatic irony at the end of the passage, too: he, the author, knows more than the text itself indicates. The most important thing about incorporating separate voices, however, is how it allows Nietzsche to represent different standpoints. Some of these standpoints might even be versions of Nietzsche himself: the speechmaker of aphorism 8 seems to have different concerns from the narrator of morality's descent, for example. The boundaries between these standpoints are often difficult to discern, however, because they are not drawn in terms of explicit claims of disagreement. Indeed, the standpoints often agree on basic historical facts and even shared cultural experience. They differ, however, in the background assumptions and implicit views that shape their reactions and can make meaningful communication difficult. Nietzsche's use of voices allows him to represent this confusing divergence of views.

The main alternative standpoint of aphorism 9 is, of course, the 'freethinker'. The freethinker – and this is part of what makes the passage initially confusing – is not that far from Nietzsche's own point of view. (The term Nietzsche uses here, *Freigeist*, is one that he associated with himself in some of his earlier works.)[17] A freethinker, in general, is someone who thinks of himself as having liberated himself from traditional forms of authority through his own power of thought.[18] As one might expect of Nietzsche, too, a freethinker is opposed to grounding authority claims in religious or metaphysical dogma, and instead roots a secular hope for humanity in his own self-produced intellectual confidence. The freethinker of aphorism 9 is cautiously ironic, too: he raises claims without asserting them, mentions terms without using them, and qualifies his conjectures. He is, in some respects, close enough to Nietzsche that Nietzsche can use his appearance to draw a contrast with himself.

The freethinker of aphorism 9 sees himself as in agreement with Nietzsche on the main details of the narrative. The values of the archaic masters have been replaced in a long social process. From a contemporary perspective this process had some unfortunate aspects; it even took a kind of Jewish or Christian

---

[17] The subtitle of *Human, All Too Human* is 'a book for *freie Geister*', and that work and the two subsequent books are sometimes thought of as the '*Freier Geist*' trilogy. See Franco 2011: ix.

[18] Here, as with the 'English psychologists', Nietzsche has particular individuals in mind, but those examples are less important than the characterisation that he provides in the text. For example, in *Ecce Homo* Nietzsche names the theologian David Strauss as the 'leading free spirit in Germany' (Nietzsche 2005: 114). But in the Preface to the second volume of *Human, All Too Human*, Nietzsche indicates that Strauss is just an example of a widespread 'inflated Germanism' (Nietzsche 1986: 209). Nietzsche may have had other contemporary thinkers in mind, too; see Ansell-Pearson 2009. Another valuable discussion is Mullin 2000. The term 'free thinker' had a currency outside of Nietzsche's use of it; see, for example, Kaiser 1985.

'poisoning' (I: 9) to shift people to the new outlook. But the costs incurred in the process are much less important than the result. Through the achievement of moral progress we have arrived at a modern, rational position that frees us from oppressive authority and allows us to embrace the institutional features of the modern world. The freethinker thus sees the descent of morality as a progressive narrative of superior values gradually gaining adherence within culture. There are still some residues of primitive belief, most notably those associated with the Church. The Church, according to the freethinker, once served the useful function of aiding in the defeat of the masters, but has since become outmoded. It can only present its values in a vulgar, unappealing form, and so no longer has any necessary task or even 'right to exist' (I: 9) at all. Apart from the Church, however, the freethinker takes the overall trend to be unequivocally positive, and this is why he cannot resist responding to Nietzsche's speech. As he sees it, Nietzsche is trying to recount the narrative while failing to note its progressive trajectory.

The freethinker began with the question, 'Why are you still talking about noble ideals?', and in thinking about where he and Nietzsche diverge, that is indeed a good place to begin. The freethinker points out that even on Nietzsche's view, noble values have been conclusively defeated. Social and maybe even physiological change have rendered them irrecoverably lost; they are not viable options for anyone to live by and, from Nietzsche's standpoint, that is a significant consideration. From the freethinker's perspective, this implies that there is no longer any reason to talk about them, and this points to the general difference with Nietzsche. In the freethinker's progressive narrative, outmoded forms of valuing are simply replaced, with new and better systems of belief and value taking over; the only drama in the story is how quickly the vestigial practices can be swept away in favour of a 'truly modern taste' (I: 9). From this perspective the only other narrative possibilities that he can imagine are turning back to the master morality, or turning back to the authority of the Church, and these are both absurd. The freethinker's narrative is, in part, a story about the originality of his own standpoint, about his own continual self-separation from the past, so the past is bound to seem both irrelevant and bad. But that is not Nietzsche's narrative.

Nietzsche's narrative is instead one of continuity, in particular that the freethinker's 'modern taste' is an extension of the standpoint that he decries. The freethinker realises that there is a causal connection there, but Nietzsche sees a substantive one. The freethinker is looking for a secularised form of 'redemption' (I: 9) and thinks that it has been found in the triumph of popular values and the social world that is built around them. Nietzsche only spells out his position with the narrative of the *Genealogy* as a whole, and he does not mention freethinkers again until III: 24. But discussing noble ideals is Nietzsche's way of representing a different trajectory than the freethinker does: one in which creating the appearance of progress is the latest link in an extended series of reactive failures. With respect to the freethinker in particular, Nietzsche characterises him as an elitist, who is contemptuous of those with 'crude and peasant-like' beliefs (I: 9) and sees himself as the vanguard of history, but has no way of making sense of his superior standing. His hope is that a 'delicate intelligence and a truly modern taste' (I: 9) effectively 'seduces' (I: 9) better than older values, but this hope is itself ungrounded.

The freethinker does convey some awareness of his connection with the religious tradition that he rejects: 'the church repels us, not its poison' (I: 9). This makes the connection incidental, however. There would be overlap, in that both the Church and the freethinker partake in 'poison', but he can still find the Church independently repellent. But what is the poison? 'Poison' and its synonym 'intoxication' recur several times, but their meaning evaporates with each appearance; there is a metonymic chain that seems to lead nowhere. At first it is almost literal, or at least a metaphor that depends closely on a literal sense. The freethinker says, without quite endorsing it, 'One might at the same time take this victory as a blood poisoning (it has mixed the races together)' (I: 9). Here the poison is harmful and physiological: the idea is presumably that race-mixing is bad for everyone's health. The freethinker does not disagree, but views the social achievement of the 'victory' as outweighing any physiological cost. Even if the poison goes through the 'entire body of humankind' (I: 9), the price is worth the reward. More than that, though, he says, 'we, too, *love the poison* . . .' (I: 9, emphasis added). The poison, whatever it is, is somehow separable from the Church, affects all of humankind, bears a physiological cost, has been successful, and now serves as the basis of a deeply impassioned commitment.

There is a feature of the 'poison' that allows it to function in such a polymorphous way, despite not signifying anything in particular. About the poisoning the freethinker says, 'its tempo and pace from now on can be ever slower, more subtle, less audible, more thoughtful – one has time, after all . . .' (I: 9). He perhaps initially conceived of the poisoning as a social breakdown brought about through intermarriage: old social identities and their associated expectations lost their standing once families no longer respected them. But now the poisoning has lost any biological connection, and is merely the forms of 'more subtle, les audible' normative regulation that are observed without explicit hierarchies or demands for obedience.[19] The poison has become the infinitely complex way in which the 'values of the common man' (I: 9) have diffused throughout modern ways of life. The freethinker calls attention to two separate aspects of this. One is a new sense of time: 'one has time, after all'. An effect of the subtle poisoning is openness to a future that is not constrained by tradition or by immediate exigencies. The other subtle aspect is 'everything is *noticeably* becoming jewified or christianized or rabbleized (what do words matter!)' (I: 9, emphasis added). Although the subtle poisoning works primarily on internalised norms and feelings, it also has a counterpart in outward practices that become homogenised as familiar categories lose their significance. The freethinker finds all this to be positive, but Nietzsche, in letting him bring it up, problematises it. Nietzsche's implicit suggestion, I take it, is that the optimistic temporal openness might just be empty and directionless. And the homogenisation might indicate that the freethinker's assumption in loving the poison, that the deeper content of values is separable from their embodied character, is wrong. If

---

[19] Cf. BGE §226: 'This world that concerns *us*, in which *we* have to fear and to love, this almost invisible, inaudible world of subtle commanding, subtle obeying, a world of "almost" in every respect [. . .]'.

the poison manifests itself not just in progressive values but also in the enervation of lived experience, then it is more harmful than he realises.

When Nietzsche's voice returns after the end of the freethinker's speech, he says, 'he had listened to me up till then and could not stand to hear me be silent. You see, there is much for me to be silent about at this point' (I: 9). The freethinker takes the silence to be about the evaluation of the descent of morality; he grows impatient waiting for Nietzsche to say that the story and its outcome is a good one, since he sees that as the whole point of telling the story. Nietzsche's suggestion, however, that there is much to be silent about implies that he is neither obtusely forgetting to say that the story is good nor craftily omitting a claim that the story is bad. He is, instead, deliberately refraining from revealing the full dimensions of a story that he is not yet ready to communicate. Nietzsche's concern here is that his readership is comprised of freethinkers, albeit less vocal ones, who are too captive of their ideals to understand what he has to say about them, at least until the story catches up to them and their commitments. Nietzsche's manifest silence, then, is not an omission or a secret, but a tacit commentary on the commitments that make genealogical inquiry approachable and comprehensible.

3
The Second Treatise: 'Guilt', 'Bad Conscience' and Related Matters

Introduction

In the Second Treatise, Nietzsche shifts his attention from what we esteem to our labour on ourselves. He considers this topic, as he does that of the First Treatise, as involving the descent of a conceptual repertory – in this case, 'guilt' and 'bad conscience'. This story is a more complex one, however, as the conceptual account is also one of social and psychological transformation, and through these transformations, novel forms of ethical experience. The shifting career of the idea of 'guilt', that is, turns out to be the story of how we make ourselves into the kinds of creatures for whom morality is important. We have, according to Nietzsche, transformed ourselves from creatures who relied on unconscious instinct into creatures who recognise and are moved by concerns that are even more powerful for us than self-preservation, including concerns about what we ourselves are. The burdens of social coexistence – having to follow rules that ensure harmony, making oneself accountable to others – force the development of 'inner' psychological life. This not only changes the meaning of 'guilt' from a failure to satisfy outward requirements to an internalised sense of irredeemable culpability, it makes for 'guilty' human beings who see themselves in terms of their moral standing and inevitable shortcomings.

Nietzsche fills his narrative with long tangents and digressions on topics such as punishment, historical meaning and suffering, but the basic story traces a path from the notion of indebtedness, through the bad conscience, to the moralised notion of guilt. Guilt, claims Nietzsche, has its roots in the notion of debt. Human beings first measured themselves against one another through the creditor–debtor relationship; creditors eventually suffered losses and sought compensation for those losses by inflicting pain on the debtors; individuals came to see themselves as debtors in relation to their communities and communities came to see themselves as debtors in relation to their ancestors and gods; the 'bad conscience', meanwhile, develops once natural instincts are directed inwards in response to social pressures; and finally guilt is drawn back into the bad conscience, making a final discharge of the creditor–debtor relationship impossible and creating the moral self-torment of humanity. The narrative, then, has two intersecting arcs. One characterises the distinctiveness of morality in terms of the emergence of its own special conception of guilt. The other shows how this distinctive form of guilt is only possible with the transformation of human psychology represented by the bad conscience. Nietzsche characterises the bad conscience as primarily harmful, since it manifests various forms of self-hostility, but also productive, in that it changes the ways in which human beings relate to themselves and thereby allows for new kinds of concerns and grounds for action.

Nietzsche begins this Treatise once again with misdirection, however, so I will discuss the beginning before proceeding to the main narrative. The story of the descent of the bad conscience and the moralised sense of 'guilt' is prefaced by a discussion that both diverges from the main narrative and at the same time makes it seems to have been somehow resolved. The first three aphorisms suggest that nature has reached its crowning achievement in the 'sovereign individual' (II: 2), the latest, ripest fruit of a long developmental process.[1] This process has been heedless and

---

[1] My discussion of the 'sovereign individual' is indebted to an extended debate in the scholarly literature, from which I have profited greatly, even where my views diverge. See Hatab 1995: esp. 37–9; Havas 1995: esp. 193–210; Owen 2002; Acampora 2006; and Ridley 2018: esp. 110–31. A view that takes some distance from the text but is close to mine can be found in Lovibond 2002: 72–85.

painful, but it has culminated in human beings – as exemplified by the sovereign individual – standing above the rest of nature, autonomous, conscious of their power and with a new capacity for self-affirmation. Nietzsche immediately undermines his apparent suggestion that humanity is the realisation of nature's plan, however, and continues to undermine it in the rest of the Treatise. The initial story promises a finished achievement, but it ends up taking away the ground for any sense of achievement or satisfaction. The painfulness of the process, furthermore, turns out not to be completed so much as deepened and extended. The trauma of becoming 'sovereign' is not so much finished as self-perpetuating.

The Treatise starts with Nietzsche specifying an end, 'to breed an animal that is *allowed to promise*' (II: 1), and then, with a pair of rhetorical questions, characterising that end as 'the paradoxical task that nature has set for itself' (II: 1) and the 'genuine problem *of* human beings' (II: 1). This topic and these questions are puzzling in at least four respects. One puzzle is why the topic of *promising* is given such pride of place; promising has no obvious connection to guilt or bad conscience. A second puzzle is what it could mean for nature to carry out a breeding programme. Even apart from personifying nature, it attributes an inherent end to natural processes. Nietzsche is not making a teleological argument or arguing for intelligent design: there is a plan, as it were, but no suggestion that the plan belongs to an intelligence or that we ought to recognise the goals of the plan as our own. But Nietzsche nevertheless represents nature as setting itself a task – indeed, a paradoxical one – that we are a part of. A third puzzle is what Nietzsche could mean by the 'problem *of* human beings'. This appears to be an objective genitive: that is, this is not human beings having a problem, but that there is something problematic about being human. The task of breeding, after all, is not *our* task, but a task involving us. But what is problematically unfulfilled about us, and how has it been fulfilled 'to a high degree' (II: 1)? Fourth, Nietzsche does not simply identify promising as the goal, but breeding an animal that is *allowed to promise*. Here the translation is somewhat misleading. Nietzsche writes of an animal that '*darf*' promise, where *darf* is a modal auxiliary, such as 'may' in English. So *darf* does indicate something like permissibility, but there is no implication that someone is *allowing* promising or that there is any source of obstruction; there is only the new modal standing towards the activity of promising. This new modal standing, rather than the activity itself, is what matters to the task.

Nietzsche does not directly address any of these puzzles, so the best approach to resolving them is to examine his account of the process by which nature carries out its end. The main process consists in the development of two contrary 'forces' or 'faculties': forgetfulness and memory. Forgetfulness, Nietzsche insists, is not merely the failure to retain impressions of one's experiences, or a passive incapacity to store information.[2] Forgetfulness, rather, is an 'active, positive faculty of repression [*Hemmungsvermögen*]' (II: 1): it is a regulatory capacity that actively moderates what is allowed to enter into or remain in consciousness. It functions purposively, that is, as a restrictive 'doorkeeper' (II: 1). Forgetting keeps psychic order, preventing unconscious processes from requiring attention, maintaining mental repose and clarity so as to prepare for new things, and allowing the 'nobler functions' (II: 1) of the mind to proceed undisturbed. Forgetting, in general, regulates mental life so that it is not always occupied by whatever might immediately confront it.

Nietzsche's general point in his discussion of forgetting is that human subjectivity is not primarily passive. Although subjectivity – or perhaps being 'ensouled' – might seem as if it proceeds simply by being affected by external stimuli, it is in fact active in its most basic operations. Even its requisite forgetting is active and purposive. By invoking forgetting in particular, Nietzsche is further claiming that human subjectivity is *temporal* in character: we become what we are by establishing a particular relationship to time. Forgetting serves health and cheerfulness, and is thus instrumentally useful, but it also makes us into a different kind of creature, for whom hope and pride are possible. Nietzsche argues, 'no *present* could exist without forgetfulness' (II: 1). A 'present', that is, is not simply 'given' to us; it must be demarcated from the momentary and identified as a discrete point in time. A contrast

---

[2] The idea of 'active forgetting' has been prominently adopted by Jacques Derrida. See, for example, Derrida 1982: 126.

with an earlier work of Nietzsche's helps to illustrate this. In his *Untimely Meditations* Nietzsche writes:

> Consider the cattle, grazing as they pass you by: they do not know what is meant by yesterday or today, they leap about, eat, rest, digest, leap about again, and so from morn till night and from day to day, fettered to the moment and its pleasure or displeasure, and thus neither melancholy nor bored. (Nietzsche 1983: 60)

Merely animal existence lives in a perpetual 'now' that does not recognise temporal relations. The cattle have no broader horizon of experience or sense that one might relate differently to time. We who actively forget have time-consciousness, however. We separate ourselves from being fettered to the moment and project a present for ourselves. We live in a 'now' that is indexed to us through forgetting.

The other main element in nature's process of breeding is the emergence of *memory*. Memory, insists Nietzsche, is a 'counter-faculty' (II: 1). Once again, that is, Nietzsche insists that memory is an active faculty rather than a mere inability to let go or a passive susceptibility to retaining impressions. In particular, in calling memory a 'counter-faculty', Nietzsche suggests that its function is in opposition to that of forgetting: it provides exemptions from forgetting for certain cases, 'namely for those cases where promises are to be made' (II: 1). This opposition by no means cancels out forgetfulness or its effects. Nietzsche's story, rather, is that the antagonism between two faculties provides temporal extension; whereas forgetting brings about an indexed present, memory brings about a past and a future. Nietzsche highlights the role of promising here because promising relates our actions to other moments in time. Making a promise extends the scope of one's present activity indefinitely into the future, at least until the promise is fulfilled or broken; keeping a promise refers the significance of one's current activity back into the past. As Nietzsche puts this, memory's exemption of promises gives us

> a willing on and on of something once willed, an actual *memory of the will*: so that between the original 'I will', 'I

will do' and the actual discharge of the will, its *act*, a world of new foreign things and circumstances, even acts of will can be unhesitatingly placed between. (II: 1)

There are other, important features of promising that I discuss below. But as Nietzsche introduces the idea, it is the medium through which memory works to transform us into creatures for whom the past and future are in some sense present – that is to say, into historical beings.

The means to produce memory in human beings – '*mnemotechnique*' (II: 3), as Nietzsche calls it – thus belong to the 'entire prehistoric labor' (II: 2) of the human race. Nietzsche emphasises two characteristics of this labour: it was dully repetitive and it was exceedingly gruesome. This is where Nietzsche's kind of naturalism arises: he wishes to understand how ahistorical animals might have come to shape themselves so as to gain recognisably human capacities, and in his account he invokes performances that do not presuppose those capacities. The main procedure for cultivating memory is what Nietzsche calls the 'morality of custom' (*Sittlichkeit der Sitte*) (II: 2). 'Morality of custom' is an awkward translation: the term that Nietzsche is using here, *Sittlichkeit*, can certainly mean 'morality', but differs from the titular word *Moral*. *Sittlichkeit* is the abstract universal of *Sitte*, 'custom' or 'tradition', and thus here literally indicates 'customariness' or 'traditionality'. What Nietzsche is claiming, then, is that we developed our capacity for memory by repeatedly conforming ourselves to custom. A single episode of conformity does not require a developed memory, but only a sense of how something is to be done; it can be an unreflective iteration of a habit. Continuously shaping one's activity according to custom, however, requires a sense of what has been and how to extend that tradition into the future. And this in turn, according to Nietzsche, requires not only the acquisition of particular cognitive abilities, but a self-transformation so as to fit into the orderly world that one represents to oneself:

> How humanity must have first learned to separate necessary from accidental occurrences in order to control the future in advance, to think causally, to see and anticipate

what is remote as if present, to posit with certainty what is the end, what is the means for this, in general to reckon and be able to calculate – how humanity itself must have first become *calculable, regular, necessary*, even to itself for its own image. (II: 1)

'Humanity' learns to engage in purposive, deliberative activity, and this requires a view of the world as predictable and regular in order to be effective. We place ourselves within this view of the world, too, to make predictions about human behaviour and to see ourselves as sustaining purposes.[3] Nietzsche, then, coordinates two ideas in his account of the morality of custom. One is that we institute modal relations into the world: we come to see not merely the passing of events, but events that are necessary, possible, allowed and so on; the other is that we ourselves become 'necessary' creatures who acknowledge these modal properties.

This brings us to the sovereign individual, as the end of this process. Nietzsche equivocates between both (English) senses of 'end': the sovereign individual is both the *terminus* of the morality of custom, and also its *telos*. If anything, Nietzsche emphasises the latter sense: the morality of custom is merely a means, and, in a standard metaphor of teleology, the sovereign individual is the ripest fruit borne by a tree. This recalls one old unresolved puzzle and provokes a new one. In what sense could the sovereign individual be the telos, the end, of a natural process, and how could the predictability and reliability established by the morality of custom bring forth the sovereign individual who, Nietzsche claims, 'has liberated himself from the morality of custom' (II: 2)? I will address the former question before building up to an answer to the latter.

Nietzsche provides his account of how the morality of custom taught liberation in terms of his story of human beings as self-relating creatures. Nietzsche offers a naturalistic story about how 'the actual labor of human beings on themselves' (II: 2) transforms

---

[3] Nietzsche's discussion seems to connect the three elements that John Searle claims are required to account for social reality: 'assignment of function, collective intentionality, and constitutive rules' (Searle 1995: 13).

what we are. The morality of custom teaches us to be active in a narrow way, in which we do things because those are the sorts of things that are done. Through work on ourselves, however, we become so complexly self-referring and self-relating that we become the authors of our deeds in new ways. Nietzsche's naturalism here consists in rejecting views of the self, or the author of deeds, as a hidden inner core, soul-substance, centre of experience or object of introspection. Instead he offers an account of how human beings transformed the character of their agency by instituting new relationships to themselves through their deeds. Some of our activity is intended to work on the person: we make ourselves more disciplined and more moderate, for example, so that we are better suited to follow custom. And some of our actions are about other actions: the fulfilling of promises, in particular, but also adhering to tradition, following commands and responding to others. This self-referential activity eventually becomes so complex and entangled that we can see ourselves in relation to the customs that we have since appropriated.[4] We can come to see ourselves as standing apart from the deeds that we may, might, must or ought to do. This is how we become authors of deeds: not as a source of pure spontaneity, but as creatures who recognise different modes of orientation to our own actions.

Note that this enlarges the significance of promising. Nietzsche initially presented promising as bringing us temporal extension, thereby transforming us into historical beings; it also fits into his story of how we became self-relating creatures, by raising the issue of what current deeds could count as satisfying the commitments it produces. Underlying both of these is a more general feature of promising, that it institutes a normative commitment where none existed before. The successful performance of an act of promising brings new things into the world: obligations and expectations. It binds an agent to her word and to others, and changes her relationship to future deeds. This is not just of interest when promises are explicitly made; Nietzsche takes promising, I think, as a model for standing by one's own deeds. 'Promising',

---

[4] One can find a discussion of similar themes in Taylor 1985.

in general, is Nietzsche's shorthand for instituting a relationship to one's own deeds, to claim them as one's own. This can change the character of *all* of one's activity, by making it into instances of satisfying, breaking, transforming or neglecting those commitments. It also, Nietzsche mentions, allows for 'trust' (II: 2) and depends on 'equals' (II: 2) and 'peers' (II: 2). Promising can help to build up complicated social arrangements that, because they depend on reliable expectations, would not be possible otherwise. This in turn creates new kinds of identities. New potentials for being become possible where persons 'promise and vouch for themselves' (II: 2), and thereby live in a distinctively social world where they interact by giving their word.

Nietzsche connects his discussion of promising and the commitments and social relations it makes possible with discussions of *conscience* and *responsibility*. The rest of the Second Treatise has the 'bad conscience' as one of its main topics, but here we have a more basic and less damaging form. This basic form of conscience is self-relating ability in general having become a 'dominating instinct' (II: 2). Self-relating activity brings about a certain kind of self-distance: the capacity to take oneself and one's actions as objects of reflection and volition.

Self-distance and self-objectification can perhaps turn into something dangerous, but Nietzsche represents it here as involving 'an actual consciousness of power and freedom' (II: 2). Being able to take oneself as an object empowers one to reconsider who one is and work on oneself. This direction of thought and activity to oneself, however ineffective or fallible it might be, allows for something like a feeling of being charge of what one is. The sovereign individual thus has a 'power over himself and fate' (II: 2), as at least the ability to take a stance on what nature and fate have done to him, no matter how causally constrained he is. This is the connection that Nietzsche makes to the 'extraordinary privilege of *responsibility*' (II: 2). Distinctively moral responsibility locates blame by identifying a source of pure spontaneity, untouched by external causes, that supports an unequivocal and involuntary claim of accountability. To claim a privilege of responsibility, by contrast, one has to put oneself in a position to claim accountability for it; and one can take this kind of responsibility especially when something unpredictable happens. But to have this kind of responsibility, one has to see oneself as the author of one's actions, one has to be able to make commitments to others and have those commitments recognised by others, whether by the force of one's subsequent deeds or by the authority of one's word. In other words, one has to be a self-relating, temporally extended promiser with a conscience, among other like creatures.

At this point I can spell out a bit more about what a sovereign individual is. A sovereign individual is a creature who has gone through a project of training (or 'breeding') so intense that he has acquired the capacity to take his own training as an issue and depart from it; he is thus autonomous and supramoral in the sense that he departs from the morality of custom in this way.[5] This, by itself, is not an ideal, but only the basic capacity to stand in one's own ethical relations and not merely those that are customary. He has mastery over himself, circumstance, nature and fate not in terms of causal control, but as being able to take a standpoint with enough distance so as to assert one's independence from them, and perhaps even to take responsibility for them. In this way, by instituting new normative commitments, he has his own standard of value in his long, unbreakable will. And in expressing this will, by mediating the influences of custom and asserting accountability, he is 'like only unto himself' (II: 2). He is no mere example of a generic type, but someone who stands in specific relationships to the past, himself and others.

Nature has set a paradoxical task and has completed it. Sovereign individuals are a culmination in the sense of the furthest extent of nature working through natural processes to make ourselves explicable in terms of natural regularities. Custom can shape incredibly complex behaviours by guiding them along diverse but predictable paths, compelling suitable responses to different situations. Human beings move from being predictable as natural creatures, to becoming predictable as natural creatures who are trained to act the same way in the same situations, but then, paradoxically, change into creatures who are not exclusively explicable in terms

---

[5] I am using the masculine pronouns 'he' and 'his' to agree with the translation here. The sovereign individual is not gender-specific.

of natural regularity or custom, but also in terms of their own consciences and the accountability that they institute for themselves. So this is end of nature: not the perfection of natural teleology, but that everyone is on their own now. There used to be guidance from nature and custom, but independence leaves everyone to settle what their own commitments should be, without anything non-human to underwrite them. At the end of nature our commitments are grounded solely by our responsibility to ourselves, and without custom no one has any idea who they are. The cost of independence turns out to be dependence and pain. There is dependence because conscience depends on social relations: for example, on claiming the privilege of responsibility and finding the appropriate 'peers' with which one exchanges promises. Having a will of one's own thus leaves one all the more dependent on others, and thus unable to resolve the sense in which a will can be one's own. And there is pain because creating and enforcing conscience – making it effective among animals such as ourselves – turns out to involve a psychological trauma that is never completed, as subsequent aphorisms show.

Nietzsche begins the Second Treatise with what superficially appears to be an optimistic, progressivist story of how humanity overcame its natural limitations in bringing about the sovereign individual. The developmental process was mindless and agonising. Animal nature had to be shaped by painful repetition into habit, and habit by painful repetition into custom and tradition. Once the goal of the process had been reached, however, it left human beings as self-determining creatures with no conflict between their free legislating and their recognition of moral demands. Tradition had been instituted as an oppressive authority, but once instituted it could be challenged by sovereign demands for legitimacy and individual claims to autonomy. Nietzsche hints at this optimism because it is a familiar one, and so as to be ready to spend the rest of this Treatise taking it apart. The process is not finished because it is never finished, either with reproducing the pains of memory or with producing some definitive guidance on who we are to become. We cannot reconcile ourselves to the demands of making ourselves moral beings, and we retain our dependence on others down to the inner depths of our souls. Nietzsche, in the opening of the Treatise, indicates that his narrative is about our accomplishments in bringing about inner depth and reflections on authority, but the process has been more treacherous and less successful than an optimistic story would allow.

The rest of this chapter will follow the same format as the preceding chapter. I will start by offering a detailed review of Nietzsche's narrative of 'guilt', the 'bad conscience' and 'related matters'. Then I will discuss some of the philosophical topics that Nietzsche raises within the narrative: in particular, historical understanding, punishment and political realism. The final section will discuss the methodology of the Second Treatise with respect to Nietzsche's historicism, and examine his rhetorical strategies in the final aphorisms of the Treatise.

The basic narrative

The third aphorism serves as a second introduction. It precedes the main narrative of bad conscience and guilt but, unlike the first two aphorisms, anticipates the ideas of the Treatise as a whole. Its narrative is the Second Treatise in miniature: it appeals to archaic social practices to account for a change in 'inner' human psychology that lies at the base of our current culture. The specific dramatic question it poses is how the human capacity for memory could have been established. 'The concept "conscience"' (II: 3), Nietzsche insists, indicates a refined, well-recognised phenomenon, but there must have been preceding stages that depended on the establishment of memory for their development. The establishment of memory, furthermore, could not have been the product of a conscious plan, because that would have itself required an advanced capacity for memory. The answer to the dramatic question is '*mnemo-technique*' (II: 3). Nietzsche lists a number of violent practices: castration, boiling in oil, flaying alive and so on. His point is that these practices were all historically conspicuous because the employment of pain was an effective technique in making people remember; pain is 'the most powerful mnemonic aid' (II: 3). Rewards and incentives might have their uses, but when it came to instilling memory into recalcitrant human beings who lacked it, inflicting pain was what worked. The infliction of horrendous suffering was so central to establishing memory and thereby regulating social order that, according to Nietzsche, all our familiar practices and ways of thinking were founded on cruelty. He writes, 'Ah, reason, seriousness, mastery over the affects, this whole gloomy business we call reflection, all these prerogatives and showpieces of the human being: how dearly they have been bought! how much blood and horror are at the bottom of all "good things"! . . .' (II: 3).

This story about the technologies of bringing about memory raises four themes that are important for the rest of the Treatise and thus worth keeping in mind as the narrative proceeds. First, and most important, is the close connection between social life and the cultivation of an 'inner' psychology. Memory was not produced intentionally, but with the imperative of making 'a few primitive demands of social coexistence' (II: 3) recognised. The social demands do not merely provide a causal prompting for something inherently asocial, either. In Nietzsche's view, memory takes the form of using representational capacities that are social in nature to anticipate others' views and expectations. The second important theme is the historicity of what we are. Nietzsche expresses this in two ways in the third aphorism. One is that a seemingly stable and determinate term such as 'conscience' in fact has a 'long history and form conversion behind it' (II: 3), so that to understand what it means and what it refers to, one has to look at its past and the various shapes it has taken. The other way in which Nietzsche expresses this theme is that these pasts still live with us. Our practices and even our sentiments have content that, outside of our conscious awareness, comes from their reiteration of old dramas. For example, on the history of asceticism, he writes, 'the longest, deepest, harshest past breathes on us and wells up in us when we become "serious"' (II: 3). This raises the third important theme: the psychological demands of social life are deeply and permanently painful.[6] Nietzsche claims

---

[6] This theme, the painful psychic costs of participation in a social order, is one of many in the *Genealogy* that Freud appropriated from Nietzsche. Compare Freud 1961: 81: 'The price we pay for our advance in civilization is a loss of happiness through the heightening of the sense of guilt.' Freud, like Nietzsche, also connects guilt with the internalisation of displaced instincts, links guilt with punishment and conscience with internalised authority, and identifies two origins of the sense of guilt.

that asceticism is the primary means for shaping human beings and that living with others imposes demands that we are not naturally disposed to accept. Social life requires not just prudent behaviour but painful self-transformation to make ourselves suitable for it. The fourth important theme is how productive inner psychological development is. Humans, like other animals, can be conditioned to behave in many ways, but once we have a reflective conscience there are infinite paths for our self-cultivation. In general, Nietzsche writes, conscience allows one 'to vouch for oneself and with pride, hence also to be *allowed [dürfen] to say yes to oneself*' (II: 3). With a conscience, that is, we change from merely being susceptible to training to having the new normative standing that comes with having an outlook on oneself.

The main narrative begins with Nietzsche's question, 'But how then did that other "gloomy thing", the consciousness of guilt, the whole "bad conscience" come into the world?' (II: 4). This calls attention to the narrative's most important element rather than stating its problematic precisely. The problematic that Nietzsche identifies is that a modern conception of *guilt* is impossibly complex and yet murky, so much so that it is hard to see how the concept could have ever come about. The idea of guilt includes culpability for some infliction of harm that could have been avoided, that is blameworthy because it was somehow chosen as wrong, that merits punishment of some kind and weighs on one's conscience, that reflects poorly on one as a moral being, and more. All this would have been inconceivable in the distant past. People in the distant past had neither the conceptual resources to assemble anything like this, nor any interest in doing so; they did not characteristically make the distinctions necessary to support such a concept or have the background practices that would give such a concept its sense. So how does such an idea come about, almost out of nothing? Nietzsche's story is that guilt must have started from conceptual resources that had been available and taken a diversity of shifting forms before arriving at its place at the centre of the conceptual framework of morality. So guilt gradually recedes from the narrative as it shifts in relation to the background of ideas about agency, blame and harm that shape it, and the bad conscience and its power to produce these changes takes on a more prominent role. The narrative, in any case, is one about the conceptual resources necessary for a contemporary sense of guilt and what kinds of social worlds and psychological structures make them possible.

The more basic conceptual resource out of which guilt emerged is the idea of indebtedness: 'The major moral concept "guilt" has its origin in the very material concept "debt"' (II: 4). Nietzsche is relying on a peculiarity of German: 'guilt' (*Schuld*) and 'debts' (*Schulden*) are the same word. But 'debts' has a good claim to playing a role here, even apart from the linguistic fact. Incurring debts is a familiar thing that human beings do.[7] It is a useful practice that is easily understood by participants and observers and that does not require deep assumptions about agency or conscience; it merely requires transactions that distribute benefits and burdens to be compensated later. Nietzsche, by calling the concept of debt 'very material', seems to be treating it as the bottom level of explanation: there is no need to try to explain debts in terms of something more fundamental.[8] The idea that one can incur a burden of repayment is available in any system of social interdependence, however primitive or sophisticated.[9] And incurring and repaying debts were the basic interactions out of which the sense of guilt emerged once the material concept was adapted for new uses.

Nietzsche offers two substantive reasons why the creditor–debtor relationship was suited for its role in the prehistory of guilt. One pertains to the reciprocal structure of debt and guilt, and the other to the transformation of indebtedness into a feeling of guilt; they share an idea of instituting equivalences for incommensurable things. First, the creditor–debtor relationship provides a

---

[7] This is not a notion of 'material' that Marx would be happy with, but having a debt is notably the main example in Anscombe 1981. For a discussion of the history of debt and Nietzsche's treatment of it, see Graeber 2014: 75–80.
[8] Compare this to what Maudemarie Clark and David Dudrick (2012: 196), following Daniel Dennett, call '"top-down" explanation', in which intentional phenomena are the bottom level of explanation.
[9] See the discussion of norms of reciprocity in Miller 1993. Although Miller focuses on gift exchanges and Nietzsche on 'contractual relationships' (II: 5), Nietzsche's account only depends on the idea of compensation for injury.

model for exacting payment where no payment can be made. A violation, such as that of a credit agreement, was accompanied by 'the idea of an equivalence of injury and pain' (II: 4), so that the creditors could inflict suffering as compensation for an unpaid debt. Strangely, Nietzsche portrays this as a means to convince the *debtor* that this is a serious matter so that the practice of lending could get started: 'The debtor, in order to inspire trust for his promise of repayment [. . .] in order to convince his own conscience that repayment is a duty, pledges something' (II: 5). A credit agreement, Nietzsche suggests, includes a 'pledge' that sets an equivalent to what has been lost when the loan is defaulted on. This equivalent, since in the case of default it cannot be a typical item of value, turns out to be injury and pain. 'Guilt' subsequently borrows the idea of an equivalence of pain while leaving aside the idea of a credit agreement. The other substantive reason is that the creditor–debtor relationship was 'the first time person confronted person [. . .] a person *measured himself* against another person' (II: 8). So this, according to Nietzsche, is where human beings first learned to understand who they were in terms of their relations to others, and they did this by putting a price on themselves: 'Setting prices, measuring values, thinking up equivalents, exchanging – this preoccupied the very first thinking of human beings to such an extent that in a certain sense it is *the* thinking per se' (II: 8). The creditor–debtor relationship was thus important in that it provided an objective metric in terms of which persons could think of themselves, and thereby introduced an intersubjective aspect into considerations of who someone was.

Nietzsche discusses each of these two reasons at greater length. The former reason, about exacting payment by inflicting pain, highlights the interdependence of the psychological and the social. Nietzsche suggests that there is, in some sense, a natural basis for the influence that pain has on human development. That we learn how to take matters seriously primarily through suffering likely stems from something in our animal nature, perhaps the urgency with which we treat pain. There is likewise a pleasure in inflicting pain that stems from our nature. The equivalence whereby the creditor extracts a pound of flesh for an unpaid debt can only function if 'the creditor is granted a kind of *pleasure* as repayment and compensation' (II: 5). Nietzsche argues that the practice of lending could not have worked as it did without a currency of pain; there must have been some store of value in the potential to inflict harm. In order to make the transaction, the creditor anticipates that even in the case of default there will be some desirable compensation. At any rate, the incentive to carry out the laborious forms of torture that Nietzsche recalls from the historical record seems to have been the instinctive pleasure in them. But whatever natural basis there is, in Nietzsche's story it is a social process in which guilt emerges. Guilt stems from the social practice of lending (or contractual agreements in general), and it thus develops through promising, cooperation, contract and commerce. Even part of the pleasure is social: it derives from the creditor having 'a foretaste of a higher rank' (II: 5) in abusing another. And this social process in turn plays a role in the cultivation of conscience, memory and deliberation.

The establishment of equivalence in pain raises another point for Nietzsche. About 'the moral conceptual world' (II: 6), he writes, 'its beginning, like the beginning of everything great on earth, was thoroughly drenched, and for a long time, in blood' (II: 6). To understand our moral outlook, we must see it as the result of a long, violent process; the creation of moral personality was accomplished in a way that our moral personality could not have endured. Nietzsche asks, furthermore, 'And might we not add that this world at bottom has never quite lost its odor of blood and torture?' (II: 6). We continue to express the same violence in a different form; an 'ever increasing spiritualization and "deification" of cruelty [. . .] runs through the entire history of higher culture' (II: 6). The story of cruelty is, in this way, not just a story about the origin of our moral framework, but also a story of what it continues to express. This is why 'Related Matters' appears in the title of this Treatise after 'guilt' and 'bad conscience'. Nietzsche never specifies what these matters related to guilt and bad conscience are because they could be almost anything. Cruelty can be expressed as punishment, guilt or, once it is 'spiritualized' in higher culture, as the humiliation of social impropriety, the belligerence of academic dispute, the discursive exclusions of politics, the aesthetic judgements of bodies and clothes, or in almost any other way. There is an infinite range of possible semantic forms for the expression of human cruelty.

In the midst of discussing cruelty, Nietzsche announces a digression. He does this in his usual way, with a dash, and later marks its conclusion by writing 'to return again to the course of our investigation' (II: 8). Although the digression departs from the main narrative and contains disturbing remarks about Negroes, hysterical educated women and vivisection, it has some value in shedding additional light on Nietzsche's treatments of cruelty, suffering and spiritualisation. The main idea of the digression is that it is not necessarily bad that the roots of our moral conceptual world and higher culture lie in cruelty. Nietzsche affirms the idea that cruelty belongs to our animal 'instincts' (II: 7), but claims, as a historical point, that in the distant past cruelty was seen as a 'genuine seduction and lure to life' (II: 7) rather than something sombre and shameful. The contemporary meaning of cruelty is that it inflicts needless suffering, which is not only bad in itself but diminishes the moral standing of everyone involved; it is worse than arbitrary, too, since it acts in order to satisfy an animal or pathological urge. Nietzsche claims, however, that this understanding of cruelty derives from an interpretation of suffering, and 'what causes indignation against suffering is not suffering itself, but the meaninglessness of suffering' (II: 7).[10] On his analysis, then, people in ancient cultures experienced suffering but could 'negate' or 'justify' (II: 7) it by interpreting it as part of a celebration of natural instincts to be played out in public spectacles; cruelty was part of the delight in expressing one's drives. In more recent times, by contrast, the merely natural human attributes are seen as shameful, and thus suffering as the subjection to merely corporeal weakness is interpreted as something that ought to be eliminated altogether. This paradoxically creates new kinds of suffering, however. The hermeneutic cost of sustaining this interpretation of suffering has been to bring about an estrangement from instincts, and this estrangement changes suffering into a different

---

[10] Arthur Danto's distinction between 'extensional suffering' and 'intensional suffering' is helpful here. See Danto 1988: esp. 21.

form. Suffering undergoes a 'sublimation and subtilization' (II: 7) as it is 'translated into the imagination and the psychical' (II: 7). The modern idea that cruelty and suffering ought to be eliminated, then, is somewhat self-deceived, since it coincides with the invention and dissemination of new, inward forms of suffering.

The second substantive reason why the creditor–debtor relationship was suited for its role in the prehistory of guilt was that it is the 'oldest and most primitive personal relationship of all' (II: 8). Part of what Nietzsche wishes to explain in the emergence of guilt is why there is a '*feeling* of guilt' (II: 8, emphasis added) even though debt does not lend itself to a felt experience in quite the same way. (There is no distinctive 'feeling of debt'.) The answer, I take it, is that guilt is personalised. Whereas being indebted is a material fact about one's balance of accounts, being guilty reflects on the person: it is a matter of 'personal responsibility' (II: 8), and how one incurs and repays one's debts indicates what sort of a person one is. Nietzsche's story is that commercial transactions were the first contexts through which individuals confronted each other with competing measures of value. These exchanges involved determinations of relative worth, the seeking of others' good judgement, and assessments of personal reliability; persons learned something about themselves by participating in these exchanges, or at any rate established views of themselves and others based on these transactions. We take on the status of persons through our interactions with others, and economic interactions are the primitive ones in which strangers interacted. In this way, Nietzsche suggests, debt slides into guilt: one's commercial standing is felt, personally, as a sense of who one is.

Debt begins to slide into guilt, and the next step in the emergence of guilt is for it to become utterly pervasive. Not everyone incurs debts, and of those who do, most pay those debts back. For guilt to function as part of the moral conceptual world, however, it must be everywhere; otherwise, most persons would reside outside of that conceptual world and it would not have morality's scope. Nietzsche continues to appeal to the creditor–debtor relation here. In his account the expansion of guilt took place when individuals came to see themselves as debtors in relation to their communities: 'The community stands to its members in that important basic relationship of the creditor to his debtors' (II: 9). The community furnishes benefits, in terms of security, prosperity and sociability, and in return those who enjoy those benefits pledge themselves to the support of the community. Community members thus see themselves in a condition of indebtedness. They also see each other in such a condition and seek to enforce those debts when they are not properly acknowledged: primitive forms of punishment develop for those who fail to make appropriate use of the benefits of communal life. Those guilty of not repaying their debt to the community are reminded of its value by being viciously deprived of everything – property, bodily integrity, friendship – that the community secured.

Thinking of indebtedness as part of belonging to a community extends the eligibility for guilt, but it does not advance its conceptual development. If rule breakers are tortured and destroyed as a way of extracting their obligation to the community, then 'guilt' cannot signify more than the condition of a defeated enemy: it is the status of someone whom all the community must hate in order to claim their due reciprocity. And it is a non-status, since the guilty party must quickly die or depart. So for guilt to take on a deeper meaning, there needs to be a pathway for the guilty party to be reintegrated, while maintaining his guilt, back into the life of the community. This can take place when the community is sufficiently large and stable that individual transgressions do not threaten to bring it into chaos. Then, claims Nietzsche, punishment can shift from retaliation against an aggressor who should have been grateful, to a strategy for containing the anger against the violator. There need to be ways, that is, to convince aggrieved individuals to subsume their desire for vengeance into the limited retribution sanctioned by the community. There are a number of practical and conceptual strategies for doing this; Nietzsche mentions as especially significant the idea of taking 'every transgression as dischargeable' (II: 10) and '*isolating* the criminal and his deed from each other' (II: 10). That is, the community can treat particular deeds, rather than the transgressor, as the primary objects of retribution. This allows the community to set equivalents to crimes rather than treat transgressors as hostile. Of course, the transgressors still have to bear the burden of punishment, but they can be individuals associated with misdeeds rather than enemies to all. According to Nietzsche, one could even imagine a community powerful enough that they let their offenders go unpunished altogether; there would be no need for vengeance beyond the recognition of guilt. The important thing for the history of guilt, however, is that it furnishes a way for the guilty to continue to belong to the community while persisting in their guilt.

At this point in the narrative, Nietzsche begins a series of digressions, which he again indicates with dashes and other signposts (e.g., 'To return now to the subject', II: 13). These digressions discuss approaches to understanding justice, punishment and historical method, and I will return to them in the next section. By aphorism 14, however, Nietzsche's reflections on punishment have returned to addressing the history of 'guilt', if only negatively. He writes, 'Punishment is alleged to have the value of awakening the *feeling of guilt* in the guilty party, in it is sought the actual *instrumentum* of that psychical reaction called "bad conscience", and "sting of conscience"' (II: 14). The next step in the narrative, that is, is the story of how guilt became internalised as the painful bad conscience. Guilt has emerged out of debt by becoming personalised; it has become pervasive by being seen in relation to one's community as a whole; it became persistent by becoming potentially redeemable; and now the feeling of guilty status is to be awakened into a 'psychical reaction' that conveys 'inner anguish' (II: 14). Nietzsche takes note of one hypothesis, that *punishment* produced this psychical reaction by forcing an acknowledgement of the communal viewpoint, and argues that it is wrong. For the hypothesis to be correct, punishment would have to encourage the sympathetic engagement with others, deepening one's processes of reflection and decision making, and motivating the internalisation of a shared point of view. But punishment does the opposite of these things. It afflicts one's sentiments and vigour, it fosters resentment and alienation, and, rather than producing sympathy and depth, it merely sharpens the prudence needed to avoid future punishment. In general, it creates a barrier between the one being punished and those who are inflicting harm. Since punishment by others generates resistance to guilt taking the form of internalised self-punishment, Nietzsche looks for a different account of what happened.

The next step in the descent of guilt comes with the creation of the bad conscience. Nietzsche frequently shifts his account of what, precisely, he means by 'bad conscience'. Sometimes it is consciousness of guilt, or self-inflicted psychic cruelty, or a kind of sickness, but the account of its emergence is relatively clear: 'I regard bad conscience as the deep sickness to which humans had to succumb under the pressure of that most fundamental of all changes they could ever experience – that change of finding themselves locked once and for all under the spell of society and of peace' (II: 16). Nietzsche's story is that life in urban settlements, as advantageous as it was, brought about the 'most fundamental' change possible in human existence. Prior to living in organised, settled communities, human beings could rely on 'regulating drives' (II: 16) and unconscious instincts to guide them; there was no need for conscious reflection or resisting one's immediate impulses. Life in complex societies turns out to make intense psychological demands of everyone, however. Members of society live in close proximity to one another, are mutually interdependent even for basic necessities, and need to manage long-standing relationships with familiars rather than worry about external threats. In such a situation, members need reliable expectations, personal security and coordination of complex tasks. In order for social order to be maintained, individuals' aggressive and violent instincts, in particular, needed to be repressed, since they would otherwise threaten cohesion and stability. These repressed instincts did not die away, however; they found an outlet by turning backwards 'against the possessors of such instincts' (II: 16).

The invention of the bad conscience thus brings about the 'internalisation' of humankind: 'All instincts that do not discharge themselves externally now *turn inward* – this is what I call the internalization of human beings: now for the first time human beings grow what is later called the "soul"' (II: 16). Bad conscience emerges when the repression of violent instincts brings about their inward redirection. To live in a peaceful society, organised according to rules and without enemies against whom to target aggression, human beings had to distance themselves from their instincts. They did this by turning their instincts against themselves, opening up space to interpose new reflections and concerns between instincts and actions. So human beings appeared to be rule-following, orderly, sociable creatures rather than instinctual ones, but in fact they became rule-following creatures by becoming aggressively self-hostile ones. This hostility can manifest as physical self-harm, but more typically it takes a psychological form. Paradigmatically, this is the 'bite' of conscience directing scorn against oneself, but the bad conscience can deliver self-torment in a variety of inner forms: attacks on self-esteem or self-confidence, instilling self-destructive attitudes or self-undermining dispositions, disgust or loathing of oneself, and even self-hatred, anxiety and rage, for example.

As painful and awkward as all this is, the internal conflict of instincts opens up 'the whole inner world' (II: 16). Human beings who lose the immediacy of unrestrained instincts gain the capacity to have thoughts and feelings that are in some sense private and independently important; thought can take on the character of a silent discourse with oneself; and one's 'soul', as Nietzsche writes here, can be identified with this private discursive subject that becomes itself an object of attention and care. We become deep, reflective beings with an infinite range of sentiments and concerns, and all of this, for Nietzsche, is made possible by psychic self-harm.

Nietzsche thus calls the advent of the bad conscience 'a leap and a plunge as it were into new situations and conditions of existence' (II: 16). There was an abrupt change: the bad conscience did not come about as part of a gradual process by which human beings adapted to their environment for reproductive success. In general, the kinds of explanation offered for its emergence do not fit with those offered for biological nature, and it alters the kinds of explanation that human behaviour is susceptible to. Before the bad conscience, human beings could act in complex ways that successfully negotiated their circumstances, or that performed ingrained habits, but these behaviours would always be expressions of naturally determined drives, or attempts to satisfy biologically given needs. The emergence of bad conscience, by contrast, does not come about as a product of such behaviours, but rather requires an active adjustment of oneself to social demands. And once it emerges and sets instincts against each other, human behaviour is open to explanation in terms of new kinds of reasons and concerns: social standing, religion, politics and love, for example, can take on new meanings and offer new motivations. So the bad conscience represents a radical break in what sorts of considerations move us and how social authority can be regulated. Here, as elsewhere in the narrative, inner psychology depends on social transformation. Social life prompts us to undertake the psychic labour on ourselves through which we participate in a new form of existence. Having an inner life, in this story, is an extension of the outer one: we train ourselves to take seriously ideas and norms that supplant the importance of natural determinants in leading a life. We make our inner lives possible, that is, by actively sustaining our responsiveness to the considerations that arise in social life, and we make it important by granting it importance as part of the logic of our activities.

Nietzsche's narrative emphasises the emergence of bad conscience as a response to distinctively social existence, but he also, briefly, offers an account of how organised social existence itself arose. He writes, 'The shaping of a previously unrestricted and unformed population into a fixed form, inasmuch as its beginning was an act of force, was only brought to completion by sheer acts of force [. . .] the oldest "state" accordingly emerged and continued to function as a terrible tyranny' (II: 17). The state was not a gradual development out of pre-existing forms of cooperation and it was not based on the conscious intention to recognise political norms. The state, rather, was created by 'blond beasts of prey' (II: 17) who employed violence to shape a social order. 'Their work', according to Nietzsche, 'is an instinctive creating of form, imposing of form; they are the most involuntary, unconscious artists in existence' (II: 17). In terms of the main narrative, there is little point in Nietzsche bringing them up. Although the emergence of the bad conscience is centrally important, the emergence of the conditions for the emergence of the bad conscience is not. Bringing up the blond beasts of prey does allow Nietzsche to make two points, however. It allows him to identify a natural *explanans*, an '*instinct of freedom*' (II: 17) that expresses itself in form-giving violence. And it allows Nietzsche to claim that this very *explanans* lies behind the bad conscience: 'this instinct of freedom repressed, pushed back, and venting itself only on itself: this, and only this is *bad conscience* in its beginnings' (II: 17).

To some extent, Nietzsche's attention to the 'instinct of freedom' merely reiterates his common theme, that changes in human beings, and in particular changes in human psychology, invariably require a painful process. It requires a kind of ascetic labour to produce the bad conscience; indeed, the bad conscience just *is* a repetition of ascetic labour. This appeal to the instinct of freedom is distinctive in three ways, however. First, Nietzsche identifies the instinct of freedom with 'the will to power', which relates it to some of his other discussions;[11] in the Second Treatise, 'will to power' relates to form giving, interpreting and meaning, and in the Third Treatise to life-affirmation and assertions of collective authority. Second, the instinct of freedom is directed 'at humanity itself' (II: 18). That is, the instinct of freedom is the form of bad conscience that makes human nature as such its object. So rather than instituting particular forms of training or discipline, the bad conscience allows for more profound changes in what it is and might mean to be human. Once the 'entire animal ancient self' (II: 18) is put in question, it opens the possibility of thinking of oneself in new ways. Third, the instinct of freedom creates 'negative ideals' (II: 18) and thus new normative possibilities. Nietzsche's story is very compressed, but he recounts some of it here:

> This whole *active* 'bad conscience', as the genuine womb of all ideal and imaginative events has ultimately [. . .] also brought to light a plenitude of strange new beauty and affirmation, perhaps even beauty *itself* . . . For what would 'beautiful' be if contradiction had not first risen to consciousness of itself, if the ugly had not first said to itself: 'I am ugly'? (II: 18)

---

[11] This passage is one of the few places where Nietzsche's famous phrase 'will to power' appears in this text. His identification of it with the 'instinct of freedom' may be an interesting gloss on the other appearances, or it may be inconsistent with them. In any case, one does not need knowledge of a theory of will to power to understand the present narrative. Many of Nietzsche's discussions of will to power are in his unpublished notebooks, but there is also an important discussion in *Beyond Good and Evil*; see BGE §36.

The story seems to be that one form of the bad conscience's self-hostility is thinking badly of oneself. The bad conscience furthermore becomes active when it creates 'negative ideals', such as ugliness; psychic self-harm can then take the form of attributing these qualities to oneself. These self-attributions raise the question, however, of how accurate they are, of what counts as 'ugly', for example, and how one might satisfy or fail to satisfy the criteria. Nietzsche's suggestion, then, is that these questions open up the possibility for ideals in general: reflection can proceed to what would count as avoiding the negative altogether, to contrary ideals, to what would be genuinely valuable. The negative work of inventing new ways to denigrate oneself is what creates potentially more affirming normative reflection.

In Nietzsche's portrayal, then, the bad conscience, like every other element in his presentation of the descent of morality, is deeply ambiguous. The bad conscience is the 'greatest and uncanniest sickness' (II: 16); it ruins health; it deprives persons of the basis of strength and joy; it corrupts the affects, undermines self-confidence and causes unnecessary suffering. As 'the suffering of humans *from humans, from themselves*' (II: 16), furthermore, it is unavoidably harmful, since the source and subject of the malady are the same. Nietzsche has a favoured metaphor for expressing the ambiguous character of this sickness, however: 'It is a sickness, bad conscience, this is not subject to doubt, but a sickness as pregnancy is a sickness' (II: 19). He does not specify what the metaphor means or why he thinks that pregnancy is a sickness, but pregnancy, however uncomfortable and dangerous, at least brings forth something new. The bad conscience 'brought about on earth something so new, so profound, unheard of, enigmatic, contradictory *and full of future* that the aspect of the earth changed essentially as a result' (II: 16). The ambiguity is deeply embedded here. Not only are the effects of bad conscience ambiguous, since they both cause harm and produce valuable results, but they are necessarily ambiguous, since the process that generates them is itself driven by internal oppositions, and they are ambiguous on multiple levels, since everything that comes out of this process is 'enigmatic and contradictory'. The narrative of the bad conscience does not provide a verdict on the conceptual or psychological roots of morality, in part because its role is so equivocal. The narrative can merely show how profoundly we are tied up with it.

Only two steps in the narrative of the Second Treatise now remain: to show how the bad conscience reaches its 'sublime pinnacle' (II: 19) and to account for the moralisation of guilt through its push back into the bad conscience. To account for the intensification of the bad conscience, Nietzsche reverts to discussing the creditor–debtor relationship. The two processes, the transformation of 'debt' into 'guilt' and the development of bad conscience, converge, with a sense of extreme indebtedness accounting for the intensification of bad conscience. Bad conscience intensifies when one feels a sense of indebtedness not to a particular creditor, or even to one's community as a whole, but to one's ancestors. Then it becomes possible to feel indebted not just for the identifiable benefits of social life but also for the whole circumstance of one's existence, which is something that one cannot have done anything to merit. Past generations sacrificed immediate satisfaction in order to build up civilisation, and cannot receive reciprocal benefits. As civilisation flourishes, then, the unreciprocated benefits are magnified. According to Nietzsche, ancient cultures even believed in the continued existence of ancestors as powerful figures who granted new advantages to present generations. One could make sacrifices to them, and offer other observances, but these could never suffice to relieve the burden of debt.

The logic of this process is that the more successfully socialisation proceeds, the more the sense of indebtedness is exacerbated, even as this requires new explanations for the basis of immense debt. So, Nietzsche writes:

> this crude kind of logic should be thought to its conclusion: ultimately the ancestors of the *mightiest* tribes must have grown to prodigious proportions through the imagination of growing fear, and they must have been pushed back into the darkness of a divine uncanniness and inconceivability – in the end the ancestor is necessarily transfigured into a *god*.

Perhaps here we have even the origin of the gods, hence an origin from *fear*! (II: 19)[12]

Gods were invented, Nietzsche hypothesises, so as to imagine magnitudes of debt that even ancestors could not have been owed – magnitudes that inspire fear. Debts to gods, furthermore, are not contingent on blood relations, unlike those of tribal ancestors. The invention of gods thus permits an unlimited range of debt and its disconnection from any particular form of social formation. This process concludes with 'the rise of the Christian God as the maximal god achieved to date' (II: 20), which elicits 'a maximum of guilt feeling on earth' (II: 20).

This maximum feeling of guilt places increasing strains on belief, however. In order for the psychic harm to be sustained, one has to believe increasingly abstract stories about an all-powerful and yet remote God, while social complexity leaves less and less time for fostering such beliefs. The process of guilt might tend to diminish as it depends on theological belief. Here is where the 'actual moralization' (II: 21) of 'guilt' and 'duty' takes place, with the effect of preventing the sense of guilt and duty from withering away from a loss of faith. According to Nietzsche, 'With the moralization of the concepts guilt and duty, with their being pushed back into the *bad* conscience we actually have the attempt to *reverse* the development just described [. . .] now precisely the prospect of an ultimate discharge once and for all is *supposed* to be pessimistically closed' (II: 21). The notion of guilt has many senses, from a status of having committed an offence to a feeling that one has failed in an obligation. The psychology of the bad conscience makes the distinctive 'moralisation' of guilt possible, however. When guilt is 'pushed back' into the bad conscience, it does not need to be connected to any external reciprocal relation. There does not need to be a specific obligation that one has failed to discharge,

---

[12] Although Durkheim's approach to early religion differs significantly from Nietzsche's account – for example, regarding the role of fear – there is an interesting parallel between Nietzsche's line of analysis here and Durkheim's famous claim (actually posed as a rhetorical question) that 'god and the society are one and the same' (Durkheim 1995: 208).

or a wrongful harm that one has committed; there can be merely one's hostile relationship to oneself, punishing oneself for being someone deserving of punishment. With moralisation, that is, all the adjudication and enforcement takes place within the psyche, so one can be guilty all the time, regardless of anything one has done. The bad conscience can attach a feeling of guilt to anyone, however they conceive of themselves in relation to the positions of creditor and debtor, and since this feeling is not grounded in anything in particular, nothing could suffice to alleviate it. Guilt becomes irredeemable.

Nietzsche claims that the 'stroke of genius of *Christianity*' (II: 21) is to offer a symbolic interpretation of the irredeemability of guilt. He means both that Christianity offered an after-the-fact interpretation of a psychological process that had already taken place, and that the religious interpretation intensifies this process: 'this human of bad conscience has taken over the presupposition of religion in order to drive his self-torture to its most gruesome harshness and sharpness' (II: 22). Christianity's main myth, Nietzsche claims, is God as creditor sacrificing himself for the sake of his debtor. Human beings are so wretched that they cannot redeem their own sinfulness, so they depend on the exemplary self-sacrifice of the creditor who, out of love, suffers on the cross to redeem them. According to Nietzsche, this myth provided a 'temporary relief' (II: 21) to those who suffered from guilt, since it promised a possible future redemption. But it also intensified guilt in a 'paradoxical and horrifying way' (II: 21), since it created a new, unfathomable debt out of unwarranted sacrifice that it would be inconceivable to repay. Holding out the chance to be saved from sin offers hope, but it also emphasises the ineffaceability of sin and the utter dependence on salvation.

The story of the bad conscience and the conceptual development of guilt thus turns out to be a story of how human beings, as a condition of social existence, became so skilled at directing their aggressive instincts inward that we have produced endless guilt, not grounded in anything in particular, and without any hope for relief. Since the bad conscience was invented, we sustain it in order to accommodate ourselves to the difficulties of animal natures living in modern, rule-governed, interdependent societies. Nietzsche characterises the effect of moralisation as one of making life as a whole a condition of punishment:

> the *will* of a human being to find himself guilty and reprehensible to the point of unatonability, his *will* to imagine himself punished without the possibility of the punishment ever being equivalent to the guilt, his *will* to infect the deepest ground of things with the problem of punishment and guilt. (II: 22)

Nietzsche is, of course, not claiming that everyone consciously thinks in terms of punishment and guilt, but rather that the conceptualisation of moral guilt allows it to be internalised, pervasive and permanent, all the while retaining its connection with the material practices of punishment. Moral guilt imposes demands that do not need to be made explicit, that relate to what we are and how we feel as much as to anything we might do, and that can never be fully satisfied. Every aspect of life can be the occasion for 'psychic cruelty' (II: 22) that we experience in some way as punishment because we inflict it on ourselves, and that has few practical limitations for the same reason.

Before concluding, Nietzsche offers a contrast between two ways in which gods have been conceptualised and the different psychological functions these conceptualisations have served. Nietzsche's point is that there are ways of thinking about the divine other than the one that has contributed to the emergence of irredeemable debt and moral guilt. The Christian 'holy God' (II: 23) furnishes 'antitheses' to human existence, so that one can feel 'guilt before *God*' (II: 22). The idea of God, that is, is constructed out of a contrast with natural human limitations and failings. These contrasts are then idealised so that human beings can interpret themselves as sinful in their natural constitution. The nominal role of God is as saviour, but the conceptual place of God is to provide a model against which persons can compare themselves and find themselves to be infinitely inferior; the effect is to produce self-contempt. Greek gods, by contrast, were invented 'as reflections of noble and autocratic human beings in whom the *animal* in humans felt deified' (II: 23). The Greek gods manifested natural human qualities in exaggerated forms; they were imperfect and typically foolish, but also robust and joyful, and thus they allowed the Greeks to glorify qualities recognisable from their own lives. As flawed but powerful, the Greek gods could also be blamed for human failings and misfortunes, rather than functioning as an unattainable standard.

Nietzsche uses the last two aphorisms as a conclusion for the Treatise; I will return to these in the final section of this chapter. The narrative has already ended, however, and it had two protagonists. One was the bad conscience. Nietzsche's story depends on the idea that urbanisation produced a profound change in human psychology, and that this change worked in tandem with the conceptual frameworks of memory, accountability and punishment to create an inner world of normative concern and self-harm. In the bad conscience human beings have a faculty of internalised self-scrutiny and self-torment that no other creature has. The other protagonist is the concept of guilt. It is a slippery character, mutable and indeterminate; its meaning shifts according to changing social practices and the workings of the bad conscience to generate more dissatisfaction with ourselves. Its very fluidity, however, allows it to take a leading role in shaping our self-understanding as moral beings. The story of the Second Treatise is how the conceptual and psychological world we live in grants us a depth of moral concern and also makes these concerns painful and unresolvable. Our moral experience is sustained by a repressed guilt that perpetually afflicts us.

Philosophical arguments

In the Second Treatise, Nietzsche occasionally interrupts his narrative to offer arguments on a range of philosophical topics. These arguments, although diverging from the main narrative, elaborate on his discussion by offering higher-order reflections on the concerns of the narrative, in particular by extending his treatment of the significance of memory and morality. In this section, I will discuss his treatment of three intersecting topics: historical understanding, punishment and political realism. But first I will briefly review his treatment of a philosophical topic that runs so fully through the course of the narrative that it is inseparable from it. One could indeed almost ignore the role of morality and read the narrative as an extended meditation on this topic, the nature of the 'inner'.

Modern philosophy placed an account of the mind at the centre of its enterprise. According to typical versions of this account, the mind is a unified, conscious awareness that brings together the various aspects of the self with immediate, transparent access to its own representations. The mind, then, encompasses the self, and is perfectly private and inner. 'Within' the mind, as it were, are contents and capacities, some of which are perhaps innately present, and all of which are available to self-scrutiny but closed off to anyone outside; thinking consists in having representations enclosed within this space. There are, of course, variations, especially metaphysical ones that relate the mind to material or immaterial substance, and epistemological ones that differ on the reliability of thought and the scope of the mind's native powers. On the overall picture, however, to be someone at all is to be a mind; the mind is in some way prior to social, embodied existence, and, because of this priority, one's self and one's thoughts are independent of others.

Nietzsche, in the course of the Second Treatise, rejects every aspect of this account. He does not offer his own systematic account, but he relates a series of claims according to which the self is not coextensive with the mind; we lack fully privileged, private access to our 'inner' life; and the inner is not the distinguishing characteristic of mind but rather a late, social development. He is especially concerned to argue that various dimensions of inner life did not come fully formed as part of human animal nature, but have histories, in which they develop and change in response to social interactions. In the main narrative, for example, memory develops through ascetic practices and the repetition of what is customary, seriousness comes about through painful social sanctions, thinking in general initially takes the form of persons measuring themselves against one another in terms of prices, and the expansion of inner life takes place when instincts are forced into opposition with one another through social imperatives.[13] In all of

---

[13] In a passage in *The Gay Science* that was written at about the same time as the *Genealogy*, Nietzsche also claims that 'Consciousness is really just a net connecting one person with another' (GS §354).

these examples, inner life is not the core of what someone is, but an extension of social practices that are typically directed 'outside'. Various kinds of bodily and social training over long periods of time were needed to produce the capacities that are characteristic of inner life. Nietzsche's account, however, is not just about how these capacities were (and are) produced, but about what they are like. One aspect of inner life, for example, takes the form of monologues, or possibly dialogues with oneself. In Nietzsche's picture, this is an extension of a capacity originally developed to communicate with others in urgent situations; this capacity can be adapted to other occasions and refined so that it does not need an external addressee. It remains, in some ways, the same capacity, however. Discourse with oneself still has the character of discourse, and thus employs language in ways that reproduce the means and requirements of communication with others. Inner reflections depend on shared linguistic resources and their performative force, and are thus shaped by interactions with others. Even when inner reflections are not directly about relations to others, they can express the separateness of one's own standpoint and how it might be reintegrated with others' once discourse is brought into the open again. Nietzsche characterises inner depth not as an empty vessel for representations, but as interaction in a very secluded part of the social world, one where attitudes and expectations of others are formed.

One of the particular philosophical topics that Nietzsche takes up in a long digression is the nature of *historical understanding*. This digression appears amid a discussion of punishment, but Nietzsche's interest in the nature of historical understanding is not exclusive to punishment. He identifies a wide range of other phenomena for which historical inquiry is especially apt. He specifically mentions law and legal institutions, social customs, political practice, forms of art and religious cults, and even suggests that physiological organs and 'all occurrences in the organic world' (II: 12) demand a historical form of understanding. The domain of history is expansive and includes morality, in any case, so Nietzsche does not trouble himself to determine its precise limits so much as to address how to understand any activity or practice with its own past.

Nietzsche sees standard approaches as caught between two failed options: appeal to prior intentions and appeal to mechanistic principles.[14] He takes the latter option less seriously; he insults it as a reconciliation with the 'mechanistic absurdity of all events' (II: 12) or censures it as ethically deficient more than he argues against it. The lack of sustained argumentation reflects Nietzsche's position, however. He does not take it as a defective or mistaken mode of understanding so much as an evasion of understanding. Appeals to mechanistic principles explain events by referring them to lawlike regularities: when a set of conditions is met, a certain kind of event is bound to take place. Activities, then, can be accounted for without reference to aims or purposes by treating them simply as movements that are regularly produced. For Nietzsche, however, the kinds of questions that one might ask about punishment, for example, are why it happens, why it happens in the way that it does, and how it happened to take the form that it does. But mechanistic principles at best indicate that when one thing happens, then another thing follows. This can be important for making predictions or identifying causal factors, but whatever cognitive interest this holds, it does not address the questions that Nietzsche takes to be necessary to make sense of punishment. So he dismisses mechanism out of hand, as not making a relevant contribution to historical understanding.

The other option that Nietzsche considers is that historical phenomena are to be understood in terms of the antecedent intentions that produce them. Historical phenomena, on this view, are purposive, so in order to understand them, we look to the states of mind that instituted their aims and set them into motion. For example, 'we imagined punishment as invented for punishing' (II: 12); the practice was invented when someone formed the intention to bring it about. Activities and practices are the external realisation of the inner content furnished by the mental state. Nietzsche, however, argues that there is no such mental state, and even if there were, it could have neither the appropriate content nor causal efficacy. According to Nietzsche,

---

[14] One can find a similar discussion of the 'false dilemma' of 'mechanism and finalism' in Pierre Bourdieu's *Outline of a Theory of Practice* (1972: 72).

'the cause of the emergence of a thing and its ultimate utility, its actual application and integration into a system of purposes lie apart *toto coelo*' (II: 12). He accepts part of the standard position: historical understanding consists in reconstructing the purposes of an activity or practice; we understand historical things by understanding what they are for, or what aims they serve. But he insists on distinguishing purposes from the 'cause of the emergence of a thing'; purposes do not function to initiate events. They do not even have a separate and determinate existence before the fact. A 'thing', Nietzsche writes, requires 'application and integration into a system of purposes' to take on its purposive character. Purposes, that is, are not independent entities that generate or direct things that they govern; rather, they are a function of the system in which particular things have interconnected roles. So a prior intention to punish, for example, could not explain the invention of the practice of punishment, because the prior intention would not have any content until the practice exists and its activities are carried out. And once the practice exists, further intentions to punish depend on the past and future of the practice for their content. Purposes do not take shape by themselves, as antecedent mental states, but appear within a broader context of activity that can be made sense of retrospectively.

Nietzsche's favoured position on historical understanding, then, is that it proceeds by identifying the succession of aims and purposes that are imposed after the fact. Activities make sense as moves in ongoing practices, so to understand particular performances one has to understand the history of the practices that provide their context. Practices, furthermore, do not have stable purposes, but have their own history of shifting aims that extend into the future; practices are transformed by the attempts to extend or understand them. The meaning of a practice is not, then, available in the initial move, but only with its integration into a system of purposes. This integration, furthermore, takes place through power relations. Indeed, for Nietzsche, this integration is exemplary of what power relations are:

> Something that has somehow come into being is always interpreted for new views, newly appropriated, transformed

and reorganized for a new purpose by a superior power [. . .] all occurrences in the organic world are an *overpowering*, a becoming-master and [. . .] in turn all overpowering and becoming-master are a new interpreting. (II: 12)[15]

Historical understanding thus does not primarily involve how particular events came about, but how ongoing practices are reshaped to serve new ends through 'processes of overpowering' (II: 12).

One potential objection to taking historical understanding to be retrospective in this way is that it seems to focus more on an arbitrary imposition of meaning than on what actually happened. The theoretical appeal to thinking of purposes as antecedent mental states is that the *explanans* is self-contained and completed; everything needed to understand a historical phenomenon is potentially available by the time it takes place. If, by contrast, one thinks of purposes as continuously subject to changing power relations, then it might seem as if the object of understanding is the power relations rather than the historical phenomenon itself. Nietzsche's response to this is that, for historical phenomena, the meaning is partly constitutive of what they are. With promising or punishing, for example, the performances fall under descriptions that make them what they are. Punishment, as such, can only take place in a context where it is seen as inflicting a harm in response to a perceived wrong, and so on; it has to be carried out *as* punishment or it is some other kind of infliction of harm. To punish, then, involves a 'whole synthesis of meanings' (II: 13) that make what one does an incident of punishing, but that are not settled in advance by prior intentions or anything else. Discussion of this line of thought will resume in the final section of this chapter, but Nietzsche's point is that understanding meaningful activity requires attention to the

---

[15] Michel Foucault's conception of power relations as 'both intentional and nonsubjective' borrows from Nietzsche's discussion. See, for example, *The History of Sexuality, Volume I*: 'If in fact [power relations] are intelligible, this is not because they are the effect of another instance that "explains" them, but rather because they are imbued, through and through, with calculation: there is no power that is exercised without a series of aims and objectives. But this does not mean that it results from the choice or decision of an individual subject' (Foucault 1978: 94–5).

meaning of the activity, and that is not something that is settled in the scope of a single drama. The activity itself involves a 'continuous sign-chain of ever new interpretations and contrivances' (II: 12) with no principled limit.

Another philosophical topic that Nietzsche takes up in the Second Treatise is *punishment*. Punishment has a complex role in his discussion. It lies at the conceptual root of morality, even where it is not explicitly invoked. Nietzsche's overall story of morality is one of creating the conceptual resources to see guilt as utterly pervasive and independent of any particular social institution, and punishment follows the whole arc of this story. It first arises in a number of 'material' forms and later appears in 'internalized' or 'spiritualized' ones; punishment in all its variety is what gives sense to human beings seeing their existence as a 'guilty' condition. At the same time, punishment is a particular social practice subject to moral concern. Indeed, it is almost paradigmatically the sort of thing that one can have moral concerns about, since it involves ascriptions of blame or responsibility, deliberate infliction of harm against an unwilling other, and judgement about what is proportionate or at least commensurate with the magnitude of the wrong committed. So in addition to structuring moral self-understanding as a whole, punishment also provides an occasion for reflection on how certain kinds of considerations have moral salience.

Punishment as an object of moral concern is the sort of thing one might like to have a theory about. One might like, that is, an account of precisely what punishment consists in and under what conditions it is appropriate, and some principled basis for determining what kind or how much punishment is right for particular cases. One could then, for example, adopt a retributivist theory and devote attention to the wrongfulness of past actions and their suitable penalties, or utilitarian theory, and focus more on the expected benefits of carrying out different forms of punishment. Nietzsche argues, however, that we cannot even begin to theorise punishment because we cannot even say what we are doing when we punish; the enterprise of normative theory cannot get started because there is no way of identifying what the theory would be about. Nietzsche's case, furthermore, is not specifically about punishment. Punishment is especially well-suited for his point, which he illustrates elaborately, but he takes a more general anti-theoretical stance in ethics.[16]

When someone punishes, according to Nietzsche, they do so under the description of punishment. They have some concept of punishment available to them, and at least potentially take their action to be an instance of punishment and thus to satisfy the concept. Nietzsche claims, however, that the content of the concept depends on how it has been used in the past: what actions have fallen under it, what purposes they have served, and how these purposes have shifted over time. The meaning of punishment, that is, comes from the history of punishment as a whole, and Nietzsche argues that this history is incoherent. He makes his case with a 'relatively small and random sample' (II: 13) of approximately twelve purposes that punishment has served and thus senses of what punishment is: 'punishment as rendering harmless [. . .] as repayment to the injured party [. . .] as instilling fear of those who determine and carry out punishment' (II: 13) and so on. Punishment, Nietzsche writes, comes to form a kind of unity in that there is a single activity, punishing, that many people take themselves to be doing at many different points in time. But this unity contains many contrary and irreconcilable aims, and does not determine any particular thing that one is doing in punishing. As a result, Nietzsche claims, 'Today it is impossible to say with any certainty *why* people punish: all concepts in which an entire process summarizes itself semiotically elude definition; only that which has no history is definable' (II: 13). Someone punishing acts according to the concept of punishment, but the concept of punishment is undefinable and, as a result, we cannot say what someone punishing is doing. The enterprise of normative theory cannot get started here, then, because specifying when and how someone should punish depends on first knowing what the activity is for, and that knowledge is unavailable.

---

[16] Nietzsche's interest here, although not his particular arguments, thus overlaps with an anti-theoretical strand in philosophical ethics, such as represented by Bernard Williams, among others, and with opposition to 'ideal theory', as represented by Charles Mills, among others. See, for example, Williams 1985: esp. 110–12; and Mills 1997: esp. 121–3.

Nietzsche's argument is based on not knowing what we are doing when we punish, and one could respond that we do not need to know that in order to have a normative theory. The question of what we are doing and the question of what we ought to do are separable: one could try to specify what we ought to do regardless of what anyone is doing. So, for example, we could have a theory according to which rightness in punishment is a function of its effectiveness in incapacitating criminals from future crimes; the standard of rightness would be independent of the actions that are actually performed. This response is correct, in that the normative question is indeed separable from knowing what we are doing. Nietzsche is not denying that we can have a normative theory, however; he is denying that we can have a normative theory of *punishment*. An incapacitation theory would be a theory of some practice other than our practice of punishment, or alternately an attempt to change what the existing practice is about. What it prescribes is not how we ought to punish, but how we ought to do something else. There may be strong grounds for adopting the new practice, but it would be a new practice. So, on one hand, such a theory would not be offering guidance in our practices, but innovation for circumstances in which history is abstracted away. And, on the other hand, trying to adopt its prescriptions would not foreclose the question of what we are doing. We could still wonder whether we were not extending the old practice, with all the old motivations, but only a new pretext. Nietzsche has little to say on the feasibility of normative theory, then, but insists that it is too far removed from any actual practice to provide practical guidance.

A third philosophical topic that Nietzsche takes up might be called *political realism*. By this term I mean to indicate a form of reflection about politics, namely that it should proceed by considering the available social resources for managing the particular forms of potential disaster that happen to present themselves. This contrasts with political idealism, according to which political reflection should proceed by considering the ideals that are specific to the political domain and that ought to be collectively pursued. On such an approach, political reflection starts by articulating the values expressed in shared commitments to political life, formulates ideals based on these values, and recommends that these ideals guide political practice. Nietzsche does not denounce the formulation of ideals, but suggests that it offers little help in guiding political practice. The operation of politics does not leave room for instruction from ideals: choices in politics are too deeply constrained and dependent on contingent circumstances for ideals to be informative.[17]

Realism is, of course, not the focus of the Second Treatise. Indeed, the nature of the position is such that it is unlikely to be the centre of attention; if Nietzsche were advocating any other '-ism' than realism then it would call for an energetic defence. Realism nevertheless occasionally makes an appearance, such as in this digression from recounting the origin of the bad conscience: 'That is indeed how the "state" begins on earth: I think we have gotten beyond that wishful fantasy that has it beginning with a "contract". Whoever can command, whoever is by nature "master", whoever behaves violently in deed and gesture – what does he care about contracts!' (II: 17). Nietzsche is contrasting his story of the violent origins of the state with social contract theory. He is arguably confused here: social contract theory is not a historical account of the origin of the state, and it does not purport to describe how politics actually works. Social contract theory typically imagines a hypothesised pre-political condition in order to present the legitimacy of political institutions as a function of the choice to enter into political society and how that choice is constrained by normative commitments. In other words, it does not imagine that the state in fact begins with a contract, but assesses legitimacy by reflecting on what conditions would have to be built into such a contract. Nietzsche's rejection of social contract theory, although careless, is genuine, however. His argument, I take it, is that the mechanisms of state power are incompatible with the kinds of deliverances that a social contract theory, or any kind of political idealism, can provide.

---

[17] For this discussion I am relying on Raymond Geuss's treatment of Nietzsche and realism in *Philosophy and Real Politics*. See, for example: 'Politics as we know it is a matter of differential choice: opting for A *rather than* B. Thus politics is not about doing what is good or rational or beneficial *simpliciter* [. . .] but about the pursuit of what is good in a particular concrete case by agents with limited powers and resources, where choice of one thing to pursue means failure to choose and pursue another' (Geuss 2008: 30–1).

Nietzsche paints with a broad brush, and his digression is about the origin of states rather than their ongoing operation, but his general point seems to be that political life 'on earth' (II: 17) is rooted in superior power, control over the use of violence, and the disposition to be 'master' (II: 17). Established institutions can regulate themselves to some extent by 'grounds, reasons, consideration' (II: 17), but having political authority at all depends on an assertion of power that manages to make itself recognised. This is not to say that politics must take power as its own end or glorify violence; it is only to say that the ends of politics are achieved in an ultimately non-rational manner. Nietzsche's case for realism, then, offers a pair of contrasts. Political idealism depends on being able to structure institutions so that they function according to public norms, but, in Nietzsche's view, these norms would not be *effective* in motivating political actors or shifting the character of institutions, and they would be *too abstract* to have clear applications in political decision making. Nietzsche thinks, by contrast, that political realism, by starting with an account of how power operates, is better suited to raise considerations that would be effective in guiding political action and that are applicable in concrete cases. (In Nietzsche's metaphor, the political actor is a sculptor imposing form on material: meaningful results come about by producing specific effects on specific material.) Reflection, then, for Nietzsche, should take the form of attentiveness to what effects are possible and desirable given the material that is available to work with. Political idealism can propose its own criteria of assessment, but these might never inform practice.

Methodological and rhetorical issues

The first part of this section is devoted to continuing the argument from the previous chapter about Nietzsche's methodology. I argue that Nietzsche, in the Second Treatise, shifts his naturalistic approach into a historicist one. In terms of both expressed methodology and characteristic claims, he uses this Treatise to make a case for a historical understanding of morality. The second part of this section reviews the final two aphorisms, where Nietzsche offers a coda to the Second Treatise. His concluding remarks are strangely disconnected from the ostensible argument of the Treatise, but they are rhetorically rich and connect the Treatise to the project of the Genealogy as a whole. So I will discuss some of Nietzsche's rhetorical strategies and how they relate to his philosophical claims.

In the previous chapter I argued that Nietzsche's naturalist understanding of morality required an appeal to semantic content because it turned out that the emergence of morality turned on the availability of moral concepts. The First Treatise, I claimed, laid out a case for how creatures without a moral vocabulary made one available for themselves; aside from the specific content of the Treatise, it was meant to make the methodological point that naturalism involves meaning. Now I want to argue that the aim of the Second Treatise is, apart from conveying its specific content about guilt and bad conscience, to make the methodological point that understanding meaning involves historicism. That is, one should approach the understanding of content with a distinctively historical account by appealing to past practices in which the content emerged. Understanding these practices, furthermore, amounts to reconstructing the participants' standpoints, not in the sense of recapturing lost mental states, but in the sense of reconstructing the shifting systems of purposes that the practices served.

Nietzsche expresses the need for a historical account through his claim that the concepts relevant to morality are undefinable:

> The concept 'punishment' in a very late stage of culture [. . .] in fact no longer represents one meaning at all, but a whole synthesis of 'meanings': the previous history of punishment generally, the history of its exploitation for the most diverse purposes, ultimately crystallizes into a kind of unity that is difficult to sort out, difficult to analyze and, it must be emphasized, entirely *undefinable*. (II: 13)

Understanding morality requires a historical account because it necessitates understanding concepts, such as 'punishment', that are undefinable. Where no satisfactory definition is available, understanding the concept relies on locating its use in the context of past social practices, and thus constructing a historical account of what it means. Nietzsche does leave open the possibility that there are some concepts whose content is so determinate and simple that one would need no historical account to understand them. At the same time, however, the conditions for not needing a historical account are demanding: a concept must never have been used before, or at least never employed towards any end, and its conditions of application must be unambiguously specifiable. For culturally embedded concepts that are tied up with human ends, a historical account is needed to make sense of their content.

We might still ask ourselves several questions about the nature of the difficulty here, however. How can the entire previous history of a concept be contained in its present usage? Why can its content not be explicated in terms of what it means at a given moment of time? And even if the meanings are tangled and difficult to analyse, why can they not be specified as definitions, however complex and compound those definitions might have to be?

In his claim about undefinability, Nietzsche gives two indications of his answer to these questions. One is that punishment has become a 'synthesis', that it has crystallised into a kind of unity. That is, punishment develops with its own independent logic. To be sure, the idea of punishment contains, in some way, ideas of retribution, deterrence and so on, and thus its meaning depends on the content of those other ideas. One of Nietzsche's points here, however, is that how those other bits of content relate to the content of 'punishment' depends on how punishment in fact functions. Once punishment is crystallised, as it were, into a unity, then it becomes possible to punish for its own sake: one can form an intention to punish and act on that basis. Punishment takes on its own meaning, which is not reducible to a complex of more basic parts, even though it relies on a connection with those elements of past practices for its continued sense.

This relates to the other indication that Nietzsche gives in his claim about undefinability: 'punishment', among other things, is not to be treated as a fixed semantic unit, but as an ongoing practice. To understand the meaning of something such as punishment, Nietzsche insists, is not to identify some discrete unit available for inspection; there is no determinate bit of content to be uncovered. Later in the *Genealogy*, Nietzsche complains that a semantic '*in-itself*' would just 'stand there dumb for all eternity, like every thing-in-itself' (III: 7);[18] that is to say, such a notion of content could not contribute to anyone's understanding. To understand what something means, rather, involves situating it in the context of a practice, the 'history of its employment for various ends'. When someone acts under the description of punishing, the practice of punishment is being reinterpreted and extended; the legacy of the practice is being appropriated in a particular way, and a direction for the future of the practice is being set. Nietzsche discusses the resulting 'fluidity' of meaning in terms of '*signs* that a will to power has become master over something' (II: 12). Explaining the meaning of something, then, is more like accounting for how criteria of salience are being adapted and transformed than it is providing definitions.

This might seem to suggest that one only needs a historical account to understand a practice as a whole, but that individual occasions might be more readily understood. One might concede, for example, that punishing in general, or the contemporary meaning of punishment, is opaque for historical reasons, but nevertheless insist that, if one is only interested in a single occasion in the past, one ought to be able to explain what it meant to punish someone. Even on a single occasion, however, acting under the description of punishment takes up the ongoing synthesis of meanings, so the particular performance cannot be disentangled from the practice as a whole. And the practice as a whole is not determinate moment by moment. What counts as punishing needs to be open-ended for future expressions to be possible. The meaning of punishment only gets settled through its expression, and so only after the fact, at which point the question of what now counts as punishing is renewed. To be sure there are ways of

---

[18] I have modified this translation slightly. The Del Caro translation has '*in himself*' for the German *an sich* and 'stupidly' for the German *dumm*. I have replaced the '*in himself*' with the neuter '*in itself*' because it refers to a neuter 'fact' rather than a person, and I have replaced 'stupidly' with 'dumb' because Nietzsche's point is not that the fact is unintelligent, but that it is, by itself, silent or mute. Here is the passage in context, with my modifications: 'What does that *mean*? For this fact first has to be interpreted: *in itself* it stands there dumb for all eternity, like every "thing in itself"' (III: 7).

understanding single events that are different, but the understanding of meanings and intentions has a historical form.

Nietzsche illustrated this earlier with the example of the drive for purity.[19] He claims that 'pure' and 'impure', like all concepts, were originally meant only literally: the criterion in that case was whether or not one was covered in filth. But, Nietzsche writes, 'it becomes clear from the whole nature of an essentially priestly aristocracy why [. . .] valuation opposites could soon become internalized and sharpened in a dangerous manner' (I: 6). Elsewhere he discusses a similar process by which 'a drive learns to cower and submit, but also to *purify* and *sharpen* itself' (BGE §189). In the process that Nietzsche describes, at least some people have a drive for purity; to understand those people, then, might require understanding that they have this drive and what this drive means. But this is a potentially impossible task because what it means at one moment may be completely different from what it means at another: the content of the drive is susceptible to internalisation, sharpening, purification and possibly 'spiritualization' (II: 6). In that case, what had been about being covered in filth can be about sex, or ritual, or innocence, or adulteration in some sense, with the historical process of development as the tenuous but enduring linkage between these senses.

The content of a psychological drive for or ideal of purity can undergo radical shifts, from the skin to the soul. But a historical account can show how disparate instances can all count as examples of one and the same thing, undergoing change while preserving its unity. We can understand these diverse instances as examples or manifestations of the same thing by taking a participant standpoint seriously: washing one's feet and not uttering certain words, for example, belong together from a viewpoint that sees them both as satisfying a demand for purity. Similarly with punishment, what counts as an offence or as a penalty depends on the relevant standpoint. In taking up a historical account, we are not using our present judgement of salience to determine what

---

[19] Haidt and Joseph 2004 discuss purity in a similar way, in their case as a basic foundation of morality. See also *Monty Python and the Holy Grail*, on how to recognise who the king is (Chapman and Cleese 2002: 5).

belongs together; in the case of purity, we might not even have a concept that is similar enough to apply. Nor do we treat instances as senseless movements that happen to have properties in common. We take on, as it were, the standpoints of drives and ideals, and identify how they fit in a system of aims and purposes.[20]

I will take up the methodological argument again in the next chapter, but I now turn to address the rhetorical features of the end of the Second Treatise. Nietzsche effects an abrupt change in both tone and content here. Most of the Treatise, apart from a few interruptions, recounts its narrative in a straightforward manner. With aphorism 24, however, the tone shifts from that of a temperate analysis to the urgent consideration of problems. The discussion suddenly becomes personal and pressing, and yet ironic and dense with rhetorical figures. Many of Nietzsche's typical tropes appear: there is, for example, ellipsis, metonymy and marked silence. The most distinctive feature of the discussion, however, is its shift from the story of the conceptual framework of guilt and its concomitant psychological changes to a series of rhetorical questions. These rhetorical questions are asked in different voices: the first is posed to Nietzsche by a hypothetical interlocutor, whereas the next two seem to come from Nietzsche himself. Rhetorical questions allow for the absence of explicit answers, and by remarking that his asking the questions is 'plain to see' (II: 24), Nietzsche conjures a shared confidence with his audience, as if they have been aware of the subtext of his discussions all along. The rhetorical questions differ in kind, but they all appear as part of a conversation about the ultimate aims in working on a genealogy of morality. The function of Nietzsche's rhetoric here, then, is to induce reflection on how his historical narratives connect to an implicit normative project.

There are three rhetorical questions that Nietzsche privileges as comprising the conclusion to this Treatise. The first connects the historical narrative to his normative project by calling attention

---

[20] Nietzsche seems to treat psychological features, such as drives, and axiological ones, such as ideals, as being interchangeable: drives are purposive standpoints, and having an ideal is a function of the purposive structure of one's drives. See, for example, Nietzsche's notebooks, where he claims that each of our basic drives has a 'perspectival assessment' (Nietzsche 1988: 25).

to ideals as historical possibilities. The question is posed to Nietzsche: 'Is an ideal being erected here or is one being broken down?' (II: 24). Nietzsche's response seems to reject the framing of the question, since he answers with another question rather than accepting either of the offered alternatives. There are good reasons to reject the alternatives, since the Treatise was not about either erecting or breaking down ideals. Indeed, there is no clear referent for the ideals in question. Guilt and bad conscience are the prominent topics in the narrative, but these are not ideals; other possible candidates, such as 'great health' and 'the holy God', appear later in the aphorism, but these have not been named in the Treatise up to now. The basis for raising this question is not the prior discussion of specific ideals, but a background assumption that the aim of the narrative is somehow to replace existing ideals with new ones. The first rhetorical question takes this as obvious, and wonders at the absence of a preferred new ideal, since that is presumably how a process of changing ideals should culminate.

By avoiding a direct response, Nietzsche accepts the change in topic, even while rejecting the offered alternatives. The first question sets out two activities that one can take up in relation to ideals: either building them up or breaking them down. What it means to perform these activities remains unclear, but the question does treat ideals as a human creation: they are constructed or destroyed through some kind of purposive activity. Later in the aphorism, Nietzsche accepts the characterisation of ideals as constructed, but rejects the idea that there are discrete processes of erecting and destroying that one is free to take up. He makes this claim enigmatically, using anaphora to create an imitation proverb: 'In order for a temple to be erected *a temple must be destroyed*: that is the law' (II: 24). 'Temple' is presumably a metonym for 'ideal' here, since it too can be erected or destroyed. Nietzsche, then, is replacing the false alternative of the rhetorical question with a pseudo-lawlike process of ideal creation. He gives no evidence to support a law; the point of the proverb is not to convey information, but to issue a reminder that a realistic process of ideal formation is constrained by historical and psychological limitations. Ideal creation is not like inventing a band name or imagining a utopia, and destroying an ideal is more involved than deprecating it. Either activity requires rendering human beings suited to recognising the ideal, having a vocabulary in which to make sense of it, and leading a way of life in which it can (or cannot) be embodied. The historical narratives, rather than the proverb itself, provide guidance on such processes. The proverb, then, might point to metaphorical obstruction: as the Second Temple was built on the same site as Solomon's Temple, new ideals might need to be cleared of interference from old ones. Or the proverb might be pointing to a more dialectical process, in which new ideals are built out of the remnants of old ones, as 'guilt' was constructed out of 'debts'. The narrative, in any case, points to limits in the range of historical possibility, and this is what the first rhetorical question calls attention to.

The second rhetorical question offers a way of thinking about how to assess historical possibilities. With this question an answer is beside the point: 'But have you ever asked yourselves sufficiently how dearly the erecting of *every* ideal on earth had to be purchased?' (II: 24). This is Nietzsche's rejoinder, in his own voice and with an implication of superior knowledge, to the first question. The answer is presumably 'no', but that does not matter: the aim of the question is not to extract information but to carry out the performative task of calling attention to the costliness of ideals. In particular, Nietzsche takes 'you' to be concerned with 'erecting' ideals, and therefore encourages 'you' to reflect sufficiently on what the costs of doing so have been. This furnishes some context to the historical narratives: they can be reconsidered as treatments of the construction of ideals through purposive activity. Although this activity was not guided by any overarching intention, we can weigh whether the activity had benefits that potentially outweighed the costs. There is a prospective inference to be made here, too: one is presumably supposed to infer from past events that the future erecting of ideals will be costly, too. This is Nietzsche's recommendation for thinking about the historical possibilities of ideals, in terms of their costs. But what is the currency of costs, and who incurs them? If the costs are located in the past, with the invention of old ideals, then we can perhaps discount them, but the 'you' of the question suggests that the costs are personal and contemporary. From the first rhetorical question we might think that the cost is the sacrifice of old ideals, that our loss is the ideals we can no longer have. The narratives suggest psychological costs, too, however: the self-hostility of bad conscience, and perhaps susceptibility to anxiety, fear, resentment and hypocrisy.

Later in the aphorism Nietzsche offers some guidance as to the nature of the costs. He emphasises the psychological costs, and with a noteworthy temporality: 'We modern human beings, we are the heirs of thousands of years of conscience-vivisection and self-animal-cruelty: in this we have our longest practice, perhaps our artistry, in any case our subtlety, our pampered taste' (II: 24). Nietzsche uses the first-person plural here. 'We' are, of course, located in the present, but related to the past as its heirs. The costs of ideal creation are to be measured in terms of self-inflicted cruelty, and in particular the internalised cruelty of conscience. These costs, although incurred in the past, somehow continue in us to this day. They have been incorporated into our 'artistry' and our 'taste', so that we continue to inflict them on ourselves. The costs of ideal creation seem to be perpetual, then: they are incurred not just in effecting a transition, but afterwards in us because they are a part of our 'longest practice'. This still leaves the costs of erecting future ideals unclear, however. They could extend and intensify the psychological costs of past ideal creation, or they could be entirely new ones, which either supplant the old harms or add to them.

The third rhetorical question retains the idea that creating new ideals is costly, but introduces a new set of costs. Nietzsche asks, 'How much reality always had to be slandered and denied, how much lying sanctified, how much conscience disturbed, how much "God" sacrificed each time?' (II: 24). He once again calls for an inference from the past to the future, but this time in terms of a set of new, somewhat mysterious costs. Slandering reality and sanctifying lies imposes some sort of burden on us, but 'God' is a metonym for something unspecified, and it is not clear why these costs are costly, or how we might measure them against anything else. The end of the aphorism, furthermore, introduces more costs of the 'previous ideal': 'the great nausea [. . .] the will to nothingness [. . .] nihilism' (II: 24).

At the beginning of II: 24, Nietzsche declared that he was concluding with three question marks. The function of the ensuing rhetorical questions was to convey an underlying agenda in offering historical narratives; that agenda was to make sense of the historical possibility of new ideals in terms of how costly they might be; these costs are unclear but involve psychological or spiritual harms sustained not only initially, but on an ongoing basis. After the initial three rhetorical questions, Nietzsche adds a second set. A series of new questions concern possible courses of action to undertake in response to the historical lessons about the costliness of new ideals. The first brings up the idea of a 'reverse attempt':

> A reverse attempt would be possible *in itself* – but who is strong enough for it? – namely to wed to bad conscience the *unnatural* inclinations, all those aspirations to the Beyond, to what is counter to the senses, instincts, nature, animal, in short, the previous ideals, all of which are ideals hostile to life, ideals that slander the world. (II: 24)

This gives a description of the ideal or ideals that are subject to being broken down: they are hostile to life and they slander the world. The ideals, that is, denigrate our senses and other features of our animal nature, and orient our sense of what is important to something that is imagined to lie outside human experience. Holding these ideals, then, dissociates us from our natural constitution. A 'reverse attempt' would thus take the psychological resources that accompany anti-natural ideals, in particular the bad conscience, and 'wed' them to the anti-natural ideals themselves. This is strange, though, because it sounds more like a means for effecting change than a final end. This counter-project reinforces the idea that destruction is needed for the erection of a new ideal, perhaps, but seemingly falls short of providing a new ideal.

Nietzsche nevertheless indicates that he seeks not just an antidote, as it were, to past harms, but a *'redemption* of this reality' (II: 24): some way to consider the natural things that have been devalued as genuinely valuable. He does not furnish an ideal to bring about this redemption, however. The best candidate in the aphorism is perhaps the 'great health' (II: 24). Here Nietzsche associates the great health with 'a kind of sublime malice itself, a final superlatively self-confident mischief of knowledge' (II: 24), but he does not say what it is. The best evidence for what he means by 'great health' comes from another work, written at roughly the same time. In *The Gay Science*, Nietzsche writes that great health is 'a health that one doesn't only have, but also acquires continually and must acquire because one gives it up again and again, and must give it up!'[21] 'Great health', then, sounds almost like an ideal: 'health' is paradigmatic of something valuable for its own sake, and 'great' implies intensity and importance. But great health is an ironic ideal at best. One could call it an ideal, but it is not a perfected end state that could govern one's aspirations and indeed cannot be an end state at all: one has to acquire it continuously and give it up repeatedly. The associations with 'sublime malice' and 'mischief of knowledge', furthermore, imply ironic distance. The would-be possessor of great health does not identify with health or as healthy, but instead takes a playful attitude towards it: she knows about it and what it takes to achieve it, but does not commit to acquiring it. Great health, then, does not appear to be action-guiding, since it is only available to someone who already has it and is continually losing it. Great health is less of an ideal than a characterisation of a process of successfully pursuing ideals.

Great health does not supply an ideal for human beings to measure themselves against, but a warning about the form of reflective ethical practice. Morality, beyond the specific demands that it makes, carries with it a model of ethical success. Success is a matter of arriving at the correct ideal, making particular judgements by reference to this ideal, and living in accordance with those judgements. Morality's hold on us can be such that, even if we reject specific moral demands, we might still think we need to find a solution of this form in order to carry out ethical reflection at all. Nietzsche's warning, then, is not to reinstitute morality with a novel content that obliges us in some mysterious way. The unfulfilled promise of a 'great health' is that there is some way

---

[21] GS §382. Nietzsche also quotes this passage in the section of *Ecce Homo*, 'Why I Write Such Good Books', during his discussion of *Thus Spoke Zarathustra* (Nietzsche 2005: 125).

to redeem our values without appealing to a new and conclusive answer to the problems of leading a life.

The second set of rhetorical questions also gives an indication of how Nietzsche sees his practical task by *personalising* it. About the 'reverse attempt' Nietzsche asks, 'who is strong enough for it?', and 'To whom should we come today with such hopes and demands?' (II: 24); and he answers, 'a *different kind* of spirit would be needed than is possible in this age of ours' (II: 24). This might make it seem as if what is needed is a particular personality type, and this type is not presently available, so the philosophical project of creating ideals consists in waiting for the right individual to arrive. Personalising the task is not a way of taking a passive role or placing all of one's hopes on a saviour-figure, however. It functions instead to elicit an implication from the narrative, that ideals are psychologically demanding and thus depend on suitable personalities. The process by which ideals emerged was not one of arriving at the conclusion of an argument, but one of ideals becoming embodied in a way of life. To see ideal creation as seeking 'a different kind of spirit', then, serves to emphasise the importance of the psychological transformations whereby human beings make themselves suited to new ideals and make new ideals meaningful for themselves.

There is another reason why Nietzsche frames his philosophical task as a search for a novel kind of personality. He does this to indicate that he does not see his task as something akin to seeking moral progress, whereby improvements are made in light of an existing moral vocabulary. For his project, he writes, 'we would have precisely the *good* people against us; additionally, as is only fair, the comfortable, the reconciled, the vain, the fanatical, the weary' (II: 24). He is pointing to a lack of conceptual resources for making sense of changes that he would recommend. The narrative arguments were about the emergence of the conceptual and psychological conditions for moral guilt. If we take Nietzsche, as the hypothetical interlocutor of the first rhetorical question does, to be rejecting that conceptual framework, then this leaves him without any obvious way to articulate an alternative. At least in terms of the existing vocabulary, there is no way to account for a new ideal, so instituting change will seem pathological or defective: those who are regarded as 'good', as well as the complacent and the fanatical, will be against it. Radical change has to come from those who, because they do not meet current standards of goodness, can only appear as moral failures. Of course, Nietzsche's point is not that this is an accurate way of classifying them, but that this is the only readily available framework for doing so; we lack a vocabulary suitable for understanding our situation. Personalising his philosophical task, then, is a way for Nietzsche to account for the nature of a change in ideals when there is a lack of present means for expressing what its content will be.

Nietzsche does not just personalise his philosophical task by representing it as the search for a different kind of spirit; he also personifies it as something to be carried out by a single individual. Nietzsche starts with a very long definite description before naming the individual: 'he must really come to us, the *redeeming* human being of great love and contempt, the creative spirit who time and again is driven away from any aloofness or Beyond by his surging strength' (II: 24). In the next aphorism Nietzsche identifies this future individual as '*Zarathustra the godless*' (II: 25). This leaves us to wonder why Nietzsche chose to use personification, and why he chose Zarathustra, the ancient founder of Zoroastrianism, to fill this role. Nietzsche gives no hints to the latter question here, but offers an answer in a later work, *Ecce Homo*:

> Zarathustra was the first to see the struggle of good and evil as the true wheel in the machinery of things, – morality translated into metaphysics as force, cause, goal in itself, is *his* work. But this question essentially answered itself. Zarathustra *created* this fateful error of morality: this means that he has to be the first to *recognize* it. Not only has he spent longer and had more experience here than any other thinker – the whole of history is in fact the experimental refutation of the principle of the so-called 'moral world-order' – : more importantly, Zarathustra is more truthful than any other thinker [. . .] The self-overcoming of morality from out of truthfulness, the self-overcoming of moralists into their opposite – *into me* – that is what the name Zarathustra means coming from my mouth. (EH 'Why I am a Destiny' §3)

In short, Nietzsche ascribes the invention of the 'moral world order' to Zarathustra, and thus attributes the first recognition of the error of morality to him, too. This helps little in understanding Nietzsche's use of personification, but it does indicate that he sees his narrative as conveying a historical drama in which failed human pursuits eventually come to light. Morality, in particular, as a human invention falls apart through 'experimental refutation' when its own advocacy produces its 'self-overcoming'. Zarathustra's role in this drama is to replace a focus on the 'Beyond' with 'a great love and contempt'. Personification thus works to emphasise the importance of contingent, qualified human emotions over that of transcendent ideals.

Nietzsche's trope of silence returns in the final aphorism of the Second Treatise: 'At this point only one thing befits me, to be silent . . .' (II: 25). By this point, the meaning of this silence is starting to take shape. Nietzsche is using this demonstrative silence, first, to claim superior knowledge. He could speak to matters that are critical for understanding his philosophical project, but he is deliberately withholding his knowledge; it is, for some reason, unsuitable to reveal at this moment. At any rate, *he* is unsuited to reveal it. A second use of silence, then, is to indicate Nietzsche's limited efficacy in the process of ethical transformation. He is powerless at effecting change or even formulating new ideals; he limits his role to spelling out the dynamics of the process as it has transpired in the past. Third, Nietzsche uses silence to call attention, again, to the shortcomings in the conceptual resources for expressing what an alternative to moral ideals might be. There is no conceptual space for a new ideal; anything one articulated would appear merely as a form of moral failure. Nietzsche accordingly claims that it is fitting to be silent 'at this point', implying that this will soon change. The next Treatise, he suggests, will supply some resources for thinking about what an alternative might look like, or at least further specify the difficulties of formulating an alternative.

4
The Third Treatise: What Do Ascetic Ideals Mean?

Introduction

Nietzsche, in the Third Treatise, still makes use of his tropes of objectivity: he still claims, for example, to be setting out 'the real state of affairs' (III: 13). But one can see from the start that the form of his discussion has changed. The opening is, in a way, unusually clear. The title and the first aphorism identify a topic of inquiry, provide a preliminary answer, and discuss the implications of this answer. There is no familiar explanatory task, as in the previous two Treatises, however, and even less is there a recognisable normative task. No history of the emergence of distinctively moral concepts seems to be on offer, and there is no apparent call for a new set of ethical values or the destruction of an old one. The Treatise instead begins with an open-ended hermeneutic question about an unfamiliar notion, 'What do ascetic ideals mean?' (III: 1), and then proceeds to offer a series of wide-ranging narratives that do not revert back to the genealogy of morality or even the titular hermeneutic question until the end. The very character or goal of Nietzsche's philosophical enterprise here remains unclear. Yet this is the most important part of the book: the *Genealogy* culminates in the Third Treatise. Nietzsche brings together his earlier ideas into a single, all-encompassing narrative that contextualises morality and the will to truth in an account of the role of ideals in sustaining human agency. In this account, furthermore, Nietzsche argues that the familiar forms of our self-understanding have collapsed, leaving behind a bare insight into human will: 'it would sooner will *nothingness* than *not* will' (III: 1).

The main narrative once again has a straightforward overall structure. After some reflections on the figures of the artist and the philosopher, as represented primarily by Richard Wagner and Arthur Schopenhauer, respectively, Nietzsche turns to the figure of the priest. He portrays the priest as tending to his sickly flock, which is suffering from '*degenerating life*' (III: 13) or 'physiological obstruction and exhaustion' (III: 13). The priest administers various remedies, including 'the "guilty" kind' of 'priestly medication' (III: 21), that is to say, he encourages the '*feeling of guilt*' (III: 20) to such a degree that it provokes an '*excess of feeling*' (III: 19) that temporarily alleviates suffering. In order to accomplish this, the priest changes 'the direction of *ressentiment*' (III: 15): he convinces his suffering flock that someone is to blame for their suffering, but then tells them '*you alone are to blame for yourself*' (III: 15). Having turned his people's own impotent, vengeful hostility against them, the priest succeeds in providing an explanation for their suffering, and this 'contrivance' (III: 13) provides them with some comfort. But the self-blame induced by the priest produces the 'ascetic ideal', which not only attributes value to practices that happen to be painful, but values activities and ends precisely because they are self-abnegating. The ascetic ideal gives purpose to those who would otherwise suffer from its lack, but invariably makes them sicker, thereby requiring greater asceticism to serve its purpose, and thereby making them sicker still. This process of intensifying ascetic cruelty advances until it culminates in 'nihilism': after having given up more and more for the sake of finer and finer subtleties, there was nothing left to do but give up everything for the sake of nothing. The ascetic ideal finally turns against itself, taking away even its own contrivances, so that nothing appears to be left. Modern science offers itself as a potential replacement for the ascetic ideal, but turns out to be its most extreme form.

This story of the genesis, flourishing and seemingly endless death throes of the ascetic ideal takes its importance from the existential questions that Nietzsche anchors in it, however. By framing his inquiry in terms of what ascetic ideals *mean*, Nietzsche identifies his primary concern as the significance that our lives and what we have made of ourselves have taken on. The basic claims of the Third Treatise are that we need to have a sense of purpose to carry on in our lives; we feel this need most acutely when we suffer; when we lack a sense of purpose one can be manufactured through asceticism; this asceticism is harmful, however, and the self-distance it opens up in our souls leads us to confusion about ourselves; furthermore, its effectiveness in manufacturing purposes eventually exhausts itself; and yet, although it is costly and exhausted, there is nothing to take its place. Nietzsche's ultimate argument is that we have yet to conceive of a way of thinking about our lives that is not a form of commitment to the ascetic ideal. All of our conceptual space for making sense of how life might be worthwhile is filled with ways of dedicating ourselves to ideals that are painful and alienating for us.

Morality has a privileged place in this account, as exemplifying the problems that Nietzsche attributes to the ascetic ideal. Nietzsche's ultimate argument is not primarily about the content, status or authority of moral values, however, but about human psychology and the constitution of meaning. The long history of asceticism reveals, for Nietzsche, the dependence of human agency on having a sense of purpose. This is not merely to say that individual actions are purposive, but that we need to see ourselves as aspiring towards something and overcoming obstacles in order to make sense of our endeavours, and making sense of our endeavours is a condition, for us, of sustaining activity. This distinctive feature of human agency is complemented by our ability to manufacture meaning through the self-infliction of suffering. Harming ourselves has turned out to be astonishingly productive, so that our sense of purpose has been sustained by asserting power over life's suffering through imposing it on ourselves, for example, or by creating the appearance of a 'higher purpose' by disrupting immediate satisfactions. Since these techniques respond to suffering by creating more, they generate a self-exacerbating process, but one that has nevertheless been effective.

Nietzsche's discussion of the ascetic ideal allows him to situate morality within a psychological and historical process characterised by intensifying suffering. This process is also a self-destructive one. Here it is important to see Nietzsche's story as a psychological account that proceeds, within the narrative, as if it concerns the truth of ideals. The participants in Nietzsche's narrative wish to discover metaphysical truth about values so that they could be governed by the right ideals and thereby relieve their existential worries. At some point the pursuit of the correct ideal turns into the positivist claim that there is no sense to be given to getting ideals right, and thus no such thing as a correct ideal. Inside this story, as it were, this is a drama about what ideal, if any, requires our allegiance. The process that Nietzsche thereby depicts, however, is about the psychological uses of pursuing ideals, and how the pursuits involved in sustaining the will produce an ultimate form of asceticism. For Nietzsche, positivist science preserves the form of being governed by something outside of oneself while discarding the benefit of sustaining purposes; it is an asceticism that turns our capacity for generating new meanings into depriving ourselves of them. The *Genealogy* thus comes to an anti-climactic ending in which both the pursuit of ideals and their dismissal are implicated in the history of asceticism.

With the beginning of this Treatise, as with the previous ones, Nietzsche manages to mislead about its content and nevertheless summarise it in a cryptic, compressed fashion. This Treatise, uniquely, starts with an epigraph, a slightly altered quotation from the section 'On Reading and Writing' in Nietzsche's dramatic-philosophical work, *Thus Spoke Zarathustra*. The significance of this epigraph is initially unclear, so I will postpone discussion of it until the end of this section. The very first aphorism, however, provides a self-contained introduction to the entire Treatise. It misleads: it appears merely to raise a side issue that digresses from the task of understanding and criticising moral values. Not morality, but the meaning of ascetic ideals is the central topic; holiness and faith appear here, but so do seductiveness and boredom. Nevertheless, what Nietzsche introduces here is not a small distraction, but the more comprehensive issue that sets the terms for understanding morality as one player in a much bigger drama about the human will.

The first aphorism summarises the Treatise as a whole by suggesting the case that Nietzsche is about to make: *all* of our ideals are deeply ascetic, they have become painful and empty, and yet we can neither imagine any alternative to them nor give them up. Nietzsche's scattered catalogue of personae is meant to illustrate that not only moral ideals, but those from science, art, culture and religion are deeply ascetic; they do not merely involve some pain and difficulty in their pursuit, but represent a compulsion to understand ideals as having an exacting, compulsory force over us that alienates us from our desires. Although such ideals are painful and self-estranging, we nevertheless rely on them to make sense of who we are and what our place in the world is. Ideals are no longer effective in fulfilling this function, however. The process by which they function has required them to be increasingly demanding, but at the same time come to seem arbitrary or empty. As a result, ascetic ideals no longer work for us, except as a form of self-inflicted cruelty. Yet we cannot give up on them, for lack of any alternative way to think about who we are and what our deepest commitments ought to be.

The first aphorism starts by using an unfamiliar new term, 'ascetic ideals', as if it were familiar. After the initial question, 'What do ascetic ideals mean?', most of the aphorism is taken up with the catalogue of personae and what ascetic ideals mean for them. Nietzsche derives one general lesson, a 'basic fact of the human will' (III: 1), from this catalogue of meanings, and he concludes with an imaginary conversation that leads into the rest of the Treatise.

Nietzsche never defines 'ascetic ideal'. It involves asceticism, of course: depriving oneself of comforts, or even imposing harm on oneself, for some disciplinary or spiritual purpose. Ascetic ideals must be more than particular ascetic practices, however. Nietzsche is claiming that a wide range of familiar ideals include ascetic components. With ascetic ideals, asceticism is valorised for its own sake, so that ultimate standards of value include self-denial or self-harm. Nietzsche initially refers to ascetic ideals in the plural, and treats them as if they appear in many forms, but by the end of the aphorism he refers to the singular 'ascetic ideal', as if the diverse forms are all variations on one overarching ideal.

There are six categories of personae. Artists, philosophers and priests are treated at length later in the Treatise. Nietzsche discusses saints in other works.¹ So in this section I shall focus on 'physiological failures' (III: 1) and 'women' (III: 1). The meanings vary in each case, according to the purposes served through the ascetic ideal; in Nietzsche's analysis, a distinctive feature of the ascetic ideal is how flexible it is, operating differently according to its context. What all versions of the ascetic ideal have in common, however, is that that they are conceived of as forms of self-subordination. They call for directing cruelty towards oneself, out of submission to purposes that lie outside of oneself.

In the case of the 'physiological failures and the depressed' (III: 1), the ascetic ideals mean 'an attempt to appear to themselves as "too good" for this world, a holy form of excess, their major weapon in the battle against [. . .] boredom' (III: 1). Nietzsche is merely sketching the outline of a story here, but his suggestion is that for some people who are fundamentally and irremediably dissatisfied with life, their belief in ascetic ideals serves as consolation. Since ordinary forms of satisfaction are unavailable, they disavow them in a kind of existential sour grapes. The disavowal, that is, functions to show commitment to otherworldly values that cannot be directly endorsed. Denying themselves accessible pleasures gives them a claim to accessing something purportedly more valuable.

There are four basic features of the mechanism that Nietzsche identifies. First, ascetic ideals have a meaning because they are *purposive*: in Nietzsche's words, they are an 'attempt' or even a 'weapon'. In this case, they reconcile unhappy people to their lives by creating a value commitment to something imaginary or inaccessible. Second, the purposiveness is not consciously available as such. Since the physiological failures 'appear to themselves as "too good" for this world', the ascetic ideal works for them through self-deception. The effectiveness depends on creating an otherworldly meaning for their lives that they can identify with, rather than on seeing the psychological purpose for what it is. Third, although the purposiveness may not be consciously available, the asceticism must be self-imposed. For the physiological

---

[1] BGE §51 is particularly relevant. But Nietzsche discusses saints and the meaning of saintliness in many other passages. See, for example, HAH §141 and §143.

failures to appear as 'too good' for the world and not merely as deficient, they have to *deprive themselves* of worldly satisfaction; they need to show that their lack is a preference. Fourth, this also works as a 'holy form of excess'. Ascetic pursuits can in themselves be psychologically satisfying; one can revel in one's self-denial and gain gratification from that alone. Unlike other forms of psychological excess, it is disconnected from pleasure and self-interest, and can thus be pursued without provoking moral conscience.

For some women, in Nietzsche's telling, ascetic ideals mean 'one *more* charming trait of seduction, a bit of *morbidezza* on lovely flesh, the angelical appearance of a pretty, plump animal' (III: 1). Nietzsche is even more perplexing here, since ascetic ideals convey both seductiveness and angelic appearance. What he seems to have in mind, however, are the ascetic ways of regulating one's body so as to conform to norms of self-presentation. Managing one's appearance through diet and exercise, hair and skin care, and clothing and footwear can be difficult, demanding and even painful, and yet take place according to norms that are so deeply internalised that they are not even consciously available. For Nietzsche, the ascetic ideal is in this case, as with the physiological failures, ambiguous. On one hand, ascetic ideals demand a self-subordination to standards given by society: in self-presentation, one is constrained by what others count as appropriate or successful in appearance. But on the other hand, this subordination allows for new possibilities of self-expression: women, in this way, take control over their appearance and can present themselves as they wish to be seen. Nietzsche, furthermore, characterises the asceticism as self-imposed by describing the appearance as of a 'pretty, plump animal'. That is, one appears as an animal nature that expresses its own vigour and self-regulation and can thus identify with its self-fashioning, rather than merely as a pretty appearance or as an animal without expressive capacities. Thus here, as in the case of the physiological failures, ascetic ideals can be both purposive and unconscious, and harmful and expressive.

The other personae offer variations on the productiveness of the ascetic ideal, but collectively they characterise a process that is effective but empty. The ascetic ideal is effective: it has purposes and those purposes are, for the most part, realised. It enables new meanings to be created, and those meanings change persons' relationships to their own deeds and selves; they can not only appear differently, and feel differently about themselves, but also become something different – assume new kinds of identity – through ascetic ideals. As Nietzsche intends his catalogue of meanings to show, the ascetic ideal is immensely open-ended. The only limits to what it can mean are the range of purposes that it might serve, the contexts in which it might arise, and the possible objects of ascetic self-denial or pain. Asceticism can make anything seem important, but at the same time this flexibility derives from its emptiness. Nietzsche's point here is that the ascetic ideal is effective because it does not need to track anything independent: it institutes new appearances, and functions psychologically, but is not grounded in anything else. As a result, it can be arbitrary at the same time as it is demanding – indeed, all the more demanding on account of its emptiness, because it has nothing to sustain it other than the sacrifices it calls for.

The ascetic ideal's diversity of possible meanings, its history of effectiveness and its ultimate emptiness afford the general lesson that Nietzsche presents in the Third Treatise. He identifies in the first aphorism, as a fundamental concern calling for interpretation, 'that the ascetic ideal has meant so much to humanity generally' (III: 1). The ascetic ideal's wide range of meanings, its effectiveness in furnishing them and its pervasiveness in human culture are remarkable enough that they call for a deeper understanding. These phenomena show something fundamental about us, which Nietzsche spends the rest of the Treatise elaborating. They betoken the 'basic fact of the human will, its *horror vacui: it needs a goal* – and it would sooner will *nothingness* than not will' (III: 1). Ascetic ideals have been historically prominent because they match the needs of the human will; the ascetic ideal comes in so many forms because the will has a 'horror' of emptiness and so 'would sooner will *nothingness* than not will'. We can see what Nietzsche means here in terms of a historical process in which human beings sustain their activity by making use of the ascetic ideal. In this process, we need to have goals that seem significant and that we can identify with, and the ascetic ideal supplies goals that give sense to people's lives. When a sense of purpose is lacking, we respond by adopting purposes supplied by the ascetic ideal, and, when we find that these purposes are ultimately empty or dissatisfying, search for and produce newer purposes. This process culminates in a stark set of alternatives, however: either try to adopt 'nothingness' itself, a self-aware lack of purpose, as one's final commitment, or give up on agency altogether.

The story of the Third Treatise is how we have arrived at this impasse, and how the main sources of authority in our culture – science, religion, art, morality – are all stuck firmly there. With this in mind, then, we are in a somewhat better position to consider the epigraph. Analysed somewhat crudely, the epigraph contains these claims: wisdom is a woman; as a woman she loves only warriors; warriors are heedless, mocking and violent; and therefore wisdom wants us to be heedless, mocking and violent. The epigraph is about *wisdom*, as opposed to science or knowledge. The cognitive ideal that Nietzsche proposes as relevant here does not invoke demonstrable truth or an accumulated body of evidence produced by systematic inquiry, but something more like a personal capacity for insight and understanding. Nietzsche characterises wisdom as a *woman*. Wisdom is a woman in *Thus Spoke Zarathustra*, and elsewhere he personifies truth, too.[2] Personifying wisdom as a woman is Nietzsche's way of indicating that wisdom responds to human relationships of trust and persuasion, rather than being compelled by the necessary force of arguments. The figure of 'woman' here is of someone self-possessed and wilful, who is moved by the considerations that she judges to be important. Nietzsche's approach to wisdom thus reverses the traditional trope, in which women are to be acquired or possessed; here, rather, the hope is that wisdom might want and love us.[3]

---

[2] On wisdom as a woman, see especially 'The Dancing Song' in *Thus Spoke Zarathustra* (Nietzsche 1978: 107–10). On truth as a woman, see GS Preface §4, and BGE, Preface §1 and §220.

[3] Nietzsche is likely indebted to Machiavelli's version of the traditional trope, in which 'fortune' is personified. 'I am certainly convinced of this: that it is better to be impetuous than cautious, because fortune is a woman, and it is necessary, in order to keep her down, to beat her and to struggle with her. And it is seen that she more often allows herself to be taken over by men who are impetuous than by those who makes cold advances' (Machiavelli 1984: 84).

The last main trope here is that of the *warrior*. With this trope, consideration of the original context, Zarathustra's speech about reading and writing, helps somewhat. To be 'heedless, mocking, violent' is associated there, above all, with laughter and with accomplishments won by refusing to take things too seriously.[4] A warrior, then, effects change – even 'violent' change – by mocking, shifting the meaning of inimical values, rather than by engaging with them on their own terms. Applied to the current context, Nietzsche is suggesting that a cautious, methodical approach to the ascetic ideal is not suitable. The ascetic ideal has worked by positing something compelling and real outside of human purposes and then trying to demonstrate why it must govern us; trying to refute this ideal reiterates it, by insisting that our commitments be settled by some kind of objective compulsion. So the better approach is to defeat it by establishing a new meaning for it. We take this 'warrior's' approach by changing how we relate to our values and to each other, and thereby putting ourselves in a position to laugh at it.

The basic narrative

Whereas the first two Treatises each offer, albeit with digressions, a single long narrative presenting the history of the emergence of some conceptual elements of morality, the Third Treatise offers something more like a series of vignettes: first about artists, then about philosophers, and then the most important one, about priests. These vignettes contextualise the various figures that Nietzsche discusses rather than contributing to a single, linear history. Nietzsche appeals to these vignettes, however, in his concluding reflections on meaning, ideals, self-knowledge, art, comedy and the 'will to truth'. These final reflections suggest that the vignettes are intended to provide a history of the present, recounting an emergence-story of several aspects of who we are.

---

[4] The original version uses the word 'brave' (*muthig*) rather than 'heedless' (*unbekümmert*). See TSZ, 'On Reading and Writing' (Nietzsche 1978: 41).

The *artist* was the first entry in Nietzsche's catalogue of personae, and that is where his vignettes begin. Nietzsche moves back and forth between general and particular: although he aims at a fuller response to the opening question, what do ascetic ideals mean in the case of artists?, his discussion is focused on an individual, the composer Richard Wagner. Wagner was at one point a close acquaintance of Nietzsche's, and his analysis doubtless bears the traces of personal grudges against him, but Wagner also stands in here for the modern condition of the artist.[5] According to Nietzsche, Wagner's career as an artist divides itself into early and late periods. In the early period, Wagner's operas present a contest between the competing attractions of sensuous, earthly love and sacred, spiritual love; his theoretical writings insist on the importance of integrating music with the dramatic representation of human events and the revolutionary potential of art. In Wagner's late period, there are no longer competing sources of value, as self-renunciation, pity and chastity are unequivocally heroic and sensuousness is unequivocally dangerous. The theoretical writings, meanwhile, combine reactionary politics with a new primacy for the metaphysical significance of music, at the expense of its dramatic context. So, Nietzsche asks, finding a new idealisation of asceticism in Wagner's music, 'What does it mean when an artist switches over into his opposite?' (III: 2).

Note that Nietzsche is offering an analysis of *artists* rather than, at least directly, of art. His claim is that modern artists use ascetic ideals to search for a kind of redemption – a complete, conclusive vindication of life from outside of ordinary experience. In Wagner's case, there is a straightforward, if perhaps uncommon way in which he uses ascetic ideals: he 'pays homage to chastity' (III: 2) in his works. But this, Nietzsche is suggesting, is just an especially literal example of how artists use ascetic ideals. Ascetic ideals are an avenue through which artists set themselves apart

---

[5] Wagner was a far more prominent cultural figure than Nietzsche in their lifetimes, and was an important early personal influence on him. After an early period of admiration, Nietzsche treated Wagner as a significant rival or opponent in his writing, even after Wagner ceased to take notice of him. There is an extensive literature on their relationship. For a sophisticated historical and philosophical treatment, see Prange 2013.

from quotidian concerns in order to occupy themselves with aesthetic creation, out of hope for an extraordinary, transformative experience that redeems an otherwise empty world. Artists set aesthetic creation above and apart from practical concerns, and use this self-separation 'from the "real", from the actual' (III: 4) to create works that themselves may or may not have ascetic content; for Wagner, the ascetic conditions of production eventually produce an ascetic outlook. Nietzsche discusses this in terms of how Wagner conceived of the role of the musician:

> He [the musician] became an oracle, a priest, indeed more than a priest, a mouthpiece of the 'in-itself' of things, a telephone of the Beyond – henceforth he spoke not only music, this ventriloquist of God – he spoke metaphysics: is it any wonder that finally one day he spoke *ascetic ideals*? (III: 5)

According to Nietzsche, then, the Wagnerian artist produces, in a manner detached from ordinary life, art that purports to have a metaphysical significance and that thereby stakes a claim to value as a 'telephone of the Beyond'. This is already ascetic, in its separation from and devaluation of material comfort, and thus it fits well with explicitly 'speaking' ascetic ideals, for example by praising chastity.

When he returns to the opening question, Nietzsche claims that artists' ascetic ideals mean '*nothing at all* . . . Or so many things that it is as good as nothing at all' (III: 5). Art that purports to have a metaphysical, redemptive significance becomes disconnected from the ordinary, sensuous conditions of its presentation: it claims to signify more than it seems to be. The connection to the metaphysical is arbitrary, however. There is no telephone of the Beyond, or at any rate the telephone does not link to anything; the claims of metaphysical significance are not constrained by anything outside of themselves. Just as ascetic ideals in general function to produce meaning, so artistic effects can attach significance to any sensuous representation. If anything can be accorded deep significance, however, then nothing is especially significant. Nietzsche's point, then, is that ascetic ideals in artists can mean *too many* things in that their meanings are furnished by the metaphysical stories that they appeal to, and this amounts to 'nothing at all' in that attributions of meaning thus seem merely arbitrary. If different artworks can communicate different, incompatible metaphysical commitments with no basis for ascribing superior accuracy to any of them, there is no reason for taking their metaphysical meanings seriously. Artworks can, of course, be important in non-metaphysical ways, and ascetic ideals might foster creativity, but the ascetic ideals of artists turn out to be empty.

Nietzsche's accounts of how artists use ascetic ideals and of how they turn out to be arbitrary or empty furnish his answer to the other question he posed, about what it means when an artist switches over to his opposite. Nietzsche viewed Wagner as initially grappling with the appeal of the sensuous aspects of life, and how to integrate them with more spiritual values, but then coming to renounce all sensuality. The reversal takes place when the attempt at integration exhausts itself and the hope for redemption through art turns into discouragement or despair. When an artist attempting to make use of ascetic ideals confronts their arbitrariness, worldly redemption through art seems impossible. Artists can still be productive when they aim at a redemption that they cannot have, but their art then turns to the unattainability of sensuous satisfaction, the devaluation of the familiar, and the hope for a saving force from outside. Nietzsche is not criticising, at least not here, the resulting artworks, so much as their conditions of creation. They come out of an orientation that takes basic conditions of life, such as conflict between incommensurable values or the limitedness of satisfaction, as objectionable and needing to be overcome. This orientation can be self-destructive, in that it fosters hostility to one's life, and it can force misunderstanding, as it leads to neglect of local, contingent matters of interest. Nietzsche frames these issues in terms of how the conflict between 'chastity' and 'sensuality' relates to one's 'existence': 'There is no necessary opposition between chastity and sensuality [. . .] even where there really is that opposition between chastity and sensuality, fortunately it need not by any means be a tragic opposition [. . .] Just such "contradictions" seduce us to existence' (III: 2). Ascetic ideals in art, Nietzsche suggests, come from suffering from the tensions that we ordinarily face. We are better off, however, and relate better to our own condition when we live with such contradictions, or find ways to transcend rather than revoke them. Nietzsche named 'philosophers and scholars' as his second category in the first aphorism, but the next vignette exclusively names *philosophers* as its subject matter.[6] Once again, Nietzsche uses a single figure, at least initially, to stand in for the category as a whole. Arthur Schopenhauer had come up already in passing, as the philosophical pretext for Wagner's ascetic turn. Here Nietzsche moves from a particular observation about Schopenhauer's approach in aesthetic theory to offering a series of claims about the uses that philosophers make of ascetic ideals, identifying and answering an interpretative 'problem' about understanding them, and connecting philosophers' ascetic ideals to modern personality in general.

Nietzsche's approach is strange: not only is he appealing to an idiosyncratic position of an idiosyncratic philosopher to make his point, but he is taking a philosophical position as an *explanandum*, something that requires explanation, without reference to its underlying arguments. When Nietzsche calls attention to Schopenhauer's 'use of the Kantian version of the aesthetic problem' (III: 6), he does not so much as mention what 'the aesthetic problem' is. Indeed, in might not mean anything in particular, since Nietzsche uses it to encompass both issues about the quality of sensations and those about the nature of artistic creation. What Nietzsche seems to have in mind as 'the Kantian version', however, is something like this. In our judgements of sensuous experience, a fundamental norm is that of *beauty*. But beauty is perplexing, in that it seems to involve both subjective feelings of pleasure and claims to universal validity: beauty is in the eye of the beholder, but some things simply are beautiful, and anyone who perceives them adequately ought to take them as such – indeed, ought to take pleasure from them. So the specifically Kantian version of this problem seeks to explain how these features of aesthetic judgements could be combined, and in Nietzsche's telling

---

[6] For those concerned about the neglect of scholars, there is a chapter of *Beyond Good and Evil* called 'We Scholars' (BGE §§204–39).

this requires identifying a form of subjective experience characterised by 'impersonality and universality' (III: 6). The Kantian solution is to take judgements of beauty as *disinterested*. That is, they involve no conceptual determination whereby the subject might take the object as serving a particular interest or gratifying a particular desire; the aesthetic object, rather, engages the free play of one's faculties without reference to any further end.

Schopenhauer's use of ascetic ideals, then, is to apply impersonality and disinterestedness to the understanding of beauty: pleasing sensuous experience only attains its ideal when completely disengaged from usefulness or desire. According to Nietzsche, however, Schopenhauer's appropriation of Kant was peculiar: 'he interpreted the words "without interest" in the most personal way possible, on the basis of an experience that must have been among his most routine' (III: 6). Nietzsche's approach to philosophical theory, at least in this case, is not to engage with substance, but to treat it as psychologically revealing. He is not treating Schopenhauer's theory as a legitimate candidate for rational acceptance, but rather as a cultural phenomenon that stands in need of interpretation.[7] According to Nietzsche, 'Schopenhauer speaks about few things as certainly as he does about the effect of aesthetic contemplation: of it he says that it counteracts precisely *sexual* "interestedness"' (III: 6). One can conceivably regard an image of a nude, for example, merely as a sight whose formal properties appeals to the senses and then, perhaps, one perceives beauty as separate from any further interest. Schopenhauer, Nietzsche is claiming, sees this disinterested gaze as an opposition to and quieting of sexual desire, and takes this as the fundamental nature of beauty.

For Schopenhauer, beauty has a metaphysical significance, and its effectiveness in counteracting sexual desire is an incidental, if telling, feature. For Nietzsche, however, this shows how philosophers use ascetic ideals. Beauty is compelling because it antagonises one's

---

[7] Nietzsche often takes this approach. Randall Havas makes this claim in discussing one of Nietzsche's previous works: 'Thus, because Nietzsche seeks in this way a diagnosis of the impulse to philosophy, he is much less interested in the content of specific philosophical claims than in what he thinks our tendency to make such claims shows about us' (Havas 1995: 88).

own desires; it is a form of ascetic self-denial. And Schopenhauer is eager to embrace it precisely on account of its ascetic character, because it serves his own needs to do so. From this, Nietzsche identifies two preliminary interpretations of what ascetic ideals mean in the case of philosophers. This is one answer: 'And, returning to our first question, "What does it *mean* when a philosopher pays homage to the ascetic ideal?" – here at least we get a first hint: he wants *to break free of a torture*' (III: 6). Schopenhauer 'pays homage' to the ascetic ideal because he was tormented by his own desires; he conceives of beauty as something that quiets those desires, as a means of gaining relief from them. This answer is preliminary because it is too specific to Schopenhauer's case. The second answer, likewise, appeals to something particular to Schopenhauer: 'his enemies held on to him, his enemies seduced him again and again into existence' (III: 7). Schopenhauer 'treated sexuality as a personal enemy' (III: 7) because it gave him a way of seeing himself as the protagonist in a perpetual conflict. Having an enemy gave him something to complain about and a framework for making sense of his life, and sexuality is a convenient enemy because it does not need to be sought out – it is always available for ascetic struggle.

Nietzsche's excursus on Schopenhauer's aesthetic theory and sexual frustrations was intended to raise larger points, however: 'So much with respect to what is most personal in the case of Schopenhauer; on the other hand there is also something typical about him – and only here do we come to our problem' (III: 7). Nietzsche does not explain what he means by 'our problem', but it seems to be the task of understanding the 'philosophers' prejudice and cordiality with respect to the entire ascetic ideal' (III: 7). The embrace of the ascetic ideal presents a paradox: asceticism is self-hostile and unpleasant, and yet it is adopted, at least among philosophers, widely and with enthusiasm. The solution to the problem is that ascetic ideals provide philosophers with 'an optimum of favorable conditions': 'Every animal, and thus also *la bête philosophe*, strives instinctively for an optimum of favorable conditions under which it can completely let out its power and reach its maximum feeling of power' (III: 7). Ascetic ideals, in general, enable philosophers to reach their 'maximum feeling of power'. This by itself only indicates what Nietzsche takes to be the basic task of explanation here: to account for how ascetic ideals have the ability to summon internal motivation for pursuing them, and indeed to provide not only specific motivations but an overall increase in motivation, even though these are ideals of self-denial. Nietzsche explains how ascetic ideals accomplish this by identifying three uses to which philosophers put them.

The first use is the most straightforward. Nietzsche claims that 'a genuine philosophers' irritability and rancor has existed against sensuality' (III: 7), and philosophers' ascetic ideals are a way of expressing this. Philosophers, that is, are the sorts of people who are naturally disposed to be hostile towards sensual pleasures, and this comes out in the ideals they express. When Socrates, for example, asked, 'Do you think it befits a philosophical nature to be keen about the so-called pleasures of [. . .] food and drink?' (Plato, *Phaedo* 64d), he was expecting a negative answer, as he did with all the other questions that he asked about bodily pleasures, and his metaphysics and his value commitments turn out to reflect this outlook. This is what Nietzsche took Schopenhauer to typify. The specific form of his anxieties about sexual desire may have been unusual, but philosophers, in general, use ascetic ideals to express their own tendencies. Nietzsche thus claims that 'philosophers are not exactly unimpeachable witnesses and judges of the *value* of the ascetic ideal' (III: 8). His point is not merely that philosophers make biased evaluations. It is that the very way in which philosophical claims of universal or objective purport are formulated is a means of self-expression for them. Ascetic views are framed as metaphysical not because they have an authoritative ground, but because it serves philosophers to present them that way; precisely where they claim impersonality, philosophers are in it for themselves.

The second use of the ascetic ideal, according to Nietzsche, is that it furnishes an 'optimum of conditions of highest and boldest spirituality':

What accordingly does the ascetic ideal mean in a philosopher? My answer is [. . .] the philosopher smiles at the sight of it, seeing it as an optimum of the conditions of highest and boldest spirituality – he does not deny 'existence' this way, on the contrary in doing this he affirms *his* existence and *only* his existence. (III: 7)

Later Nietzsche refers to the ascetic ideal as providing 'the most authentic and natural conditions of their *best* existence, their *most beautiful* fruitfulness' (III: 8). Asceticism, conceived of as neglect of worldly involvement and bodily comforts, might seem like a form of self-harm: one is forsaking advantages that could otherwise be enjoyed. But the forms of self-denial that it requires are ones that eliminate distractions from the pursuit of 'spiritual' aims. For someone leading a 'life of the mind' – filled with abstract concerns, the need to cultivate one's intellect, and attention to ideas and theories – asceticism provides favourable conditions for self-cultivation. Nietzsche, incidentally, places himself here, as someone who needs the metaphorical 'desert' (III: 8) of the ascetic hermit.[8] Ascetic ideals might impede many forms of development, but philosophers' use of them make them suitable for flourishing.

The third philosophical use of the ascetic ideal is that it made philosophy possible. According to Nietzsche there is an ancient historical 'bond' (III: 9) between philosophy and the ascetic ideal because it gave contemplative individuals the confidence to engage in systematic reflection. In Nietzsche's picture, ancient societies were organised primarily around meeting urgent needs, and thus prioritised things such as physical strength, martial skill, control of resources and political leadership. In this context, there would be no place for reflection that was not directed to immediate goals; it would have seemed, if anything, like lassitude or indolence. But ascetic ideals gave contemplative persons descriptions that they could fit their reflective activity under, and ones that made them seem fearsome rather than feckless. They could be communing with higher powers, seeking mystical insight or aligning hidden energies. Adherents of ascetic ideals could, at the very least to

---

[8] There are a few references in III: 8 that indicate that Nietzsche includes himself among those whose optimum conditions are ascetic. First, he refers to 'my most beautiful study'. Second, he refers to 'we philosophers'. Third, he has a long description of 'mountains for company' that corresponds to where he carried out much of his summertime writing.

themselves, appear as bold practitioners of esoteric activities who rigorously practised self-denial as part of their vocation. So even if engaging in philosophical reflection rather than appearing as fearsome ascetics was their primary aim, embracing ascetic ideals gave proto-philosophers a role that they could identify with.

In the same way that ascetic ideals furnished the conditions for individual philosophical self-confidence, they also furnished the social conditions of the possibility of philosophers. What philosophers did was, presumably, incomprehensible to everyone else. Consider this illustration of philosophical activity from Ludwig Wittgenstein: 'I am sitting with a philosopher in the garden; he says again and again "I know that that's a tree", pointing to a tree that is near us. Someone else arrives and hears this, and I tell him: "This fellow isn't insane. We are only doing philosophy"' (Wittgenstein 1972: 61, §467). Philosophical activity, when it is not classified as 'philosophy', seems like delusional or insane versions of ordinary speech. Once philosophers are seen as ascetic practitioners, however, they are still incomprehensible to everyone else, but they are perhaps not seen as pathological. They can be acknowledged as having an established role that merits forbearance and the presumption of competence. The creation of this social role, furthermore, allows it to be elaborated. Philosophers can move from isolated reflections to sustained debates, schools of thought and traditions of argumentation, and articles in double-blind peer-reviewed journals. The ascetic ideal plays a deceptive role in these processes:

> the *ascetic ideal* long served the philosopher as a form of appearance, as a precondition of existence – he had to *represent* it in order to be a philosopher, and he had to *believe* in it to represent it. The peculiar aloof stance of philosophers, world-denying, hostile to life, not believing in the senses, de-sensualized, which has been maintained into most recent times and therefore has emerged as practically the *philosophical attitude in itself* – it is above all a consequence of the distressed conditions under which philosophy arose and survived at all: since philosophy would *not have been possible at all* for the longest time without an ascetic wrap and cloak, without an ascetic self-misunderstanding. (III: 10)

For Nietzsche, the ascetic ideal deceives so well that it demands self-deception among the philosophers, who have to believe in the ascetic image of what they are doing when they are creating a social role for themselves. But it is in any case an effective self-deception, which opens up a role for philosophy and the 'philosophical attitude' that they would not otherwise have.

One meaning of the ascetic ideal, then, is that it creates the conceptual and social space for philosophers to be themselves, and thus provides the conditions for the flourishing of a certain type of personality. Although Nietzsche includes himself here, his interest in this is not purely self-regarding. Philosophers are the prime movers of this process but, in Nietzsche's telling, the operation of the ascetic ideal is important because the philosophers' history is the history of *everyone*. This is Nietzsche's list of the philosophers' characteristic 'drives': 'his doubting drive, his negating drive, his wait-and-see ("ephectic") drive, his analytic drive, his exploring, seeking, venturing drive, his comparing, balancing drive [. . .]' (III: 9). This list is informative of Nietzsche's conception of a psychological 'drive', since these examples seem less like individual, biologically basic urges than overlapping motivations to engage in culturally specific forms of activity.[9] But what is noteworthy here is that these distinctive characteristics of philosophers are familiar aspects of any modern, mature personality. For anyone open to new experiences, unsure of who they might become, living in a world with competing and unreliable pulls of influence, and needing to make complex decisions to manage everyday affairs, all of these traits are going to contribute, to some extent, to navigating one's days. These traits would have been out of place in a traditional society with defined social roles and little room for individual discretion, but now they are widespread. Nietzsche makes this point dramatically, by associating these philosophical traits, in their modern forms, with 'pure hubris and godlessness': 'Even when measured against the standard of the ancient Greeks our whole modern being, insofar as it is not weakness but power and consciousness of power, smacks of pure hubris and godlessness'

---

[9] For discussions of Nietzsche's concept of a 'drive', see Stern 2015; Katsafanas 2013.

(III: 9). Philosophers' ascetic ideals, although not intended as such, were the basis for the modern self-arrogation of authority and the changes in personality that they entailed. Nietzsche indeed characterises these changes in personality not just as incidental effects of social change, but as something more like the invention of self-shaping. Ascetic philosophy, at any rate, created the conceptual resources for thinking of ourselves rather than non-human nature as in charge, somehow, of what we are like. Thus when Nietzsche expands on 'hubris', the outrageous insolence of our modern being, he writes, 'hubris today is our stance on *ourselves* – for we experiment with ourselves as we would not permit with any animals, gleefully and curiously slitting open our souls while our bodies are still alive' (III: 9). Splitting souls open, for Nietzsche, seems to amount to disrupting our sense of what is important so that we make ourselves responsive to new kinds of 'spiritual' (III: 9) concerns, and making these concerns central to who we are. This change in 'spirit' is nevertheless momentous:

> Now we violate ourselves, there is no doubt of it, we nutcrackers of the soul, we questioners and questionable ones, as if life were nothing but nutcracking; and for this very reason we must necessarily become ever more questionable each day, *worthier* of questioning, and perhaps therewith also worthier – of living? (III: 9)

'Worthier of living' echoes Immanuel Kant's phrase 'worthiness to be happy' (Kant 1997: 7 [4: 393]). Both phrases suggest that there is a kind of value, incommensurable with the naturally but contingently available appealing ones, that we can make available to ourselves and that confers a distinctive status on us.

The ascetic ideal takes on many meanings for philosophers. It expresses their intrinsic hostility to sensuality, it creates the categorial possibility of philosophy and, above all, it furnishes the optimum conditions for their 'spiritual' growth. This last meaning for philosophers, in particular, is worth considering because it has become so widely shared. The importance of the ascetic ideal lies not only in its role in shaping the specifically moral features of our personality, if there are any such features. Its role, rather, has been to shape human personality in general, including some features that might normally escape notice because they seem so widespread and unbound by duty. We are more than our suitability for submitting to moral commands, and our personalities have been shaped by the ascetic ideal in complex ways that have not yet been fully accounted for. Nietzsche suggests, at any rate, that we are all philosophers now, who question and experiment on ourselves; likewise, we can surmise, we are all artists, who strive after a redemptive experience that we may never find.

The discussion of the *ascetic priest* is the longest and most important of the Third Treatise, but its importance reflects the priest as having the least distinctive character. Being an artist or a philosopher involves specific abilities and practices, but Nietzsche treats the ascetic priest as the personification (or 'incarnation') of the ascetic ideal in general. The story here is not one of discrete individuals who happen to take up the ascetic ideal, but rather of an instrument through which the ascetic ideal implements and diffuses itself. The ascetic priest and the ascetic ideal are inseparable: 'his *right* to existence stands and falls with that ideal' (III: 11). Nietzsche presents no historical exemplars who have their own quirks and eccentricities. He instead conveys the psychological dynamics of the ascetic ideal and its institutions in human culture. The figure of the priest is used to present the issue of the Treatise as a whole:

> Only now, after we have caught sight of the *ascetic priest*, do we seriously come to grips with our problem: what does the ascetic ideal mean? – only now does it get 'serious': now the actual *representative of seriousness* stands facing us. 'What does all seriousness mean?' – perhaps this even more fundamental question is already on our lips here. (III: 11)

Nietzsche promises to address 'our problem', the meaning of the ascetic ideal, not just for particular personae, but for human life in general.

One main claim of this Treatise is that the ascetic ideal has acquired such a general role in human life. This took place through the priests, who advocated religious practices in ways that privileged ascetic ideals and extended their scope to every aspect of life. Ascetic ideals, Nietzsche is claiming, trumped or co-opted other considerations, until only ascetic ideals were left; the plurality of different kinds of values that contributed to organising different aspects of people's lives all came to be filtered through an ascetic outlook. The importance of the priest, then, is not so much as a religious figure but as the 'representative of seriousness'. Theological expressions were just a way of effecting a novel relationship to value. The priests brought about seriousness by formulating ideals, rather than piecemeal and partial collections of values, and demanding reflection on what those ideals mean, how overridingly important they are, and how we personally fail to live up to them. So this new, serious relationship to value involves persons coming to think of themselves as, fundamentally, failures, who understand themselves in terms of ideals that they remain perpetually remote from.

'Seriousness' initially took religious forms of expression. But Nietzsche pays almost no attention to the particularities of these forms. Myths, metaphysical doctrines and customary rituals are not investigated; he does not try to demonstrate that a certain being does not exist or that an imperative would be unwise to obey. He does not regard the differences between traditions as important, either; the ascetic priest in every case used these traditions to express an ascetic 'manner of valuation' (III: 11). Natural human existence is treated as intrinsically worthless, ruined by transience or the corruption of matter. Some 'completely different existence' (III: 11) is posited and esteemed, and then ascetic practice is called for, either to make earthly existence as much like the other kind as possible, or to render it a 'bridge to that other existence' (III: 11). The ascetic priest disseminates a negative '*valuation* of our life' (III: 11), and Nietzsche's enterprise is to understand this valuation: what it means, what purpose it serves, its psychological function and its effects.

The task of understanding the ascetic valuation of life is challenging because it does not make sense on its own terms. It calls for a form of life that is disgusted with itself, lauds its own failures, and sustains itself in its own profound dissatisfaction. Choosing one's suffering in asceticism is already difficult to understand, but treating all of life as an occasion for deliberate asceticism is 'paradoxical to the highest degree' (III: 11). And yet, Nietzsche writes, 'Such a monstrous mode of valuation is not inscribed into the history of mankind as an exception and a curiosity: it is one of the broadest and longest facts there is' (III: 11). The ascetic ideal is so pervasive that it cannot be a random aberration; not only is it prevalent everywhere, but it seems to have been adopted independently in different places and at different points in time. There must be some reason for its success, then, one that does not appeal merely to the surface description of the ideal.

According to Nietzsche, 'it must surely be an *interest of life itself*' (III: 11) that the ascetic form of life is so prevalent. So he refers to the ascetic ideal as a 'means' (III: 11), a 'tool' (III: 13) and an 'artifice' (III: 11), for example; his explanation of this interest appeals to the ideal itself as fulfilling a function, rather than to the psychological states of believers. 'The interest of life' is not something that individuals aspire to serve. Indeed, the success of ascetic self-descriptions depends on individuals misunderstanding their own conditions. Their belief *in* the ideal serves the interest, not their particular beliefs, in roughly the way that a trusting nature or paranoia might be instrumentally useful even where it leads to some defective beliefs. The surface content of the ascetic ideal is that it expresses antipathy to life, but its functioning, according to Nietzsche, is contrary to that surface content. It serves the purpose of supporting 'the *preservation* of life' (III: 13).

From the standpoint of the ascetic priests and those whom they lead, ascetic ideals are not purposeful. They are ideals: they offer standards or models of goodness, which may be action-guiding, but which also might suggest forms of perfection that are unavailable to human beings. Their character, in any case, is not as *useful* things, but as expressing what would count as flawless and complete. Nietzsche insists, however, that to understand the role of the ascetic ideal in human life, especially its prevalence and endurance, one has to see it as fulfilling an important purpose. At this point, then, Nietzsche declares what he takes that purpose to be, points out some of its main side effects, and identifies the five main psychological means by which the priests instituted it in societies. This is the main task of Nietzsche's account of the ascetic priest, and by extension that of the Third Treatise. His aim is not to refute the ascetic ideal, furnish an alternative ideal, prove that priests' views are false, or locate the historical pathways of the ascetic ideal's transmission; these tasks are not undertaken and, as manifestations of ideal commitments to theoretical truth, they even fall under the scope of the phenomenon that he is investigating. His aim, more simply, is to come to terms with the nature of our commitments to the ascetic ideal: above all, what it does for us, what it does to us and how it works on us. In this way, since the effects of the ascetic priests are still with us, we might gain a better position to understand ourselves and reassess the role of ideals in our lives.

The general form of Nietzsche's account is that hostility to life is an unconscious strategy for sustaining engagement with it. This is similar to his account of Schopenhauer's aesthetics. Here he presents the strategy as the ascetic ideal bringing about a 'desire for a different mode of being' that serves as a 'fetter that binds' us to existence:

> The ascetic priest is the incarnate desire for a different mode of being [. . .] but the very *power* of his desire is the fetter that binds him here, it is the very thing that makes him a tool that must work on creating more favorable conditions for being-here and being-human – with this very *power* he binds to existence the entire herd of people who are deformed, depressed, underprivileged, failures, and those of every kind who suffer from themselves, by instinctively walking ahead of them as shepherd. (III: 13)

The ascetic priest transmutes apathy and misery into the conviction that our whole existence is fundamentally defective – indeed, that *we* are fundamentally defective. Sense is given to this defectiveness by contrast with an ideal: some superior mode of being that we might aspire to inhabit. For Nietzsche, this hostility to life on the part of the priests functions as among 'the very great *conserving* and *Yes-creating forces* of life' (III: 13). The ascetic priests suggest that our whole lives ought to be fundamentally altered, or at least acknowledged in their profound shortcomings. This creates a project. It instils a desire for life to be otherwise, even impossibly, incoherently otherwise. It institutes subjects who, if nothing else, can both direct and at the same time be targets of blame. And it prepares persons to oppose their own standpoints: to be uncomfortable enough in their own skins that they reflect on the corruption of their judgements and consider occupying different standpoints.[10] All of this self-doubt and antipathy makes us 'sicker' (III: 13), insists Nietzsche. It leaves everyone more uncertain and dissatisfied than before. But it also 'magically brings to light an abundance of tender Yeses' (III: 13) by giving sense to new hopes and aspirations that sustain an attachment to life.

Before turning to the psychological mechanisms through which the ascetic ideal operates, Nietzsche discusses one general side effect of its employment. He expresses it in terms of some portentous-sounding notions – 'will to power', 'nihilism', 'pathos of distance' (III: 14) – but the problem is social. The problem, that is, is that sustaining attachment to life through the ascetic ideal engenders a form of social arrangement in which cohesion depends on shared sickness, and thus 'disgust' and 'compassion' (III: 14) are the prevailing social emotions. This is a problem because it crowds out alternatives, including forms of flourishing. As Nietzsche characterises the situation, those who validate their lives by appeal to the ascetic ideal depend on seeing themselves as *solely* taking up the appropriate response to their condition. 'We alone are the good, the just' (III: 14), Nietzsche has them saying; others are defective by failing to live like them. This is the 'will of the sick to represent *any* form of superiority, their instinct for secret paths that lead to a tyranny over the healthy' (III: 14): it is a form of social solidarity that depends on diminishing others, or even '*shoving into the conscience* of the happy their own misery' (III: 14). There is nothing wrong *per se* with the strategy of the 'good' and the 'just', except that it depends on invidious comparison and closes off alternative possibilities.

With aphorism 15, Nietzsche begins something like a narrative history of the ascetic priest. Even then, the discussion is not

---

[10] Nietzsche's famous treatment of perspectivism (III: 12) appears at this point in his discussion, and it relates to this theme, but I will not discuss it until the next section.

chronologically structured or connected to any particular historical tradition. Instead, Nietzsche refers to himself repeatedly as a 'psychologist' (III: 19, 20), or alternatively claims 'physiological' (III: 15) insights, and in these terms offers a study of the ascetic priest's effectiveness. Nietzsche's story, such as it is, presents something like a phenomenology of religious practice to show how ascetic ideals work. His discussion is not directed to assessing either beliefs or value schemes; there are some value claims and some claims of falsity, but these are not the main point. Nietzsche, rather, identifies psychological processes and their effects.

Nietzsche divides his discussion of the psychological means by which priests instituted the ascetic ideal into four 'innocent' ones and one set of 'guilty' ones, but this appears to be a largely nominal division. He is not casting moral judgement on them; the guilty one, rather, functions by eliciting a feeling of guilt, whereas the innocent ones do not.[11] The most important means of the innocent category is the '*anesthetization of pain through affect*' (III: 15). This is more complicated than it sounds, since it involves the sufferer's 'discharging of affects' (III: 15) against one perceived to be the cause of their suffering. Nietzsche claims that everyone who suffers instinctively looks for someone to blame, and experiences relief when they can lash out, either physically or somehow symbolically, against the perceived source. The genius of the ascetic priest was to simultaneously facilitate and contain this lashing out. They facilitated it by making a target always available; they contained it by making the retribution socially harmless. Accomplishing both of these desiderata at once required changing the direction of *ressentiment*:

> 'I suffer: someone must be to blame for this' – thus thinks every diseased sheep. But its shepherd, the ascetic priest, says to it: 'Right you are, my sheep! someone must be to blame for it: but you yourself are this someone, you

---

[11] The 'guilty' means also cause harms that the innocent ones do not, and therefore Nietzsche writes, 'This kind of pain remedy measured by modern standards is a "guilty" kind' (III: 19). Even here, Nietzsche is mentioning but not endorsing a guilty/innocent distinction.

alone are to blame – *you alone are to blame for yourself*!' . . .
That is bold enough, false enough: but at least one thing
is achieved with it, like I said, the direction of *ressentiment*
is – *changed*. (III: 15)

The priests invented a discourse that contributed to a psychological end: anaesthetising suffering and exploiting the bad instincts of sufferers. This discourse – perhaps including such concepts as 'guilt', 'sin', 'corruption' and 'damnation' (III: 16) – furnished a way for sufferers to think of themselves as to blame for their suffering. This, Nietzsche claims, is false but effective. It allows the 'healing artistic instinct of life [. . .] through the ascetic priest [. . .] to thus *exploit* the bad instincts of all suffering people for the purpose of self-discipline, self-surveillance, self-overcoming' (III: 16).

Before reviewing the other means, Nietzsche offers an aside about his working presupposition:

> In this treatise, as one sees, I proceed from the presupposition that I do not first need to justify, given readers as I need them: that 'sinfulness' in humans is not a fact, rather only the interpretation of a fact, namely of a physiological depression – the latter seen from a moral-religious perspective that is no longer binding on us. (III: 16)

This departs from the discussion of the ascetic priests, but raises a few interesting points about Nietzsche's approach. First, this is a warning about having the wrong conceptual framework in place for understanding phenomena – even ourselves. In this case, we are bound to get this wrong if we view ourselves in light of moral categories such as 'sinfulness'. We may need to understand others' conception of 'sin', but from a framework that does not employ that concept. Second, we can be in the grip of concepts in ways that we might not be able to anticipate or acknowledge. They might seem 'binding' on us, and yet this can shift through cultural change. Third, Nietzsche speaks frequently of 'depression' in this part of the Treatise, and he almost certainly does not mean a psychiatric mood disorder, which had not been fully theorised in his time, but a 'physiological' sense of diminished vitality. Fourth, although Nietzsche writes that sinfulness is 'only the interpretation of fact, namely of a physiological depression', he also claims, implicitly, to be 'the strictest opponent of all materialism' (III: 16). He does not define 'materialism' here, so it could be the position that only matter (including perhaps 'physiological' entities) exists, or that events can only be explained in material terms. His position seems to be, then, that although attributions of 'sinfulness' are misinterpretations of physiological states, his own account is that the very conceptualisation of 'sin' explains profound changes in human beings. Interpretations explain what we are.

The other three 'innocent' psychological means are 'mechanical activity' (III: 18), the 'small joy' (III: 18) and the '*formation of* a herd' (III: 18). None of these have the dramatic effects of anaesthetisation; they do not lead everyone to reconceive of themselves as sinful and blameworthy. Nietzsche suggests, however, that they are familiar, conducive to social regulation and relatively easy to induce. Mechanical activity works on the principle that attention is limited and repetitive work distracts from suffering. Nietzsche's broader point here is that this functions as a 'training for "impersonality"' (III: 18). In the performance of mechanical tasks, that is, one becomes detached from one's own ends, in favour of fulfilling the task's purpose. As detachment this is ascetic, but it also initiates a process of learning to take an objective stance.[12] The 'prescription of a small joy' that is easily accessible and can be made into a routine leads Nietzsche to discuss the 'joy of giving joy' (III: 18) in terms of the '*will to power*' (III: 18). His claim is that beneficent deeds do not stem from pure altruism or unegoistic detachment, but rather represent a small assertion of superiority. Helping others can be an expression of power, but can be encouraged for its own sake because it is a socially productive way of asserting power. Nietzsche refers to the formation of a herd as 'an essential step and victory in the battle with depression' (III: 18). This, Nietzsche says, expresses a shared will to power,

---

[12] This is similar to the points that Hegel makes about 'service' and 'work' in the development of the 'unhappy consciousness' in *The Phenomenology of Spirit* (Hegel 2018: 115, §195).

whereby individuals take pleasure in their banding together. The members of such a herd avert their self-aversion through 'arousal of the community's feeling of power' (III: 19).

The 'guilty' means works as a topsy-turvy version of anaesthetisation. The ascetic priest provokes an '*excess of feeling*' (III: 19) in order that this might counteract depression and alleviate suffering. Nietzsche claims that 'all great affects' (III: 20) can be provoked to excess so as to serve this end, and that the ascetic priests make use of all of them. However, 'The main trick the ascetic priest allowed himself for making the human soul resound with heart-rending, ecstatic music of all kinds [. . .] was his exploitation of the *feeling of guilt*' (III: 20). Out of all the intense feelings that they could make use of, the feeling of guilt is the one most reliably available since it does not depend on anything external. Unlike revenge or lust, it carries little danger to social harmony. And most importantly, it can be elicited through an interpretation that makes guilt into a state of being rather than something transient. Acetic priests operate through reinterpretation, and they convince sufferers that they are the source of their own suffering, and indeed that they should understand suffering itself as a '*state of punishment*' (III: 20).

Nietzsche's story here is that the ascetic ideal serves its function by providing an explanation of life in terms of the meaning of suffering. This meaning is that suffering is a form of merited punishment. This is not a good interpretation, but it nevertheless served as an especially durable and generally applicable form of explanation: it has coloured how we think about ourselves, and in particular shaped our views on blame and desert. It was effective, too: it succeeded in provoking emotional excess. Doing so helped in coping with suffering by making sense of that suffering in terms of reasons to explain it, and 'reasons relieve' (III: 20), even bad ones. It was also amazingly productive, since it provides the impetus for its own acceleration: its provocation of guilt causes more guilty suffering, which it can in turn explain as punishment, which causes more suffering, and so on.

This productivity is why Nietzsche claims that '"Sin" – for this is what the priestly reinterpretation calls the animal "bad conscience" [. . .] – has so far been the greatest event in the history of the sick soul' (III: 20). The great event is the reinterpretation of suffering, through the conceptualisation of sin, for the exploitation of guilty feelings. As 'medication' (III: 21) through interpretation, it succeeded: it alleviated suffering by assigning a reason for it. It created a basic form of self-misunderstanding, since it ascribed a metaphysical significance to an 'animal' drive and treated it as central to the 'soul'. The intensification of guilt also made everyone sicker, insists Nietzsche. And yet, 'With respect to *this* entire kind of priestly medication, the "guilty" kind, any word of criticism is too much' (III: 21). Not only did the 'priestly medication' provide a remedy, it transformed the nature of human experience. The meaning of having a soul expanded from suffering from the physiology of despair to responsiveness to infinite possibilities of concern: 'life itself became interesting again' (III: 21). The effect of the exploitation of guilt was 'to put the human soul for once completely out of joint, to immerse it in terrors, frosts, embers and ecstasies until it is freed of all the smallness and pettiness of malaise, dullness, depression as if by a stroke of lightning' (III: 20). This was unsettling in a way that, on one hand, prepared people for self-discipline and self-overcoming, and, on the other hand, made it possible for such self-relating activity to be directed to any purpose that seemed compelling. This changed what life could be about, albeit by making everyone unsure of who they were and what they wanted. The ascetic ideal introduced perpetual self-transformation into human life, at the cost of perpetual self-misunderstanding.

In the rest of his treatment of the ascetic priest, Nietzsche identifies two additional ways in which self-misunderstanding is perpetuated, and makes this comment about morality:

> On the whole, the ascetic ideal and its sublime-moral cult, this most ingenious, unscrupulous and dangerous systematization of all means of emotional excess under the aegis of holy intentions has inscribed itself in a terrible and unforgettable way on the entire history of humanity and unfortunately *not only* on its history. . . (III: 21)

Nietzsche treats morality as merely a 'cult' of the ascetic ideal here. Morality is not an independent topic that identifies particular demands or values separate from their cultural meaning. Morality, rather, is a subset of the ascetic ideal, and thus the proper terms for analysing it are the ones that clarify its psychological uses and effects. Nietzsche is claiming here that morality has been and remains a way of systematising the 'guilty' means of providing relief: morality convinces people they are bad, so as to alleviate some of their suffering by explaining it. He is not objecting to a particular theory of morality or claim about the content of morality, and he is certainly not arguing in favour of a different content. He is pointing to the 'dangerous' psychological means and ends of a practice, the effects of which endure regardless of what theory of morality we might hold.

The two remaining forms of self-misunderstanding that Nietzsche discusses in his treatment of the ascetic priest are temporal distortion and a form of bad taste. As part of the exploitation of guilt, Nietzsche claims, one sees 'everywhere the past regurgitated, the deed distorted, the "green eye" for all action; everywhere *wanting*-to-misunderstand suffering gets made into the content of life' (III: 20). Once someone sees themselves as 'guilty', they cannot help but look back to the choices they have made and deeds they have done and see some of those as culpable; they seek out long-ago faults in order to understand their current condition. Their sense of self, then, shifts from who they are in the present and their future potential to an excessive focus on the past and how they could have done things differently. They mislocate their identity in a past they are stuck in.

The other form of self-misunderstanding arises in a long discussion of the New Testament. Nietzsche writes of the 'pious little men' (III: 22) of the New Testament: 'They have an ambition that is laughable: *this* type regurgitates their most personal things, their stupidities, sorrows and loafer's worries, as if the very existence of things were bound to do something about it, *this* type never tires of dragging God himself into the tiniest misery in which they are stuck' (III: 22). Nietzsche has much more to say about this, but his basic point is that the priestly discourse that fosters guilt is also one that inflates petty matters into divinely important ones. The New Testament, in particular, takes up elements of an older vocabulary and transposes them into a new, personal, almost intimate context that is bound to confound everyone about what to take seriously in their lives.

In aphorism 23, Nietzsche begins to draw his discussion to a close. He addresses the meaning of the ascetic ideal, not just in particular contexts or for particular personae, but in general, as an expression of human will. His exposition takes on a dramatic form, with gradual and surprising reveals, until it concludes by returning to the cryptic claims of the first aphorism. There are four main points in the build-up to the conclusion: his analysis of the ascetic ideal is primarily about its meaning rather than its effects, the apparent alternatives to the ascetic ideal are in fact intensifications of it, the ascetic ideal can no longer fulfil its original purposes, and we have yet to find a way to conceive of ourselves apart from the ascetic ideal.

After noting some harmful effects of the ascetic ideal, Nietzsche insists that he is not suggesting that one weigh these costs against its benefits. To be sure, the ascetic ideal has generated effects, but Nietzsche's inquiry is aimed at accounting for its *meaning*:

> It is not what this ideal has *done* that I want to bring to light here; instead, quite simply what it *means*, what it hints at, what lies hidden behind, beneath and in it for which it is the provisional, unclear expression overloaded with question marks and misunderstandings. And only with respect to *this* purpose should I not spare my reader a glance at the enormity of its effect, and also its disastrous effects: namely in order to prepare them for the ultimate and most terrible aspect that the question of the meaning of that ideal holds for me. (III: 23)

There is a temptation to judge that the ascetic ideal is bad because it has bad effects, or is good because of its benefits. Nietzsche concedes that various kinds of damage have been sustained, but insists that more important than weighing outcomes is understanding something about *ourselves* that the ascetic ideal expresses; we need to know who we are before we can judge what trade-offs we are willing to make. There are two general features of Nietzsche's analysis. First, the idea of meaning is connected to something 'hidden behind' the ascetic ideal. This is remarkable: Nietzsche is already treating specific forms of religious belief and even morality as superficial phenomena, as particular ways in which the ascetic ideal manifests itself, and now he is suggesting that the ascetic ideal, too, is superficial. We need an analysis that shows who we are and why we make use of the ascetic ideal in order to come to terms with it. The other main feature of Nietzsche's analysis here is that the idea of meaning is connected to that of 'purpose'. To understand the ascetic ideal is, at least in part, to understand what it is *for*, and only in light of this purpose can one appreciate how disastrous it has been.

The efficacy of the ascetic ideal, as Nietzsche thus characterises it, is primarily interpretative rather than causal. Its effects follow from its influence on how we make sense of everything:

> What does the very *power* of this ideal mean, the *enormity* of its power? Why has it been given space to this extent? why was no better resistance offered? The ascetic ideal expresses a will: *where* is the counterwill in which a *counterideal* expresses itself? The ascetic ideal has a *goal* – it is universal enough that measured against it all other interests of human existence appear petty and narrow; it relentlessly interprets ages, people, human beings according to this single goal; it allows no other interpretation, no other goal to stand, it rejects, denies, affirms, and confirms only in the sense of *its* interpretation [. . .] Where is the *counterpart* to this closed system of will, goal, and interpretation? (III: 23)

This is Nietzsche's conception of enormous 'power': the shaping of interpretations. The power of the ascetic ideal is thus that it assigns a meaning to everything else, including ourselves and potentially competing ideals. Since it expresses an effective 'will', it drives interpretation according to *its* 'goal' rather than those of individuals. There are other goals and interpretative resources that might inform our understanding of things, but these are all subject to narrow, contextual application; the ascetic ideal interprets everything. It is a 'closed system of will, goal, and interpretation' that co-opts or subsumes any competition. As a closed system it cannot be challenged; points of resistance to particular beliefs can arise, but there are no genuine alternatives to the ideal itself. And thus it can foster misunderstandings so profound that they cannot even be recognised or open to question.

The ascetic ideal offers an evaluation of everything, leaving no domain in which it does not assert its authority. Of course, it seems as if there are alternatives. There is a rough narrative that, in one version or another, seems intuitively correct. In this narrative, primitive cultures held superstitious beliefs that led them to the self-infliction of harms; they made sacrifices that they would not have made, had their myths not valorised them. Organised religion, depending on one's point of view, either adopted and exacerbated the asceticism of these primitive myths, or represented an advance by putting them in a civilised form that was compatible with social progress. Now, however, we can recognise that a legacy of Enlightenment is to have left behind the benighted past and its ascetic values. Above all, 'modern science' (III: 23) is an alternative to the ascetic ideal and the superstitious myths that supported it.

Modern science initially appears not only to offer an alternative to the ascetic ideal, but even to have defeated it, since it dispels the ascetic ideal's religious interpretation of existence: it 'has gotten along well enough without God, the Beyond, and the negating virtues' (III: 23). But according to Nietzsche, 'the scientific conscience is an abyss' (III: 23) and science is not an opponent to the ascetic ideal but rather its *latest and most noble form*' (III: 23). As there were with the means of the priestly ascetic ideal, there are different versions of this claim. In one version, 'science today has absolutely *no* faith in itself, let alone an ideal *above* itself' (III: 23); this is 'science as a means of self-anesthetization' (III: 23). This version is science not as making claims about the ultimate nature of reality or the correct epistemic stance, but as delivering confidence in some instrumental success. Scientific practitioners can be indifferent as to whether science carves nature by its joints, and insist more simply that predictions will be more reliably fulfilled, and thus ends more likely satisfied, when one defers to the results of science rather than to traditional patterns of belief. For Nietzsche, however, this is 'the very *unrest* of the lack of ideals, the suffering from a *lack* of great love, the discontent with an *involuntary* contentedness' (III: 23). His view is that this version of the scientific conscience amounts to a position on what ought to be taken seriously: only what can be settled by an empirical procedure. This functions as a licence to dismiss deeper problems about ideals and ultimate ends; 'people generally *should* be satisfied' (III: 23) without engagement with these topics. Detachment of this sort is helpful in producing empirical knowledge, but anaesthetic in that it disconnects us from sources of concern that weigh on us unless we are numbed to them – and perhaps, unconsciously, even then.

The other version of science as a form of the ascetic ideal comes in many variations: at one point Nietzsche names it 'unconditional and honest atheism' (III: 27) and at another point associates it with 'free spirits' (III: 24). This version is characterised by a genuine passion. Whereas, with the other version, the claims of religion were merely ignored, the advocates of this one are the '*counter-idealists*' (III: 23) who see themselves as fighting to establish the truth in opposition to the ascetic ideal. Their self-image is of brave truth-tellers who insist on refuting superstitious beliefs. Nietzsche claims that there is something noble about these counter-idealists, and that it is the proper historical legacy of millennia of culture. For all that, it is not in opposition to the ascetic ideal, but its purest form:

> These negaters and outsiders of today, these people who are unconditional about one thing, their claim to intellectual cleanliness; these harsh, strict, abstinent, heroic spirits who constitute the honor of our age, all these pale atheists, antichristians, immoralists, nihilists, these skeptics, ephectics, *hectics* of the spirit [. . .] these last idealists of knowledge in whom alone today the intellectual conscience dwells and became incarnate – they believe themselves indeed to be as detached as possible from the ascetic ideal [. . .] this ideal is precisely *their* ideal, too, they themselves represent it today and perhaps nobody else [. . .] Those are not *free* spirits by a long shot: *for they still believe in truth*. (III: 24)

This kind of atheism (or immoralism or nihilism or scepticism), Nietzsche is claiming, is still a form of self-denial that is driven by an unwavering commitment to an ideal. The atheists deprive themselves of the comforts of belief out of a faith in a true world behind the welter of confusion; that there is no substantive content or further promise associated with this faith makes it all the purer. I will return to the faith in truth in the next section, and Nietzsche's call to bring the value of truth into question. Note here, however, that Nietzsche is not expressing opposition to truth, as if were impossible or undesirable. Sceptics are indeed one of the categories of counter-idealists, presumably because their insistence on truth's unavailability is tied up with an insistence on its importance. Nietzsche is criticising an 'overestimation of truth' (III: 25), not just in a comparative sense, in which people might take truth-seeking a little too seriously. There is a superlative ideal of truth, or an 'unconditional will to truth' (III: 24), as the positing of reality, independent of our discursive practices, from which we are deeply estranged, and which would yet answer all of our meaningful questions. This metaphysical faith in truth, Nietzsche claims, is at the centre of the ascetic ideal.

Science is thus the 'best *ally* of the ascetic ideal' (III: 25) and atheistic unbelief is its '*core*' (III: 27). Science contributes to asceticism because it binds us to 'self-contempt' (III: 25) and 'self-belittlement' (III: 25), and atheism is the core of the ascetic ideal because it is 'that ideal itself in its most rigorous, most spiritual formulation, esoteric through and through, stripped of all outworks' (III: 27). Science's role is to convince us that we are unconditionally bound to its results, and that its results diminish human importance. The nature of its claim to authority is already ascetic: it locates that authority as outside of human interests in a way that is 'guaranteed and chartered' (III: 24) by the ascetic ideal. More substantially, however, science dismantles the pretensions that human beings are especially important, that our lives are meaningful or at least meaningfully structured, or that we are worthy of dignity or self-respect. Free-spirit atheism is the core of the ascetic ideal because, after it takes away all the comforting myths, all the concrete sources of reassurance, it leaves behind nothing but a commitment to being 'strictly bound' (III: 24) by the value of truth.

Here it might be helpful to borrow a distinction from Randall Havas. Nietzsche is not objecting to the 'ordinary conditions of intelligible speech' that enable us to take responsibility for what we say (Havas 1995: 198). There is an ordinary commitment to truthfulness that comes with belonging to a culture and obedience to its norms. Through this kind of responsiveness to demands for truth, we can make ourselves intelligible to others and to ourselves. But the 'modern commitment to truthfulness', on the other hand, is ascetic in its 'unconditionality' (Havas 1995: 235). It is ascetic, that is, because it is expressed in attempts to hold ourselves accountable to standards that lie completely outside of any contingent practices. We cannot fully meet the demands of the modern commitment to truthfulness, so it provides opportunities to understand ourselves as culpable. At the same time, however, it represents an evasive lack of commitment: the standards binding on us are not *our* standards that we identify with, but something inhuman and ultimately opaque.

Science and free-spirit atheism not only fail to be alternatives to the ascetic ideal, then, they are the culmination of a process in which the ascetic ideal intensified itself. Nietzsche claims, that is, that the modern interest in truth is the pure form of the ascetic ideal, and human history manifests the 'inner development' (III: 25) that 'liberates the life of the ideal' (III: 25). The movements from simple, outward forms of asceticism to self-directed inner cruelty, to more esoteric and abstract forms of asceticism, are all part of a single process in which the ascetic ideal unfolds until it reaches its fullest realisation. Atheism, Nietzsche claims, is 'one of [the ascetic ideal's] final forms and inner logical consistencies' because it is 'the awe-inspiring *catastrophe* of a two-thousand year training in truth, that in the end forbids itself *the lie of believing in God*' (III: 27). And science, similarly, involves self-submission to the implacable, external authority of truth, where that is understood to preclude any compensatory consolation.

The process of intensification is also one of self-destruction. Nietzsche depicts modern science as the product of Christianity destroying itself: in particular, the 'concept of truthfulness' (III: 27) contained in Christian morality comes to be taken so seriously that it turns against itself. 'This is how Christianity as a *dogma* perished', Nietzsche writes, 'by its own morality; this is also how Christianity *as morality* must now perish – we are standing at the threshold of *this* event' (III: 27). Religion instils a more and more rigorous understanding of truth, to the point where that understanding is 'sublimated into scientific conscience' (III: 27), which denies the claims of religion. Morality can be separated from religious dogma and recast in secular form, but the scientific conscience carries forward the destructive process against it, too. Morality can be undermined by a number of views: that human behaviour cannot be suitably explained in terms of distinctively moral motivations, that moral belief is impossibly heterogeneous and does not converge towards a correct view, or that the very ideas of moral objectivity or moral obligation are inscrutable, for example. The scientific conscience undermines itself, too, by insisting that every belief is open to individual rational scrutiny, and at the same time not being able to account for its own authority claims. Nietzsche's time had its own forms of resistance to the claims of science; now we have creationism, homeopathy, climate change denial, antivaccine movements and more. The ascetic ideal takes away belief, including belief in itself, leaving only empty ascetic practices until those, too, collapse. But even though the ascetic ideal has turned against itself, leaving nothing of itself behind, and even though its complete self-destruction seems imminent, there remains no clear alternative – just an unstable wavering between fanaticism, cynicism and indifference.

This is what Nietzsche characterises as 'nihilism'. We can see this in his description of 'modern historiography':

> Its noblest claim now is that it aspires to be a *mirror*; it rejects all teleology; it no longer wants to 'prove' anything; it scorns playing the judge and has its good taste in this – it affirms as little as it denies, it ascertains, it 'describes' . . . All of this is ascetic to a high degree; but to an even higher degree it is *nihilistic* at the same time, let us not deceive ourselves about that! (III: 26)

For Nietzsche, historiography – the science of historical method – exemplifies a science with a directly human relevance. Its modern form is ascetic because it is self-denying: it tries to diminish its own role to nothing. Its ideal, Nietzsche claims, is to represent undistorted reality, and its conception of how to accomplish that is, *per impossibile*, to set aside human interests and judgements altogether. But this is not only ascetic, but nihilistic in that it demands adherence to an ideal that its own commitment to neutrality prevents it from endorsing. The alternative is to give up on the ideal, but then there would be no standpoint that is not arbitrary or capricious. So the nihilism here is that we make our own ideal commitments impossible to maintain, even as the integrity of one's standpoint depends on them. Here Nietzsche is using one scientific discipline as an example, but this is the general form of nihilism. As he elsewhere expresses it, it takes the form of 'the terrible Either/Or', 'either abolish your reverences or – *yourselves*!' (GS §346). The need for and insistent emptiness of 'reverences' is nihilism.

For all of Nietzsche's complaints against the ascetic ideal, then, the ultimate one is that it has drawn a conclusion against itself. The ascetic ideal, in all of its forms, served an important function:

> The meaninglessness of suffering, *not* suffering, was the curse that lay spread over humankind up till now – *and the ascetic ideal offered it a meaning*! It was the only meaning so far; any meaning is better than no meaning at all; the ascetic ideal was in every sense the all-time '*faute de mieux*' par excellence. In it suffering was interpreted; the tremendous void seemed filled; the door closed to all suicidal nihilism. (III: 28)

It was the '"*faute de mieux*" par excellence': the very best at filling the lack of anything better. It did not remove suffering or furnish an accurate or satisfying meaning to human existence, but it explained suffering, provided meaning and helped human beings make sense of our experience. It preserved the will against 'suicidal nihilism'. According to Nietzsche's historical argument, however, it has turned against itself, and can thus no longer effectively serve its functions. The ascetic ideal *was* valuable, but can no longer serve a purpose for us. If this is not already apparent, that is only because nothing has replaced it.

What remains of the ascetic ideal is just the awareness of its demise. Nietzsche frames this in terms of the 'will to truth': 'what meaning would *our* entire being have if not this, that in us the will to truth came to consciousness of itself *as a problem?*' (III: 27). Many 'meanings' have been assigned to human life. People at different times and places have believed in an order of things that demanded their adherence and gave sense to their activities. Now, Nietzsche is claiming, after dismantling all these cultural forms, we realise that there is a problem, in general, with securing the meaning of our lives by getting something absolutely right, by holding ourselves accountable to some extra-human order. Indeed, that realisation may be the primary characteristic of modern culture; 'our entire being' lacks any other meaning; the ascetic ideal has been 'the only meaning so far' (III: 28).

Nietzsche opened the Treatise by asking what ascetic ideals mean, and now, finally, he relates what *the* ascetic ideal means. He writes, '*That* is precisely what the ascetic ideal means: that something was *lacking*, that a tremendous *void* surrounded humanity – he did not know how to justify, to explain, to affirm himself, he *suffered* from the problem of his meaning' (III: 28). As soon as there was a problem of meaning, we suffered from it. The very interest in attributing meaning to one's life has been an expression of the ascetic ideal. The ascetic ideal, at any rate, emerged along with concerns over how we might provide ourselves with worthwhile goals and make sense of our lives. Its 'meaning' is just the openness to these concerns, and the openness to these concerns has become inseparable from a recognisably human life. As a result, Nietzsche, far from offering any obvious normative resolution of ethical matters, is suggesting the unavailability of any solution that is not self-undermining. The *Genealogy* does not conclude with a new, better ideal, or a refutation of all ideals. The *Genealogy* concludes with both the idea that we suffer from the lack of ideals and that ideals are the problem that we suffer from.

Nietzsche's argument in the *Genealogy* is ultimately about how we interpret our lives.[13] Morality has a primary role in this, since

---

[13] One can find a similar point in Andrew Huddleston's *Nietzsche on the Decadence and Flourishing of Culture*: 'Indeed, I think this is Nietzsche's most important legacy as a philosopher of culture. One of the central styles of critique that we see in Nietzsche's work, exemplified especially in his criticism of the Christian-moral outlook, involves interpreting social and cultural phenomena' (Huddleston 2019: 150).

it colours how we think about our values and our psychological capacities, and also, according to Nietzsche, leads us to interpret our whole existence as 'guilty' – as marked by culpable flaws and failures that merit punishment – in a way that intensifies our suffering. But morality is merely a part of the ascetic ideal's more comprehensive 'will to nothingness': 'a rejection of the most fundamental presuppositions of life' (III: 28). We have interpreted our lives in a way shot through with a hatred of life's embodied and sensuous conditions, its instabilities and confusions and unsatisfied desire; we have made sense of our existence in a way that expresses a longing to get outside human finitude altogether. Such interpretations did provide the basis on which *the will itself was saved* (III: 28). The historical role of the ascetic ideal has been to give people a sense of purpose by which they could direct their agency. It would have been better to have a way to do this that was not empty and did not work through hostility and suffering. But Nietzsche's claim here is that the ascetic ideal is the only ideal we have had; we do not even have the conceptual resources now to imagine what an alternative would be. So, Nietzsche concludes, 'to say once more what I said at the beginning: humanity would rather *will nothingness* than *not* will . . .' (III: 28).

Philosophical arguments

There are points in the Third Treatise where Nietzsche's discussion could be taken to engage with standing philosophical debates. One could reconstruct positions on the meaning of art, the status of philosophical reflection or the nature of society, for example. But the Third Treatise is, above all, where Nietzsche's discussion becomes most idiosyncratic; the terms of his analysis depart from conventional philosophical approaches. So in this section I will discuss three distinctively Nietzschean topics: perspectivism, the value of truth and self-knowledge. The first two, in particular, can easily be mistaken for interventions in familiar philosophical debates, but it is important to see how they contribute to Nietzsche's project in this Treatise.

The word 'perspectivism' does not appear in the *Genealogy*, but a passage on 'perspectival seeing' is sometimes taken as the centre of Nietzsche's epistemological theory: 'There is *only* a perspectival seeing, *only* a perspectival "knowing"; and *the more* affects we allow to express themselves on a given thing, *the more* eyes, different eyes we know how to engage for the same thing, the more perfect will be our "concept" of this thing, our "objectivity"' (III: 12). If we take Nietzsche to be concerned with offering a theory of knowledge, then this appears to be the statement of a suitably radical approach. One could take Nietzsche as denying the possibility of objective truth-claims, or alternately offering a revisionist account that is relativised to affects or 'eyes'. The details of Nietzsche's theory are presumably to be filled in by his claims in the rest of the passage and a broader understanding of his epistemological commitments.

But Nietzsche is not offering an epistemological theory. The context is worth considering here. 'Perspective seeing' arises amid Nietzsche's discussion of the ascetic priest and why promoting *ressentiment* 'over life itself' (III: 12) is only an apparent contradiction. Although this hostility to life is paradoxical, he claims, it serves the end of sustaining attachment to life by creating antagonism towards it. The ascetic priest thus plays a constructive role, and doing so by teaching self-hostility imparts the capacity for opposition to one's own affects. Such internal, affective conflict allows for responding to things not according to one's immediate sentiments, but by taking up a self-distanced standpoint. At the least, it is the first step in bringing about the possibility of a self-critical standpoint that takes alternative standpoints into consideration. The context of Nietzsche's discussion is not what is the nature of knowledge? The context, rather, is what useful end did the ascetic priest serve by contributing to the formation of an internally opposed standpoint?

Nietzsche presents two opposite characterisations of objectivity and knowing: one invoking 'the diversity of perspectives and affective interpretations' (III: 12), and another invoking the 'pure, will-less painless, timeless subject of knowledge' (III: 12).[14]

---

[14] Essential reading for a fuller understanding of Nietzsche's contrast and much else in this passage is Christopher Janaway's 'Perspectival Knowing and the Affects' (Janaway 2007: ch 12).

The ascetic ideal is useful insofar as it promotes one of these. But the pure, will-less subject is nonsense, Nietzsche insists; there is nothing there to promote because this view of objectivity is a 'non-concept and absurdity' (III: 12). This leaves the diversity of perspectives as the valuable result. This is perhaps puzzling, since the 'will-less subject' seems more in line with the ascetic ideal. The point of Nietzsche's analysis, however, is that the ascetic ideal works paradoxically. It can promote the belief in will-less knowing, as a form of ascetic detachment, while the cultivation of self-hostile affects promotes internally opposed standpoints that can incorporate a diversity of perspectives. What the ascetic ideal nominally advocates and what it actually produces diverge here. Nietzsche dismisses the philosophical ideal out of hand not because he wants to replace it with a superior one, but because he wants to pick out important psychological changes instead.

Apart from this context, there are specific reasons to think that Nietzsche is not interrupting his narrative to offer a perspectivist theory of knowledge. Consider the two different enterprises that he might be engaged in. First, he could indeed be offering a theory of knowledge. In that case, one would expect to find some account of the difference between knowledge and mere belief, perhaps with an account of justification or warrant and an explanation of how thought is adequate to reality or how truth can be distinguished from falsity. Alternatively, Nietzsche might be presupposing some familiarity with existing epistemic practices and commenting on the philosophical story of what makes them succeed. Even lacking a theory of knowledge, we have practices of weighing evidence, gathering data, deferring to expertise, employing suitable concepts and so on, and typically have no trouble certifying, as it were, certain claims as true, or even as examples of knowledge. A philosophical story about these practices might then try to vindicate aspects or results of the practices in terms of accounts of what the true claims have in common, what validates knowledge claims, and possibly how best to acquire new knowledge.

Nietzsche's discussion of perspectival knowing is the latter enterprise: he is commenting on the philosophical story – or at least a certain kind of philosophical story – about our epistemic practices. We can see this most clearly by noting that all the key terms are in scare quotes. Nietzsche does not discuss knowing, objectivity and concepts, but rather 'knowing', 'objectivity' and 'concept'; that is, he has no theory of these things themselves, or even an endorsement of a particular usage, but only a commentary on how these terms are used in our discourses. Nietzsche indicates the same point by returning to the epithet of the Preface, 'knowing ones' (III: 12; P: 1): he is referring to a characterisation of who we are in terms of our typical practices, not claiming that we have achieved a philosophical ideal.

Another reason for thinking that Nietzsche is not offering a theory of knowledge is that he treats the key terms indiscriminately. If he were offering a theory, he would need to distinguish between objectivity, conceptual adequacy and knowledge, and explain how they relate to one another. He does not. A third reason for thinking that Nietzsche is not offering a theory of knowledge is that he is giving an account of how everything always works rather than an account of a privileged status. There is only perspectival knowing because there is only perspectival seeing; he treats any alternative position as meaningless conceptual manipulation that 'cannot be thought at all' (III: 12). Nietzsche is not offering a new theoretical ideal that meaningfully contrasts with existing practices, but rather redescribing in novel terms what is already being done.

Nietzsche's treatment of perspectivism in the *Genealogy*, then, is a set of claims about how our epistemic practices function: they require affective engagement and diversity of perspectives, but not impersonal philosophical ideals. Some familiar philosophical stories are empty myths. Instances of what we call 'objectivity', for example, are not abstracted away from all human standpoints or thought in the absence of affect. They are, if anything, incorporations of many different affect-laden standpoints. This idea, of success as '*the more* eyes, different eyes', will not match up perfectly with the use of 'objectivity', if only because it is unlikely that the concept of objectivity is entirely coherent. Nietzsche does not need to be concerned about this, however, because he is neither offering a normative theory of objectivity nor a theory of regularity in concept usage. His point is that we make use of objectivity without any resort to the 'dangerous old conceptual mythmaking' (III: 12) of a philosophical ideal. This supports the claim of his narrative about the productivity of the ascetic priests. Their important contribution was not the invention of philosophical ideals, which may amount to nothing, but inducing a broad change in affective self-relation, which ultimately – perhaps unforeseeably – reshaped our epistemic practices.

The *value of truth* is another topic that can be easily misconstrued as part of an intervention in epistemology. In a sense, it is: Nietzsche's discussion, like the one about perspective seeing, aims at deflating (or demoralising) an epistemic ideal. But Nietzsche does not aim at replacing the ideal he undermines; he calls for a 'critique' rather than refounding epistemology on a new basis. He thus presents the 'value of truth' as a 'new problem':[15]

> In all of them a consciousness is lacking for the extent to which the will to truth itself first requires a justification, here every philosophy has a gap – why is that? Because so far the ascetic ideal was the *master* of all philosophy, because truth was posited as Being, as God, as supreme authority itself, but truth was not *allowed* to be a problem at all. Do you understand this 'allowed'? – From that moment when faith in the God of the ascetic ideal is denied, *there is also a new problem*: that of the *value* of truth. – The will to truth requires a critique – let us here determine our own task – the value of truth has to be for once experimentally *called into question* . . . (II: 24)

The passage is dramatic but mysterious. The value of truth is a *new* problem, one that is newly allowed to exist, and connected, somehow, to requiring a justification of the 'will to truth'. This problem gives us 'our' task, one to be carried out 'experimentally'.

If the problem of the 'value of truth' were assimilated to a somewhat conventional philosophical problem, then Nietzsche's

---

[15] The 'problem of the value of truth' has appeared previously in Nietzsche's work, in the first aphorism of *Beyond Good and Evil*.

main point would be that truth is, at best, only instrumentally valuable; his critique would be directed towards 'the belief in a *metaphysical* value, the value *in itself of truth*' (III: 24).[16] If the truth has only instrumental, non-metaphysical value, then it would be rational to inquire as to whether pursuing truth is beneficial for us. There might be considerable costs in pursuing truth. We are not in a position to assess the value of truth, in any case, until we understand the trade-offs involved, and so far these have not been taken into account. So Nietzsche, on this line of interpretation, has no position on whether there is such a thing as truth or whether it is accessible to us. His point is that we do not need to regulate our discourse in terms of truth. We should regulate our discourse – judge what is appropriate to say and believe – in whatever way is most beneficial for us. Trying to do so might raise some self-referential worries: we might wonder, for example, how to assess claims about what is beneficial other than by their truth. But presumably these worries can be resolved in the most beneficial way to do so.

Nietzsche presents the problem of the value of truth differently, however. Rather than a recommendation for greater prudence, he identifies it as a question of *meaning*, and associates it with the culmination of his narrative. In the initial presentation of the problem, he wrote that it involves a situation, that the 'will to truth' requires a critique, and a correlative task, that of calling the value of truth into question. Later he integrates the will to truth into his narrative: 'After Christian truthfulness drew one conclusion after another, in the end it will draw its *strongest conclusion*, its conclusion *against* itself; but this will happen when it asks the question: *"what does all will to truth mean?"* . . .' (III: 27). What had been 'faith in God' (III: 24) in the earlier passage now becomes 'Christian truthfulness', but in both cases Nietzsche offers a non-religious way of describing an event in terms of the will to truth. This event is a shift in the nature of the commitment to truth. This commitment had been understood to be based on accountability to what is real: to God, first, and then to reality in itself. But then it becomes, abruptly, a question of one's 'will'. That is,

---

[16] For a long, Nietzsche-inspired meditation on truth as an intrinsic value, see Williams 2004.

the commitment to truth becomes seen in psychological terms, in light of what we might hope to achieve in holding ourselves accountable in that way and what that reveals about us. This is how the problem of the value of truth fits into Nietzsche's narrative: it is the ultimate form in which the way we submit ourselves to authority becomes questionable.

This idea, that the problem of the value of truth is about the way in which we recognise authority, also appears in its initial presentation. There Nietzsche writes, 'truth was posited as [. . .] supreme authority itself' (III: 24), but it was 'not *allowed* to be a problem at all' (III: 24). The problem of the value of truth arises when the supreme authority is doubted; prior to that the authority of truth took such a form that it somehow could not be challenged. This is confirmed in Nietzsche's later clarification, in which he retracts the use of a value-term, 'overestimation': 'the same overestimation of truth (more accurately: [. . .] the same belief in the *in*estimability, *un*criticizability of truth)' (III: 25). We can loosely understand the problem as an overestimation, as one of attributing too much value, but a more accurate understanding would be in terms of 'inestimability', of value beyond all comparison, or 'uncriticizability', of status so authoritative that it cannot be subject to criticism. The overall issue that Nietzsche addresses in terms of the problem of the value of truth, then, is this. We have conceived of truth as having a form of authority that is completely beyond criticism, completely unproblematic, which we are obliged to recognise. But belief in that kind of authority depends on the ascetic ideal, since it is 'guaranteed and chartered by that ideal alone' (III: 24). So the problem comes in trying to understand what kind of authority truth has when its 'supreme' authority can no longer be sustained.

Truth has a mundane authority for us, in that we ought to regulate our assertions and especially our beliefs by it. We believe only what we take to be true, and should prefer to have more true beliefs rather than fewer; our system of beliefs should be as accurate and comprehensive as possible. Insofar as the meanings of our claims are connected to their truth-conditions, these forms of self-regulation are basic to our ability to use language and communicate with others. We can see these regulations as not especially demanding. Nietzsche makes many assertions, and it is true, for example, that water is H_2O, that penguins can swim, that demand curves slope downward, that a red light means stop, that Arsenal did not lose a league match in the 2003–4 season, and so on. As with all beliefs, these are subject to refinement and rejection. Asserting them as true makes one accountable to the facts and to one's interlocutors. Truth can hold, at least, this kind of authority.

Nietzsche's concern about 'supreme' authority, then, is that truth came to be regarded not merely as a norm that regulates our shared discourse, but as something sublime – 'truth was posited as Being, as God' (III: 24). In various forms truth came to be regarded as inestimably important, so that the worth of one's whole existence could depend on getting a few fundamental things right and eliminating falsity. And at the same time, the norm of truth became intensely demanding, so that only what is completely perspicuous and immune to doubt could be taken as true: it became so idealised as to be unattainable. The increased importance assigned to truth, that is, generated a reconceptualisation of what it is and how demanding it could be, which could support an ever greater assignment of importance, until truth became a supreme authority that is redemptive but inaccessible. Mundane and possibly inconsequential truth in a language continues to operate alongside the sublime form, leaving us with a confused or incoherent relationship to truth.

This is not just an epistemic matter. Calling the value of truth into question and critiquing the will to truth is 'our own task' (III: 24) because truth is the main exemplar of ascetic authority; truth's form of authority and the misunderstandings about it are the final form that the ascetic ideal takes. There are three problematic features of this form of authority. First, truth purports to be a form of *unconditional* regulation. Truth imposes a demand on us, beyond criticism, that cannot be overridden, and that in turn furnishes a guarantee: gaining truth counts as a non-contingent success, regardless of what consequences it brings. Second, truth purports to be a form of *impersonal* regulation. Truth seems to regulate us by itself, merely on the basis of how things are, and independently from any human authority or how we hold each other accountable for what we say and do. Third, truth purports to be a form of *universal* regulation. It offers a single, univocal answer that applies in every context to any meaningful question. These features make up a form of authority that is ascetic because it calls for accountability to something outside human experience, while imputing blame for the inevitable failures to adequately grasp it. This, and not epistemological or ontological matters, is the concern of the Third Treatise.

The 'problem of the value of truth', then, is about how to regulate ourselves when we no longer think of ourselves as regulated by 'supreme authority'. Truth is important in the narrative as the last form that supreme authority takes; as such, it is the successor to religious and other traditional forms of authority. The problem is a general one, however, about how we conceive of regulation and submit it to critique, and not merely about the assessment of propositions. And Nietzsche leaves it as a problem, one that can only be answered 'experimentally' (III: 24). For him it is an open question whether, regarding the 'will to truth' or anything else, we can make our normative self-regulation coherent and effective, to what extent it can be aspirational or idealised, or whether it can be sustained at all.

Another topic, *self-knowledge*, is not thematised as a distinct philosophical topic. Nietzsche does not present a theory or defend a method of inquiry. And yet, since the Preface opened with the declaration that 'we are unknown to ourselves', the task of the *Genealogy* has been to address this failing. So if the Third Treatise does not devote a separate discussion to self-knowledge, that is only because the Treatise as a whole is dedicated to addressing it: by revealing the 'basic fact of the human will' (III: 1), conveying the 'physiological knowledge' (III: 17) about the ascetic ideal and, above all, discussing the obstacles to and prospects for gaining adequate self-understanding. Nietzsche does not give a general account of self-knowledge, but he does argue that ideal commitments shape how we interpret our existence in general, and that ascetic modes of interpretation have shaped our views of ourselves in a destructive way: they estrange us from our wants and needs.

There are two modes of self-knowledge that the Third Treatise presents in order to discredit them. One involves an idealised picture of human capacities, including capacities for self-disclosure. Self-knowledge is available because human beings have a unique standing in the world and are endowed with faculties – consciousness, will, reason – that grant privileged access to one's own characteristics and wants. Self-knowledge, then, is the standard result of the proper employment of common faculties. The other mode of self-knowledge involves an idealised view of truth and a third-personal view of human beings: self-knowledge is then just a special case of knowledge of the world. We ourselves are among the things about which we can gain objective knowledge. But both of these modes of self-knowledge are ascetic, according to Nietzsche. They depend on self-diminishment and as a result, even when they are informative, they mislead us about ourselves. Nietzsche accordingly gives his psychological account of what is actually achieved by looking at ourselves in these ways and suggests the need for a different way of interpreting ourselves.

Nietzsche does not tell us the best way to interpret ourselves, however. He does not take it as something that falls to *him* to do; he is not well positioned to give an interpretation of what our lives are or ought to be. What he does instead is offer a number of articulations of how existing interpretations foster self-misunderstanding. Nietzsche in particular addresses *morality* and the harms that it causes through interpretation. It creates a hermeneutic situation in which individuals have no alternative but to understand themselves in moral terms; it thereby becomes impossible for anyone to articulate what they are and what they want so that they might lead their life in a satisfying way. Nietzsche's point is that there are social conditions for being able to meaningfully relate to one's own activities, emotions and drives, and so on, and morality destroys those conditions. When all of our possible self-descriptions are filtered through moral categories, persons become estranged from their own wants and needs.

In the *Genealogy*, Nietzsche makes this point in terms of 'tartuffery'. This word is his own coinage, after Molière's play *Tartuffe*. In *Tartuffe*, the titular character is a hypocrite who feigns perfect piety and uses moralising to swindle his host out of his fortune and seduce his wife. Nietzsche uses the term 'tartuffery' frequently, not to refer to the literary character, but rather to a general and diffuse hypocrisy that everyone participates in. We 'modern human beings' (II: 6) even possess a special kind of tartuffery: we are inevitable, necessary Tartuffes, whose words, deeds and selves cannot possibly cohere. Hypocrisy, for us, is not a conscious tactic we use in order to gain illicit ends or a false pretence of higher standards than we in fact observe; instead it 'belongs to our invincible "flesh and blood", [and] twists the words in our mouths, even those of us who know better'.[17] As a result of the demands of modern social life, tartuffery has become embodied in us, as part of our constitution, and also appears in our language. Our language is moralised to the extent that we lack discursive resources to make sense of ourselves; at best we can notice its inadequacy without having something better to say. This failing is not merely an inability to put our thoughts into words, but a more profound and ongoing deformation of the 'words in our mouths'. Morality thins out and empties our discourse of the specificity of cares and satisfactions, and we, pursuing misshapen ends or misrecognising our own emotions, intensify our own failures of self-understanding.

Nietzsche explains this in a long passage in the Third Treatise:

> Why should *we* budge even a single step for [tender moderns'] tartuffery of words? For us psychologists that would already constitute a tartuffery of *deeds* [. . .] For this is where a psychologist has his *good taste* [. . .] namely that he resists shamefully *over-moralized* discourse, which these days covers in slime all modern judging of humans and things. For let us not deceive ourselves here: what constitutes the most characteristic feature of modern souls and modern books is not the lie, but their ingrained *innocence* in moralistic mendacity [. . .] Our educated people of today, our 'good' people do not lie [. . .] The authentic lie, the genuine, resolute, 'honest' lie [. . .] would for them be something far too rigorous, too strong; it would demand what *must* not be demanded of them, that they open their eyes to themselves, that they know how to distinguish between 'true' and 'false' in themselves. (III: 19)

---

[17] BGE §24. I have modified the translation slightly, to give the German *selbst* a contrastive rather than a concessive sense.

Nietzsche characterises himself as a psychologist and his own psychological practice in terms of resisting 'over-moralized discourse'. The problem with this discourse is that it 'covers in slime' all of our judgements: morality seeps so deeply into our conceptual capacities that it affects how we think about persons and things in general, and not in a pleasant way. Nietzsche does not say that this problem can be avoided, but only *resisted*; we have no satisfactory alternative discourse with which to talk about ourselves. As a result of this problem, self-misunderstanding is inevitable – especially among the best, most modern, most educated people. Our self-misunderstanding – our inability to distinguish 'true' and 'false' in ourselves – is so pronounced that, according to Nietzsche, it renders us incapable of genuine lying. To lie, properly, we would have to understand ourselves and then intentionally deceive others. But we lack the ability to understand ourselves, since not only do we slime our own self-descriptions, but we have a naïve innocence about this: we are not troubled by it because we are not even aware that we are doing it.

According to Nietzsche, defective interpretations can have somatic consequences; in the case of the ascetic ideal, 'this interpretation [. . .] brought fresh suffering with it' (III: 28). But what he is asking us to consider, through his claims about the tartuffery of words and over-moralised discourse, is how vulnerable we are to failures in desire and feeling when we cannot articulate the things that we want, or inevitably have to 'slime' them in order to do so. We might falter in self-confidence and pride if we 'innocently' condemn ourselves as moral failures, or lack aims if we judge everything to be repugnant. Part of the way that moral discourse works on us is by introducing self-obscuring resentment against our lives into our judgements. Moral valuation, for Nietzsche, is rooted in a hatred of human embodiment and contingency, so the legacy of morality might be to compel a misinterpretation of our condition. And this ongoing misinterpretation could furthermore be the basis of ill-health, psychological and physiological.

Over-moralised discourse shapes the way that we understand all of our relations in the world: it can focus blame on those who suffer from misfortunes, provide exculpation for those who inflict harms, and introduce punitiveness into the logic of social institutions. The general ways in which we interpret our lives lead us to make defective judgements – innocent lies – about ourselves. And moral self-interpretation is only one aspect of a more general commitment to ascetic interpretation. What replaces it, for Nietzsche, and would contribute to less defective forms of self-knowledge, could not be new content assigned to old moral understandings, or any ascetic interpretation of ourselves as subject to some ultimate ethical vocabulary. The modern, secular idea of morality retains an older idea of decisive, articulable considerations in terms of which particular requirements could be theorised, but for Nietzsche, this idea is part of what needs to be overcome. In the place of thinking ourselves bound to unconditional answers, or as governed by lawlike regularities, self-knowledge requires attentiveness to the difficulties of even articulating matters of ethical interest and the particular, contingent and subtle ways that we respond to this. Self-knowledge, then, does not take the form of rules that are accessible to general understanding, but the complex understanding of the psychologist/philosopher who can consider the historical possibilities of the human soul and human communities.

Methodological and rhetorical issues

This section consists of two discussions. The first continues the argument from the previous chapters about Nietzsche's methodology. Previously I argued that in the Second Treatise, Nietzsche shifts his methodology to a historicist one: understanding morality requires a distinctively historical account of content. Here I argue that the Third Treatise develops a genealogical approach to making sense of the concepts used in inquiry. Genealogy, that is, comprises higher-order reflection on the categories that we as inquirers should adopt in understanding the historical contexts and contents of morality. The second discussion in this section is about departing from the ascetic ideal. Nietzsche provides no alternatives to the ascetic ideal: he does not offer a successor ideal, an authoritative new meaning of human existence or solution to normative puzzles. Indeed, he suggests that it is currently impossible to think of an alternative to the ascetic ideal even though the ascetic ideal is not viable. He does, however, offer two mysterious suggestions regarding how we might approach an alternative: through art and through comedians of the ascetic ideal.

In the previous chapter I argued that Nietzsche's historicist understanding of content required the reconstruction of past practices and the shifting systems of purposes that these practices served. The Second Treatise, I claimed, made the case that the undefinability of moral concepts necessitates a historical account of their content. Now I want to argue that the aim of the Third Treatise, apart from conveying its substantive claims about the ascetic ideal and human will, is to make the methodological point that the historical account of meaning needs to be supplemented by an account of what categories to employ in inquiry. Understanding morality, in the first instance, is a matter of reconstructing something like a participant standpoint for the practices in which moral concepts figure. But this leaves us with a higher-order task of how we are to make sense of the participant standpoint. A genealogical understanding of morality keeps the content of morality in view – not switching to an altogether different vocabulary of accounting for human behaviour – but constructs our own standpoint on it. The task of genealogy is to furnish this standpoint. And this is indeed how genealogical critique works for Nietzsche: explicating the meaning for us of morality to show where its practices are self-undermining or self-defeating.

To see the role of genealogy, consider one of Nietzsche's examples of a personal characteristic. In the *Genealogy*, Nietzsche refers to *chastity* as a non-virtuous product of a 'dominating instinct' (III: 8); elsewhere in *Thus Spoke Zarathustra*, he suggests that it may be either a virtue or something like a vice, depending on how it relates to sensuality (Nietzsche 1978: 54). In any case, there is a general quality, chastity, that manifests itself in individual psychology by motivating chaste behaviour as its particular end. To understand what all this amounts to, we might need a story about how the category of 'chastity' became available and developed, and perhaps one about how its adoption was promoted and disseminated; none of this, of course, needs to have been the result of a plan or conscious intention. A fuller understanding of chastity would enable us to understand a variety of different activities, and even absences of activity, as expressions of that virtuous or vicious characteristic. We would need to qualify and restrict our inquiry in various ways to make sure that we did not confuse chastity and chaste performances with different characteristics that manifest themselves in apparently similar ways. But one basic form of understanding would be to identify chastity by spelling out what it does and what it expresses in the contexts in which it appears.

Yet this is a strange form of understanding. We might think that chastity is not just a bad ideal to endorse but a bad concept: it does not make sense, it does not pick out any real quality, it is not a concept that we should adopt for our own use, and the motivations for including it in one's outlook are strange, or require strange metaphysical commitments. So for Nietzsche, even after we have a contextual understanding of chastity, there is an additional question of how we as inquirers are supposed to account for it, or what conceptual repertory we should bring to bear in understanding it. This latter inquiry is dependent on already succeeding in the prior one: without a correct contextual understanding of chastity one cannot get started in the higher-order one. But the latter inquiry becomes necessary once the prior one is completed. Otherwise we would have to settle with retaining 'chastity' in our own way of understanding things, when we would better incorporate it into our understanding by accounting for it in a different way.

This is why Nietzsche claims that knowledge of background 'conditions and circumstances' (P: 6) is required for a critique of moral values. The usefulness of this knowledge is not in trying to infer the worth or status of moral values from something about their origin, but in putting oneself in a better position to interpret them. Nietzsche announces this as the main task of Third Treatise when he declares the genealogical question to be 'what does this mean?' (III: 11). This question comes in more specific forms, such as 'what do ascetic ideals mean?' (III: 1). And it also has a more complex form, as in this case: 'What does this change of sense [*Sinn*] mean [*bedeuten*], this radical reversal of sense?' (III: 2). Here Nietzsche observes a terminological distinction between two levels of interpretation. The local-contextual participant understanding is 'sense' (*Sinn*), but the additional, higher-order genealogical understanding is 'meaning'. So, for example, although the sense of chastity might be understood in terms of sexual abstinence fulfilling an ideal of purity, this sense can in turn be interpreted as an attempted 'bridge for that other existence' (III: 11), and then perhaps as an abhorrence of the senses or a hostility to life. My aim here is not to give a correct interpretation of chastity, in any case, but to point out that the task of genealogy involves not only identifying the context of phenomena such as chastity, but the higher-order work of interpreting that content in light of how *we* are to understand it in the context of its background conditions.

This, furthermore, is how genealogical critique works. Nietzsche's claim in the *Genealogy* is that once we depart from first-order interpretations, our moral ideals turn out to be self-undermining and self-defeating. Critique is at once hermeneutic and internal: some ideals, once properly interpreted, can be seen to have a deeper meaning that is at odds with their nominal or apparent character. Genealogical critique thus points out a complex of practical 'self-contradiction' (III: 11; III: 13; III: 15). Ascetic practice is apparently self-hostile, but it turns out to serve a deeper purpose as an 'artifice' (III: 13) for giving meaning to persons' lives and thereby saving the will. But sustaining ascetic practice turns out to demand great self-sacrifice for the sake of imaginary goals, and intensifies to the point where sacrifice is required for the sake of nothing; the artifice becomes pointless and debilitating. So Nietzsche's critique is based on the moral phenomena that he examines actually counting as forms of the 'will to nothingness' (III: 24) and thus as having only an empty, self-destructive effectiveness.

Genealogy puts interpretation in the service of critique by pointing out internal failures. Nietzsche does not need to premise his critique on privileged perfectionist or supposedly natural values, and he does not need to argue that our values are bad because they have a defective origin. He only argues that our values' first-order character is in opposition to what the values themselves really mean, and that we can see this in how they undermine themselves. Genealogy's basic objection is merely that moral values, for example, cannot possibly be good for anything any more; it does not try to show that we should be doing something else, having adopted different values.

Our interpretative interests do not stop when we give a sense to moral values. Genealogy thus takes up where the first-order historical account leaves off by placing values in our own semantic context so that we can understand how to understand them. With the right conceptual framework in place, furthermore, critique becomes available. At least in the case of the genealogy of morality, it can function simply by pointing out internal contradictions, as in the case of a will to nothingness that is causing itself to expire.

The importance of *rhetoric* changes in the Third Treatise. Its main rhetorical feature is its narrative structure. It completes a drama that was anticipated in the earlier Treatises, and in this drama, as Aristotle said about the best form of tragedy (Aristotle, *Poetics* 1452a), there is a recognition at the same time as a reversal. Through the announcement that modern science is the latest form of the ascetic ideal, we are informed that the ascetic ideal has not, in fact, been defeated. Unlike a tragedy, however, nothing has really changed: rather than a conflict having been resolved, it turns out that there has been no genuine conflict, and we have not learned anything from this recognition. Nothing gets resolved, so the drama is ironic rather than tragic. But the Third Treatise, apart from its rhetorical features, also includes rhetoric in its discussion of alternatives to the ascetic ideal. Nietzsche does not treat rhetoric itself as an independent topic. But he does make two laconic suggestions for how alternatives might be found, and what these suggestions share is their rhetorical character.

The first suggestion that Nietzsche makes is *art*: '*Art* [. . .] in which precisely the lie sanctifies itself, in which the *will to deception* has good conscience on its side, is much more fundamentally opposed to the ascetic ideal than science' (III: 25).[18] He is only making a comparative claim here: art is *more* opposed to the ascetic ideal than science. This is a low bar, too, since he had already claimed that science is not at all opposed to the ascetic ideal. Still, its status as a member of the opposition might be

---

[18] For an interesting discussion of the role of art, see May 1999: esp. 153f.

surprising in light of what he had earlier written about artists. According to Nietzsche, 'during all ages, they have been valets of a morality or philosophy or religion' (III: 5). So one would expect them to be 'valets' of the ascetic ideal, too. Artists, that is, have no 'valuations' (III: 5) of their own; they merely dress up already dominant values in an appealing or interesting fashion. Artists, then, are not merely ineffectual as opposition, but they fail to oppose at all. So how can art stand in fundamental opposition to the ascetic ideal?

The second suggestion that Nietzsche makes is that an alternative can be found with the 'comedians of the ascetic ideal'.[19] He writes, remarkably, 'The only thing I care about having shown here is this: at present the ascetic ideal also in the more spiritual realm has only one kind of real enemy and *injurer*: the comedians of this ideal – for they arouse suspicion' (III: 27). He seems to be referring to the whole book, or at least the Third Treatise, by 'here'. So the lesson that Nietzsche most wishes to impart, from the entire work, is this: the ascetic ideal, in either its more literal or more 'spiritual' forms, is so successful at co-opting all opposition that there is no way to challenge it, except through one 'enemy' that not only challenges it but succeeds, somewhat, in doing so: the comedians of the ascetic ideal. But who are these comedians? One possibility is that they are those who make light of the ascetic ideal and undermine its authority in that way. That might be, but Nietzsche's earlier reference to comedians makes it seem otherwise. These seem to be the same comedians, or at least the same type:

> I would like to know how many shiploads of imitation idealism, of heroes' costumes and tin noisemakers of big words, how many barrels of sugared spirituous sympathy [. . .] how many comedians of the Christian-moral ideal would have to be exported today from Europe so that its air could smell fresh again. (III: 26)

---

[19] There is an important discussion of the 'comedians' in Conway 1997: 100–18.

These are idealists who unintentionally appear comical, rather than comedians who joke about ideals.[20] They are perhaps not exhaustive of the class of comedians of the ascetic ideal, but in any case they are not desirable company. They do not help to clarify how comedians of the ascetic ideal furnish opposition.

Art and the comedians of the ascetic ideal each furnish opposition in their own ways. What they have in common, however, is that they work rhetorically rather than theoretically. Opposition to the ascetic ideal does not consist in grounding a theoretical alternative: there is no decisive new answer to questions about the content of ethics or the meaning of life, and no attempt to prove the reality or superior standing of a competing ideal. The opposition that Nietzsche names instead works through rhetoric in a broad sense. By 'rhetoric' I do not mean only through performances of speech and linguistic techniques. There are two components, rather, to this broad sense of rhetoric. First, *how* things are said or otherwise represented is as important as what is represented. Nietzsche is calling attention to the forms that expressions take, what attitudes and moods they evince, and the figurative, non-literal meanings they convey. Second, how expressions persuade, captivate or otherwise engage with others is important. Rhetoric communicates not only by delivering content, but, as fundamentally social, by having an effect on an audience: making conspicuous something otherwise unnoticed, provoking emotions or effecting a shift in standpoint.

The comedians of the ascetic ideal do not offer a theoretical challenge to it; indeed, trying to do so would likely reinstitute it, as with science's challenge to it. Not only do the comedians not argue against it, but the ascetic ideal seems to be all they perform: they speak as advocates. Nietzsche claims, however, that they are the only 'real enemy and *injurer*' of the ascetic ideal because they exhibit what it amounts to, in practice, to live by the ascetic ideal. The 'comedians' are not professional performers, but the

---

[20] The word that Nietzsche uses for 'comedian', *Komödiant*, is ambiguous, but it does not have the modern sense of a professional joke-teller; that role did not exist in Nietzsche's time. It refers, rather, to an actor, especially one in the comic theatre, such as a performer in *Tartuffe*.

everyday clowns who prosecute their ideals in ridiculous ways. So their performances consist in staking claims to authority in a social world that is supposed to be regulated by ideals. They propound ideals, offer interpretations of what they mean and how they ought to be observed, and get others to listen to them and take them seriously. That is how they harm the ascetic ideal. They are laughable in their pursuits, and by showing how ascetic ideals would be implemented in a familiar world by familiar characters, they make these ideals themselves ridiculous.[21] Such comedians might also be upsetting or dangerous when they gain public authority, or they might be ineffective in their unintended purpose. But their power of raising suspicion against the ascetic ideal works through comedy, albeit a dark comedy.

The distinguishing feature of art, for Nietzsche, at least the one that makes it suitable for opposition to the ascetic ideal, is that it does not aim at accurate representation of the world. Nietzsche had a curious way of making this point, in terms of 'the lie' and the '*will to deception*'. This might make it seem as if art intentionally misrepresents the world, so that the audience gets a false picture while they presume they have an accurate one. But Nietzsche's claims were that in art the lie 'sanctifies itself' and the will to deception has a 'good conscience'. His point, then, is not that lying and deception are essential to art, but that art carries a prerogative for these activities: art authorises itself to depart from the truthful representation of how things are. This prerogative opposes the ascetic ideal more than a mandate to lie, which would require attention to the demands of truthful representation in order to flout them. It is an indirect opposition: it does not try to refute ascetic ideals so much as show that some important expressive activity can proceed without being regulated by them. By locating art within the same domain as the will to deception, furthermore, Nietzsche makes communication centrally important; art's effectiveness comes through its way of relating to others, by imparting how the world may be otherwise. Art's opposition, then, comes about by

---

[21] Compare the discussion of laughter in the first aphorism of *The Gay Science*: 'To laugh at oneself as one would have to laugh in order to laugh *from the whole truth* – for that, not even the best have had enough sense of truth' (GS §1).

displaying a different world and different experience of the world. Artists, Nietzsche thinks, may be useless, and art may accomplish many other things, but by imagining a different world it invites us to reshape our perceptions, change the meaning of our experience, and reinterpret ourselves in non-ascetic ways.

The *Genealogy* comes to a close with its main drama concluded, but few new pronouncements. There is no new table of values, and no identification of the ground of ethics or the naturalistic basis of health. The lessons from the story of asceticism and human will are few. Nietzsche's suggestions about what it would mean to depart from that story and tell a different story about ourselves are rhetorical in character. They propose making better use of the imagination, taking up different forms of communication, and laughing at what presently passes for authority. These proposals do not offer solutions, but only resources for moving towards a different sense of who we are.

Conclusion

When we read and interpret texts, we bring to bear the expectations that we have of them, however vague and unreflective these expectations might be. One set of expectations that we might bring to a 'genealogy' that is also a critique of moral values is that it works, somehow, as a debunking, and that the logical result of a debunking would be a moral free-for-all or an anti-moralism that picks out one tendency of morality, such as altruism or abstinence, and praises its opposite. We are, after all, familiar with debunking as an enterprise: the world is full of hoaxes and swindlers, and revealing them is a useful intellectual achievement that should steer us away from their intended influence. But Nietzsche's genealogy is not much concerned with debunking, and its partisanship is not for liberating ourselves from moral constraints through the spontaneous exercise of power, clear-eyed self-interest or anything like that.

For Nietzsche, debunking would be too much and not enough. It would be too much in that morality does not need to be debunked; it already has been. It is a means of social control, a by-product of evolutionary processes, a bourgeois ideology or a bit of metaphysical illusion. The idea of a single, determinate set of standards, binding on everyone, with a special sanction, plays little public role in how we regulate behaviour or justify it to one another. What is left of morality survives as a matter of personal conviction, more or less deeply felt, and insulated from public challenge. Debunking would be not enough in that it would concede something that Nietzsche takes pains to deny. Debunking only achieves something if morality's hold on us depends on our faith in its truth. But the stories of the *Genealogy* are not about discovering whether or not morality is grounded in the nature of reality; they are about how morality functions regardless of its metaphysical credentials. Nietzsche does not leave in place the idea that morality is to be judged by a metaphysical standard and then contest whether that standard is met. He aims, rather, to show that that kind of judgement does not matter and there could be a better way to make our practical judgements.

Genealogy, as I have been characterising it, functions primarily as a form of internal criticism. Instead of trying to compare a set of moral views to an independent order of things, Nietzsche starts with us and our standpoint. We are the 'knowing ones' for whom questions about how to live are compelling, who interpret ourselves in light of the psychological capacities that we ascribe to ourselves, and who want to be able to explain our concerns and have our ends somehow validated. We have some basic if indeterminate commitments and a view of ourselves that is filtered through these commitments. Genealogy attempts to show what these commitments mean and how our practices sustain them; the practical question it poses is what extending and refining these commitments might amount to. The narrative argument that Nietzsche makes, however, is that this has become impossible. Our self-image has become so confused and damaging that, without radically revising our outlook in some yet undetermined way, there is no way to advance an agenda that we can identify with. We need a new vocabulary and new practices to be able to preserve a sense of who we are.

Genealogy does not take issue with a particular set of moral imperatives, or even a particular conception of morality. Indeed, it cannot do that: it does not address specific historical agents, events or imperatives. Nietzsche intends his critique to cover a wide range of phenomena in order to consider all the ways in which morality informs and distorts our understanding of ourselves. Morality, then, is not treated as a single, stable thing, but rather as many interconnected, confused practices of valuing and ways of interpreting ourselves. And the critical aim of the narratives is to show that all of this has broken down in some irremediable, conclusive way. It cannot account for the distinctive authority of its claims, it needs to denigrate aspects of human existence in order to dignify them, it detaches persons from concern for their ultimate ends, and, in general, serves as a confounding way to organise ethical experience. The overarching story of the genealogies of morality, then, is about how psychologically demanding it is to lead a human life. Leading a life as a reflective, natural being is demanding; leading a life among others is demanding; and all of this has made it necessary to invent strange conceptualisations and to cultivate awkward inner drives in order to cope. Coping takes the form of evasions, and ways of understanding ourselves are, in Nietzsche's account, strategies for evasion. Understanding persons in such a way that everyone can qualify as an unconditional source of value, for example, contributes to avoiding a sense of human weakness and fallibility. Internalising guilt and holding oneself accountable to God, nature or truth have been strategies for avoiding accountability to others. If there is some way of being right that one is the proper arbiter of, no matter what anyone else thinks, then one can be invulnerable to the judgements of others. There is no need to persuade anyone, reach a shared viewpoint or acknowledge another's claims. In this way we can each imagine being fully in charge of our lives, by evading some of the ways we connect to others in making sense of our place in the world.

This imagination is defective, however, and its failure is why individualism is absent from the *Genealogy*. Nietzsche is sometimes taken to be advocating some form of individualism, although it is hard to see exactly where he does so. To be sure, he rejects the very idea of altruism, and also the idealisation of 'selflessness' in morality: that self-denial is inherently praiseworthy, for example, or that our lives ought to be fundamentally regulated by other-regarding duties. But it is precisely the fantasy of morality to think that we can achieve a kind of normative escape from the difficulties of social existence by conceiving of a dimension of our lives that is nothing but completely individual self-guidance. It does not matter whether this self-guidance is imagined as the untrammelled exercise of power or the observance of impersonal duties of benevolence. The problem that Nietzsche identifies is not with the specific content of imperatives – there is no discussion of such content in the *Genealogy* – but with a strategy that works to exempt individuals from the judgement of others. Both altruism and radical individualism are ways of understanding the practical demands of one's life as completely satisfiable by oneself, alone: either by domination or by independence, one tries to make an important part of oneself immune to others' regard. Nietzsche's suggestion here is not a new technique for making this work, but that all of it is pathological. The problem that worries Nietzsche is the limits of our capacity to imagine what it is to be ourselves, except by setting ourselves, in some way, completely apart from anyone.

In the stories of the *Genealogy*, human beings become what they are through their language, their practices, and indeed their whole history. There is no way to decontextualise ideals and understand them apart from the circumstances of their emergence, and no way to make sense of human beings apart from their ideals. Rather than suggesting that an individual can achieve personal authenticity through force of will, the stories aim to show that everything that makes human beings interesting is fundamentally social. Even the very possibility of raising existential questions – about who we are, what matters, how to be true to ourselves – comes about through accountability to others. If we can think of ourselves as potentially free, potentially 'sovereign' individuals, it is because we have created ways of taking responsibility for ourselves. And these ways of taking responsibility arise in a social world that we sustain and depend on for the bits of sense and opportunities for distinction that allow us to fashion identities.

The promise of ascetic ideals was that they offered a way to escape from social forms of authority, with all of their dependence on others, by submitting to some kind of impersonal authority that has its source outside the contingent conditions of human existence. We can understand what we ought to do in terms of self-submission to forms of authority more compelling than anything rooted in human practices, and we can understand who we are in terms of what we are willing to sacrifice. There is a correct way, in any case, to regulate ourselves. We might lack access to the ultimate truth, and some questions might need to be excluded from meaningful consideration. But superlative, ascetic authority points to univocal, decisive answers for the most important questions.

For Nietzsche, however, this is all misguided. Morality, and the ascetic ideal more generally, frame as susceptible to a theoretical solution questions that cannot be answered in that way; Nietzsche takes it as desperate and strange that an attempt would even be made. He asks what it would mean for a solution to be possible, and thus to be able, in principle at least, to fully and permanently meet the demands of leading a life. And he frames this question in psychological and social terms. The hope of morality then depends on there being an answer so perfect, so far outside the ordinary forms of human limitation, that it guarantees being right so fully that there is no other way of looking at things, that puts an end to doubt and regret, that compels agreement if only there are rational interlocutors, and that thus obviates the need for persuasion and negotiation. But there is no imaginable form of life like that, because there will always be new and different ways to reinterpret ourselves; we could always come to understand ourselves differently, and in that way become different kinds of persons. And the question of the best way to understand ourselves is not primarily a matter of adequacy to some independent order, but of figuring out how our self-understanding can fit with our emotional lives and practical commitments.

For this reason, Nietzsche's complaint against morality is that it fundamentally confuses this task of arriving at a satisfactory self-understanding.[1] Morality does other things, too: it induces a lot of self-inflicted suffering, for example. Its greatest harm, however, lies in framing the question of what we are as itself a moral question. Once considered as a moral question, all the particular ways that we have of making sense of ourselves – the very particular, very local desires and concerns and role and relationships – are diminished in favour of the one answer that the conceptual resources of morality inevitably lead to: we are beings who, regardless of anything else, ought to be as moral as possible. What this demands is obscure, so it amounts to cultivating the sense that we are accountable to

---

[1] This is the theme of some of Nietzsche's later writings. For example, in the *Anti-Christ*, Nietzsche refers to the 'moral world order' as 'the most deceitful of all modes of interpretation' (AC §25), and claims that 'it is indecent to be a Christian these days' in part because 'there are no words left for what used to be called "truth"' (AC §38).

something radically outside human experience that we can never get right, and that we should nevertheless, in some sense, be blamed and punished for.

This is how morality functions as a 'prejudice' (P: 2). It deforms our attempts to lead our lives by trying to align them with an impossible, incoherent source of normative authority. The idea of morality promotes an overemphasis on universal and formal claims; it conflates very different kinds of concerns by treating them as examples of the more general category of moral concern; it tends to treat practical demands as matters of private conscience; it limits the scope of reflection to what falls under the power of individual will; it focuses on obligations and duties rather than on the character of relationships and more substantive interests; and it sets such great store by avoiding partiality that it leaves little room to care about anything for oneself. As theoretical matters, each of these points can be addressed so as to refute, deny or minimise the grounds for complaint; if this does not produce a vindication, perhaps it can at least generate a muddle of moral demands.

Those modes of moral prejudice fare worse in practice, however. When they are realised in concrete practices, informing judgements and shaping the pathways for justification through their effects on public discourse, they produce an incoherence that works to efface genuine concerns and reinforce the exclusion of those already marginalised. For example, framing issues in terms of morality leads to anti-racism being called racism because, in calling attention to race, it violates formal neutrality; claims of freedom of speech and conscience are invoked to suppress critical speech; modesty in dress and killing civilians, as both falling under the mantle of morality, are treated as the same kind of general issue; avoiding ecological catastrophe is treated as a matter of personal virtue; poverty and incarceration are considered to be personal moral failings rather than systemic issues; racism is viewed as an inscrutable matter of the heart rather than something structural; education and childcare are instrumentalised whenever they do not appear distinctively moral; empathy is demanded for the powerful; and political views are aestheticised, as matters of taste that it would be disrespectful to others' autonomy to question. The workings of morality – as a set of evaluative practices and a language for managing practical demands – deform our activities and institutions so as to focus blame on the suffering and set others outside criticism.

One might wish that these were problems of implementation that would all disappear once everyone agrees on the correct theory of morality. For Nietzsche, however, the faith in a correct theory, unequivocally authoritative, that resolves all difficulties is itself part of the problem. The language and evaluative practices of morality that we have are not a yet-unsolved equation, but one particular approach to making sense of our lives, one that crowds out alternatives. This approach, in its historical emergence, has been suited to understanding life as a series of personal emergencies, the inevitability of which is rooted in our inherently corrupt nature. It may not serve us well when our most pressing problems have less to do with temptation to sin and more to do with patriarchal white supremacy, global fascism and destruction of the environment, or at the least with managing some way to find a meaningful and satisfying life in spite of all that. Whatever the pressing problems of the world may be, it is hard to imagine that they only call for everyone to be a little more moral. Nietzsche's view, in any case, is that we should not hope for moral progress but for something new that will take more courage and greater generosity than could be morally required of anyone.

Glossary of Key Terms

Ascetic ideals: ultimate standards that attribute value on an ascetic basis, i.e., because something involves the self-imposition of discipline or harms. Nietzsche claims that a wide range of familiar ideals, even ones that have no obvious moral component, are fundamentally ascetic: they demand self-sacrifice for its own sake. Nietzsche initially refers to ascetic ideals in the plural, and treats them as if they appear in many forms, but quickly switches to the singular 'ascetic ideal', as if the diverse forms are all variations on one overarching ideal.

Bad conscience: painful, internalised guilt that is produced through one's own hostile instincts being directed back against oneself. Nietzsche characterises 'conscience' in general as self-relating ability, i.e., the ability to take oneself as an object of reflection and modification. 'Bad conscience' is a painful form that conscience takes when it involves the consciousness of guilt provoked by self-directed cruelty. According to Nietzsche, the bad conscience is created when the constraints of urban living require the repression of violent instincts. Although painful, the bad conscience transforms the kinds of concerns that human beings take as important and thereby the nature of the human 'soul'.

Genealogy: the historical account of the emergence of the conditions of possibility of particular phenomena, such as moral concepts and psychological capacities. Nietzsche distinguishes his own approach to genealogy from the 'inverse and perverse kind' that he attributes to the 'English psychologists'. In his own approach, he aims to identify the background conditions and changes that made the emergence of new moral categories available; he intends these emergence stories to shed light on the meaning of these categories and the harms that are incurred by their ongoing use.

Internalisation: the process by which natural instincts are directed 'inward', i.e., back against their bearers. As part of this redirection, instincts that typically manifest themselves outwardly can take on a psychological form: aggression, for example, can come to manifest itself as pangs of conscience, self-contempt or anxiety. This process, which Nietzsche closely links to the 'bad conscience', changes the character of human personality to make private thoughts and feelings independently important and the discursive subject an object of attention and care.

Morality: a wide-ranging set of practices systematically organised around ideals. Morality can also refer, more simply, to a set of beliefs about ideals and the patterns of judgements made on their basis. Nietzsche often uses 'morality' to refer to a special set of ideals, distinguished by the centrality of the good/evil dichotomy, the praise of selflessness and compassion, and the importance of guilt and punishment. But morality also includes 'master morality', for example, and part of the aim of genealogy is to show how various forms of morality are connected by a common history.

Nihilism: the absence of a needed sense of what values or commitments are ultimately important. Nietzsche sometimes writes as if there are many varieties of nihilism (e.g., 'suicidal nihilism', atheistic nihilism), but does not catalogue them here; he suggests that he will discuss nihilism more thoroughly in a future work. (He did not write this work, but there are many notes on nihilism in his unpublished notebooks.) In one important form of nihilism, the loss of a sense of substantive importance is the result of ascetic self-deprivation, and renders our agency precariously dependent on a 'will to nothingness'.

Pathos of distance: a transient feeling of one's distance from others. This 'distance' is a metaphorical one, of superiority or relative importance. In the First Treatise Nietzsche appeals to this 'pathos', this feeling, to make the point that morality, in its most primitive form, was not based on complex articulations of value. In the Third Treatise he suggests that this pathos needs to be preserved in the modern world so that 'higher' individuals can have confidence in their tasks.

Ressentiment: a reactive sentiment, characterised by strong feelings of hostility, injury and impotence, experienced by those who suffer at the hands of others. Nietzsche uses the French word for 'resentment' primarily to explain in the First Treatise the source of the 'imaginary revenge' that produced the 'slave revolt in morality', and in the Third Treatise the priestly invention of the ascetic ideal.

Revaluation of values: a radical reconceptualisation of values, effected through a new language of value. The prefix in the German word for 'revaluation', *Um-*, does not simply mean 'again' as does the English 're-'; it can indicate, rather, alteration, especially thorough change or inversion. The main example of a revaluation of values in the *Genealogy* is the slave revolt in morality, but Nietzsche also uses the term to describe the future process by which morality will be replaced.

Slave revolt in morality: the creation of ideals centred around the good/evil dichotomy, as a vengeful response to harm inflicted by nobles. Slaves were not able to take actions to retaliate against the nobles, so as a result they invented values that inverted the nobles' self-attribution of goodness. These new, reactive values supplanted the nobles' values and, according to Nietzsche, have come to dominate evaluative thinking.

Will to power: the fundamental, telic structure of motivation that directs activity towards establishing mastery through interpretation. It is actually unclear in the *Genealogy* what the will to power is, but Nietzsche gives indications of its importance: he identifies it with the 'instinct of freedom' and the 'essence of life', and it is central to the projected but never written work that he announces. Nietzsche's claim seems to be that particular motives express a deeper interest in determining what things mean and what purposes they serve, and that accomplishing this determines what things are and in what hierarchical relations they stand.

Guide to Further Reading on *On the Genealogy of Morality*

There are several excellent commentaries on *On the Genealogy of Morality*. Lawrence Hatab's *Nietzsche's On the Genealogy of Morality: An Introduction* does more than my commentary to situate the text within a broader project in moral and political philosophy. David Owen's *Nietzsche's Genealogy of Morality* does likewise, and also attends to the development of Nietzsche's thought and competing interpretations of the *Genealogy*. Daniel Conway's *Nietzsche's 'On the Genealogy of Morals': A Reader's Guide* articulates a reading that emphasises how Nietzsche's commitments to naturalism and historicism inform his project of persuading a select audience to participate in a campaign against Christian morality.

There are also several excellent near-commentaries: that is, they offer close readings of, and deeply illuminate, parts of the text, but they do not aim to be comprehensive or they advance other agendas. Christopher Janaway's *Beyond Selflessness* uses careful historically informed exegesis to reflect on Nietzsche's broader philosophical programme; it could easily fit in the above category. Brian Leiter's *Nietzsche on Morality* offers a naturalist reading of Nietzsche that focuses primarily on the *Genealogy*. Aaron Ridley's *Nietzsche's Conscience* interprets Nietzsche's ethics in light of the character types portrayed in the *Genealogy*. Randall Havas's *Nietzsche's Genealogy* does not focus on *On the Genealogy of Morality*, but offers a reading of genealogical method in which it reveals, through problems of language and interpretation, the individual's relationship to the community.

There are three important anthologies that collect essays about *On the Genealogy of Morality*. I cited some of the essays in Christa Acampora (ed.), *Nietzsche's On the Genealogy of Morals: Critical*

Essays, despite my attempts not to appeal too much to the secondary literature. Equally worth reading are the essays in Simon May (ed.), *Nietzsche's On the Genealogy of Morality: A Critical Guide*. A slightly older collection contains a wide range of interpretations, and is still very valuable: Richard Schacht (ed.), *Nietzsche, Genealogy, Morality*.

Below are some suggestions for important articles and books, organised by topic. I have included several works that do not specifically treat the *Genealogy*, but bear on some important ideas that it contains. For those who wish to pursue further the line of interpretation presented in this commentary, some of my own writings on the *Genealogy* are listed in the bibliography.

Genealogy

Raymond Geuss, 'Nietzsche and Genealogy'.
Michel Foucault, 'Nietzsche, Genealogy, History'.
Allison Merrick, 'Of Genealogy and Transcendent Critique'.

Meaning and culture

Ken Gemes and Chris Sykes, 'The Culture of Myth and the Myth of Culture'.
Andrew Huddleston, *Nietzsche on the Decadence and Flourishing of Culture*.

Morality and politics

Keith Ansell-Pearson, *An Introduction to Nietzsche as a Political Thinker*.
Simon May, *Nietzsche's Ethics and his War on 'Morality'*.
Mark Warren, *Nietzsche and Political Thought*.

Nihilism

Kaitlyn Creasy, *The Problem of Affective Nihilism in Nietzsche*.
Bernard Reginster, *The Affirmation of Life: Nietzsche on Overcoming Nihilism*.
Alan White, *Within Nietzsche's Labyrinth*.

Psychology

Scott Jenkins, 'Ressentiment, Imaginary Revenge, and the Slave Revolt'.
Paul Katsafanas, 'Nietzsche's Philosophical Psychology'.
Robert Pippin, *Nietzsche, Psychology, and First Philosophy*.
Peter Poellner, 'Affect, Value, and Objectivity'.
Peter Sedgwick, 'The Great Economy'.

Revaluation of values

Mark Migotti, 'Not Your Grandfather's Genealogy: How to Read *GM* III'.
John Richardson, 'Nietzsche on Life's Ends'.
Aaron Ridley, 'Nietzsche and the Re-evaluation of Values'.

Bibliography

Acampora, Christa. 2006. 'On Sovereignty and Overhumanity: Why it Matters How We Read Nietzsche's Genealogy II:2', in *Nietzsche's On the Genealogy of Morals: Critical Essays*, ed. C. Acampora. Lanham, MD: Rowman and Littlefield, 147–61.

Acampora, Christa (ed.). 2006. *Nietzsche's On the Genealogy of Morals: Critical Essays*. Lanham, MD: Rowman and Littlefield.

Adkins, Arthur W. H. 1975. *Merit and Responsibility: A Study in Greek Values*. Chicago: University of Chicago Press.

Anderson, Lanier. 2011. 'On the Nobility of Nietzsche's Priests', in *Nietzsche's On the Genealogy of Morality: A Critical Guide*, ed. Simon May. Cambridge: Cambridge University Press, 24–55.

Anscombe, G. E. M. 1981. 'On Brute Facts', in *Ethics, Religion, and Politics, Collected Papers, Volume III*. Minneapolis: University of Minnesota Press, 22–5.

Ansell-Pearson, Keith. 1991. *Nietzsche contra Rousseau: Nietzsche's Moral and Political Thought*. Cambridge: Cambridge University Press.

— 1994. *An Introduction to Nietzsche as a Political Thinker*. Cambridge: Cambridge University Press.

— 2009. 'Free Spirits and Free Thinkers: Nietzsche and Guyau on the Future of Morality', in *Nietzsche, Nihilism, and the Philosophy of the Future*, ed. Jeffrey Metzger. New York: Continuum, 102–24.

Aristotle. 1987. *Poetics*, trans. Richard Janko. Indianapolis: Hackett.

Blanding, Thomas. 1971. 'Paradise Misplaced: Bronson Alcott's Fruitlands', *The Concord Saunterer*, 6.4: 2–7.

Borges, Jorge Luis. 1993. 'The Analytical Language of John Wilkins', in *Other Inquisitions 1937–1952*, trans. Ruth L. C. Simms. Austin: University of Texas Press, 101–5.
Bourdieu, Pierre. 1972. *Outline of a Theory of Practice*, trans. Richard Nice. Cambridge: Cambridge University Press.
Butler, Judith. 1990. *Gender Trouble: Feminism and the Subversion of Identity*. London: Routledge.
Chapman, Graham, and John Cleese. 2002. *Monty Python and the Holy Grail Screenplay*. London: Methuen.
Clark, Maudemarie, and David Dudrick. 2012. *The Soul of Nietzsche's Beyond Good and Evil*. Cambridge: Cambridge University Press.
Conway, Daniel. 1997. *Nietzsche and the Political*. London: Routledge.
— 2006. 'How We Became What We Are: Tracking the "Beasts of Prey"', in *Nietzsche's On the Genealogy of Morals: Critical Essays*, ed. C. Acampora. Lanham, MD: Rowman and Littlefield, 305–20.
— 2008. *Nietzsche's 'On the Genealogy of Morals': A Reader's Guide*. New York: Continuum.
Cox, Christophe. 1999. *Nietzsche, Naturalism, and Interpretation*. Berkeley: University of California Press.
Creasy, Kaitlyn. 2020. *The Problem of Affective Nihilism in Nietzsche: Thinking Differently, Feeling Differently*. London: Palgrave Macmillan.
Danto, Arthur C. 1985. *Narration and Knowledge*. New York: Columbia University Press.
— 1988. 'Some Remarks on the *Genealogy of Morals*', in *Reading Nietzsche*, ed. Robert C. Solomon and Kathleen M. Higgins. Oxford: Oxford University Press, 13–28.
Deleuze, Gilles. 1983. *Nietzsche and Philosophy*, trans. Hugh Tomlinson. New York: Columbia University Press.
Derrida, Jacques. 1982. *Margins of Philosophy*, trans. Alan Bass. Chicago: University of Chicago Press.
Dreyfus, Hubert. 1980. 'Holism and Hermeneutics', *Review of Metaphysics*, 34.1: 3–24.
Durkheim, Emile. 1995. *The Elementary Forms of Religious Life*, trans. Karen E. Fields. New York: The Free Press.

Emden, Christian. 2014. *Nietzsche's Naturalism: Philosophy and the Life Sciences in the Nineteenth Century*. Cambridge: Cambridge University Press.

Foucault, Michel. 1973. *The Order of Things: An Archaeology of the Human Sciences*. New York: Vintage.

— 1977. 'Nietzsche, Genealogy, History', in *Language, Counter-Memory, Practice*, ed. D. Bouchard. Ithaca: Cornell University Press, 139–65.

— 1978. *The History of Sexuality, Volume I: An Introduction*, trans. Robert Hurley. New York: Vintage.

Franco, Paul. 2011. *Nietzsche's Enlightenment*. Chicago: University of Chicago Press.

Freud, Sigmund. 1961. *Civilization and its Discontents*, trans. James Strachey. New York: W. W. Norton.

Fricker, Miranda. 2007. *Epistemic Injustice: Power and Ethics in Knowing*. Oxford: Oxford University Press.

Gardner, Sebastian. 2009. 'Nietzsche, the Self, and the Disunity of Philosophical Reason', in *Nietzsche on Freedom and Autonomy*, ed. K. Gemes and S. May. Oxford: Oxford University Press, 1–32.

Gemes, Ken, and Chris Sykes. 2015. 'The Culture of Myth and the Myth of Culture', in *Individual and Community in Nietzsche's Philosophy*, ed. J. Young. Cambridge: Cambridge University Press, 51–76.

Geuss, Raymond. 1999. 'Nietzsche and Genealogy', in *Morality, Culture and History*. Cambridge: Cambridge University Press, 1–28.

— 2008. *Philosophy and Real Politics*. Princeton: Princeton University Press.

Graeber, David. 2014. *Debt: The First 5000 Years*. New York: Melville House.

Griswold, Charles. 2013. 'The Nature and Ethics of Vengeful Anger', in *Passions and Emotions*, ed. James E. Fleming. New York: New York University Press, 77–124.

Guay, Robert. 2005. 'The Philosophical Function of Genealogy', in *A Companion to Nietzsche*, ed. K. Ansell-Pearson. Oxford: Blackwell, 353–71.

— 2011a. 'Genealogy as Immanent Critique: Working from the Inside', in *The Edinburgh Critical History of Nineteenth Century*

Philosophy, ed. A. Stone. Edinburgh: Edinburgh University Press, 168–86.
— 2011b. 'Genealogy and Irony', *Journal of Nietzsche Studies*, 41: 26–49.
— 2018. 'Genealogy and Social Practices', in *Routledge Philosophy Minds: Nietzsche*, ed. P. Katsafanas. London: Routledge, 347–62.
Gutting, Gary. 2005. *Foucault: A Very Short Introduction*. Oxford: Oxford University Press.
Haidt, Jonathan, and Craig Joseph. 2004. 'Intuitive Ethics: How Innately Prepared Intuition Generates Culturally Variable Virtues', *Daedalus*, 133.4: 55–66.
Hatab, Lawrence. 1995. *A Nietzschean Defense of Democracy*. Chicago: Open Court.
— 2008. *Nietzsche's On the Genealogy of Morality: An Introduction*. Cambridge: Cambridge University Press.
Havas, Randall. 1995. *Nietzsche's Genealogy: Nihilism and the Will to Knowledge*. Ithaca: Cornell University Press.
Hegel, G. W. F. 2018. *Phenomenology of Spirit*, trans. Terry Pinkard. Cambridge: Cambridge University Press.
Homer. 1951. *The Iliad*, trans. R. Lattimore. Chicago: University of Chicago Press.
Huddleston, Andrew. 2019. *Nietzsche on the Decadence and Flourishing of Culture*. Oxford: Oxford University Press.
Janaway, Christopher. 2007. *Beyond Selflessness: Reading Nietzsche's Genealogy*. Oxford: Oxford University Press.
Jenkins, Scott. 2018. 'Ressentiment, Imaginary Revenge, and the Slave Revolt', *Philosophy and Phenomenological Research*, 96.1: 192–213.
Jensen, Anthony. 2013. *Nietzsche's Philosophy of History*. Cambridge: Cambridge University Press.
Kaiser, Jochen-Christoph. 1985. 'Organisierte Religionskritik im 19. und 20. Jahrhundert', *Zeitschrift für Religions- und Geistesgeschichte*, 37.3: 203–15.
Kant, Immanuel. 1997. *Groundwork of the Metaphysics of Morals*, trans. Mary Gregor. Cambridge: Cambridge University Press.
— 1998. *Critique of Pure Reason*, trans. P. Guyer and A. Wood. Cambridge: Cambridge University Press.

Katsafanas, Paul. 2013. 'Nietzsche's Philosophical Psychology', in *The Oxford Handbook to Nietzsche*, ed. Ken Gemes and John Richardson. Oxford: Oxford University Press, 727–55.

Kaufmann, Walter. 1974. *Nietzsche: Philosophy, Psychologist, Antichrist*. Princeton: Princeton University Press.

Leiter, Brian. 2002. *Nietzsche on Morality*. London: Routledge.

Loeb, Paul S. 2018. 'The Priestly Slave Revolt in Morality', *Nietzsche-Studien*, 47.1: 100–39.

Lovibond, Sabina. 2002. *Ethical Formation*. Cambridge, MA: Harvard University Press.

Machiavelli, Niccolò. 1984. *The Prince*, trans. Peter Bondanella. Oxford: Oxford University Press.

May, Simon. 1999. *Nietzsche's Ethics and his War on 'Morality'*. Oxford: Oxford University Press.

May, Simon (ed.). 2011. *Nietzsche's On the Genealogy of Morality: A Critical Guide*. Cambridge: Cambridge University Press.

Merrick, Allison. 1996. 'Of Genealogy and Transcendent Critique', *Journal of Nietzsche Studies*, 47.2: 228–37.

Migotti, Mark. 2015. 'Not Your Grandfather's Genealogy: How to Read *GM* III', *Journal of Value Inquiry*, 49: 329–51.

Miller, William Ian. 1993. 'Requiting the Unwanted Gift', in William Ian Miller, *Humiliation*. Ithaca: Cornell University Press, 15–52.

Mills, Charles W. 1997. *The Racial Contract*, Ithaca: Cornell University Press.

Mink, Louis O. 1987. 'Narrative Form as a Cognitive Instrument', in *Historical Understanding*. Ithaca: Cornell University Press, 182–203.

Mullin, Amy. 2000. 'Nietzsche's Free Spirit', *Journal of the History of Philosophy*, 38.3: 383–405.

Neuhouser, Frederick. 2014. 'Nietzsche on Spiritual Illness and its Promise', *Journal of Nietzsche Studies*, 45.3: 293–314.

Nietzsche, Friedrich. 1967. *The Birth of Tragedy and The Case of Wagner*, trans. W. Kaufmann. New York: Vintage.

— 1978. *Thus Spoke Zarathustra*, trans. W. Kaufmann. Harmondsworth: Penguin.

— 1983. *Untimely Meditations*, trans. R. J. Hollingdale. Cambridge: Cambridge University Press.

— 1986. *Human, All Too Human*, trans. R. J. Hollingdale. Cambridge: Cambridge University Press.
— 1988. *Kritische Studienausgabe*, volume 12, ed. Giorgio Colli and Mazzino Montinari. Berlin: de Gruyter.
— 1989. *On the Genealogy of Morals and Ecce Homo*, trans. W. Kaufmann and R. J. Hollingdale. New York: Vintage.
— 1997. *Daybreak*, trans. R. J. Hollingdale. Cambridge: Cambridge University Press.
— 1998. *On the Genealogy of Morality*, trans. M. Clark and A. Swensen. Indianapolis: Hackett Publishing.
— 2001. *The Gay Science*, trans. J. Nauckhoff. Cambridge: Cambridge University Press.
— 2005. *The Anti-Christ, Ecce Homo, Twilight of the Idols and Other Writings*, trans. J. Norman. Cambridge: Cambridge University Press.
— 2014. *Beyond Good and Evil/On the Genealogy of Morality*, trans. A. Del Caro. Stanford: Stanford University Press.
Owen, David. 2002. 'Equality, Democracy, and Self-Respect: Reflections on Nietzsche's Agonal Perfectionism', *Journal of Nietzsche Studies*, 24: 113–31.
— 2007. *Nietzsche's Genealogy of Morality*. Stocksfield: Acumen.
Patton, Paul. 2004. 'Power and Right in Foucault and Nietzsche', *International Studies in Philosophy*, 36.3: 43–61.
Pippin, Robert. 1991. *Modernism as a Philosophical Problem*. Oxford: Basil Blackwell.
— 2006. 'Lightning and Flash, Agent and Deed (*GM* I:6–17)', in *Nietzsche's On the Genealogy of Morals: Critical Essays*, ed. C. Acampora. Lanham, MD: Rowman and Littlefield, 131–45.
— 2010. *Nietzsche, Psychology, and First Philosophy*. Chicago: University of Chicago Press.
Plato. 1975. *Phaedo*, trans. David Gallop. Oxford: Oxford University Press.
Poellner, Peter. 2007. 'Affect, Value, and Objectivity', in *Nietzsche on Morality*, ed. B. Leiter and N. Sinhababu. Oxford: Oxford University Press, 227–61.
Prange, Martine. 2013. *Nietzsche, Wagner, Europe*. Berlin: de Gruyter.

Reginster, Bernard. 2009. *The Affirmation of Life: Nietzsche on Overcoming Nihilism*. Cambridge, MA: Harvard University Press.

Richardson, John. 2013. 'Nietzsche on Life's Ends', in *The Oxford Handbook of Nietzsche*, ed. K. Gemes and J. Richardson. Oxford: Oxford University Press, 756–83.

Ridley, Aaron. 1998. *Nietzsche's Conscience: Six Character Studies from the 'Genealogy'*. Ithaca: Cornell University Press.

— 2005. 'Nietzsche and the Re-evaluation of Values', *Proceedings of the Aristotelian Society*, 105: 171–91.

— 2018. *The Deed is Everything: Nietzsche on Will and Action*. Oxford: Oxford University Press.

Schaberg, William H. 1995. *The Nietzsche Canon*. Chicago: University of Chicago Press.

Schacht, Richard. 2012. 'Nietzsche's Naturalism and Normativity', in *Nietzsche, Naturalism, and Normativity*, ed. C. Janaway and S. Robertson. Oxford: Oxford University Press, 236–55.

Schacht, Richard (ed.). 1994. *Nietzsche, Genealogy, Morality*. Berkeley: University of California Press.

Searle, John. 1995. *The Construction of Social Reality*. New York: The Free Press.

Sedgwick, Peter. 2007. 'The Great Economy', in *Nietzsche's Economy: Modernity, Normativity, and Futurity*. London: Palgrave Macmillan, 67–112.

Snelson, Avery. 2017. 'The History, Origin, and Meaning of Nietzsche's Slave Revolt in Morality', *Inquiry*, 60: 1–30.

Stern, David. 2003. 'The Practical Turn', in *The Blackwell Guide to the Philosophy of the Social Sciences*, ed. S. Turner and P. Roth. Oxford: Blackwell, 185–206.

Stern, Tom. 2015. 'Against Nietzsche's "Theory" of the Drives', *Journal of the American Philosophical Association*, 1.1: 121–40.

Taylor, Charles. 1985. 'Self-interpreting Animals', in *Human Agency and Language*. Cambridge: Cambridge University Press, 45–76.

Thatcher, David S. 1989. 'Zur Genealogie der Moral: Some Textual Annotations', *Nietzsche-Studien*, 18.1, 587–99.

Warren, Mark. 1988. *Nietzsche and Political Thought*. Cambridge, MA: MIT Press.

White, Alan. 1990. *Within Nietzsche's Labyrinth*. London: Routledge.
Williams, Bernard. 1985. *Ethics and the Limits of Philosophy*. Cambridge, MA: Harvard University Press.
— 1995. 'Nietzsche's Minimalist Moral Psychology', in *Making Sense of Humanity and Other Philosophical Papers*. Cambridge: Cambridge University Press, 65–76.
— 2004. *Truth and Truthfulness*. Princeton: Princeton University Press.
Wittgenstein, Ludwig. 1972. *On Certainty*, trans. Denis Paul and G. E. M. Anscombe. New York: Harper.
Zamosc, Gabriel. 2011. 'The Relation between Sovereignty and Guilt in Nietzsche's *Genealogy*', *European Journal of Philosophy*, 20.S1: e107–e142.

Index

Acampora, Christa, 84n, 209
Achilles, 40, 42
activity, 15, 23, 66, 69–70, 72,
    76, 87–91, 115–20, 130,
    139, 144, 165, 167
Adkins, Arthur, 40n
affirmation and yes-saying,
    9, 35, 40, 51, 85, 96, 107,
    154, 170, 175, 177
agency, 65–70, 90, 96, 137,
    139, 145, 178
Alcott, Bronson, 66
Anderson, Lanier, 41n
anesthetization, 163, 171–2
Anscombe, Elizabeth, 97n
Ansell-Pearson, Keith, 2n,
    14n, 78n
anti-nature, 50, 132, 159
Aquinas, 47
Aristotle, 194
art, 13, 115, 141, 145, 191,
    194–8
artists, 106, 131, 138, 146–9,
    158, 164, 195
ascetic ideal, 137–78, 180, 182,
    184–6, 189–203
    comedians of the, 191,
    195–7

asceticism, 95–6, 107, 114,
    138–43, 147–8, 152–4, 174
authority, 34, 38–9, 42, 62,
    75, 78–9, 92, 93–4, 106,
    123, 145, 157, 171,
    173–5, 182–6, 195,
    197, 202, 204–5

'bad', 29, 35, 38–41
blame and accountability, 3, 4,
    10, 47, 67–9, 71, 83, 91–3,
    96, 113, 119, 138, 162–6,
    174, 177, 183–6, 189,
    201–5
blond beast, 51–2, 106
Borges, Jorge Luis, 66
Bourdieu, Pierre, 116n
Butler, Judith, 69–70

causation, 6–7, 31, 73–5, 80,
    88, 116
Christianity, 44, 78–81,
    110–2, 174, 177n, 183,
    195, 203, 209
Clark, Maudemarie and Alan
    Swensen, 45
Clark, Maudemarie and David
    Dudrick, 23n, 97n

compassion, 20, 147, 162
conscience, 37, 65–6, 91–3,
    94–5, 98–9, 131, 162,
    171–2, 175, 194, 197
    bad conscience, 83–5, 94,
        96, 99, 103–13, 131–2,
        166
Conway, Daniel, 52n, 195n, 209
Cox, Christophe, 23n
Creasy, Kaitlyn, 210
cruelty, 95, 99–101, 104, 112,
    131, 138, 141–2, 174

Danto, Arthur, 15n, 100n
debt, 84, 97–103, 109–12
Deleuze, Gilles, 48n
depth, 9, 13, 17, 21, 41, 43, 52,
    58, 69, 85, 93–4, 102, 105,
    113, 115, 143, 193
Derrida, Jacques, 86n
Dreyfus, Hubert, 18
drives and instincts, 3, 31,
    50, 65, 83–4, 91, 100,
    104–7, 111, 114, 127–8,
    152, 156, 164, 167,
    187, 201
Durkheim, Emile, 110n

egoism, 20, 35–7
Emden, Christian, 23n
emotions and affects, 47, 65,
    163, 166, 179–80, 187
English psychologists, 30–4,
    35–7, 65, 75
enmity, 35, 44, 48–50, 60–1,
    102–4, 152, 195–6
'evil', 17, 20, 23, 29, 35, 43,
    45–6, 48, 50–1, 67, 73

falsification, 49
Foucault, Michel, 43n, 118n
Franco, Paul, 78n
freedom, 68, 85, 91–3, 106–7,
    202
freethinkers, 43, 78, 172–3
Freud, Sigmund, 95n
Fricker, Miranda, 39n

Gardner, Sebastian, 75n
genealogy, 7, 15, 17–19, 22–4,
    56–8, 59–65, 190–4,
    199–202
Geuss, Raymond, 122n, 210
God, 16, 171, 174, 201
'good', 17, 29, 35, 37–42, 50–1
Graeber, David, 97n
great health, 132–3
Griswold, Charles, 76n
guilt, 83–4, 96–113, 119, 138,
    163–8, 178, 201
    moralised guilt, 109–12
Gutting, Gary, 43n

Haidt, Jonathan and Craig
    Joseph, 127n
Hatab, Lawrence, 28n, 84n
Havas, Randall, 84n, 151n,
    173–4, 209
Hegel, G. W. F., 165n
history, 1–2, 44, 55–6, 59, 61,
    73–5, 146, 174
    historical beings, 4, 15, 88,
        90, 114
    historical sense, 35–7
    historical understanding, 33,
        115–21, 175–6
historicism, 123–8

holism, 18
Huddleston, Andrew, 177n, 210
humanity, 25–7, 43, 53, 59, 63–4, 85, 89, 98, 107, 111, 131, 144, 161, 167, 177–8, 187, 202
  the human animal, 72, 100, 114
  the human type, 26–7
Hume, David, 30n

ideals, 3, 10, 15, 23, 40, 45, 46, 49–50, 67, 71, 107–8, 112, 122, 128, 129–36, 139, 140–1, 151, 159–61, 172, 177, 180–2, 186–7, 195–7; *see also* ascetic ideal
idealists, 33, 120–3, 172–3, 196
identity, 62, 69–71, 91, 93, 98, 144, 155, 168, 202
interestingness, 31, 43, 59, 167, 202
internalisation, 4, 42, 44, 71, 81, 83, 103–5, 112–3, 119, 127, 131, 143, 201
  inner psychology, 32, 53, 83, 94–6, 105–8, 113–5, 174, 179–80
  inner states, 42, 68, 103, 153
interpretation, 10, 45, 65, 69, 100, 107, 111–2, 117–18, 126, 150, 164–7, 170–1, 176–8, 179, 186–7, 189–90, 192–4, 197–8, 200, 203
irony, 11–12, 30, 51, 77–8, 128, 133, 194

Janaway, Christopher, 30n, 179n, 209
Jenkins, Scott, 211
Jensen, Anthony, 30n
Jesus, 12, 60
Jews, 44, 78, 81

Kant, Immanuel, 34n, 150–1, 157
Katsafanas, Paul, 156n, 211
Kaufmann, Walter, 52n

language, 3, 7, 24, 37–42, 56–7, 67, 73, 115, 130, 134–5, 184, 188–9, 200, 202, 205
Leiter, Brian, 23n
life, 14, 21, 23, 25–6, 51, 132, 138, 149, 155, 157, 164, 166–7, 178–9, 201
  ascetic valuation of life, 155, 159–61, 179, 193
  interest of life, 160, 179
Loeb, Paul, 41n
love, 46, 53, 60, 67, 81, 111, 135–6, 145, 147, 171
Lovibond, Sabina, 84n

Machiavelli, Niccolò, 145n
May, Simon, 194n, 210
meaning, 2–4, 7, 10, 18, 21, 37, 51, 59, 65, 72–6, 100, 106, 107, 113, 117–20, 124–7, 139–44, 146, 148–9, 156–8, 166–7, 169–70, 173, 176–7, 183, 191–3
memory, 14, 86–8, 94–5, 113–4

Merrick, Allison, 210
Migotti, Mark, 211
Miller, William Ian, 97n
Mills, Charles, 120n
Mink, Louis O., 56
Monty Python, 127n
morality, 3, 9–10, 20, 55–6,
  62, 75, 133, 136, 139,
  167–9, 175, 177–8,
  187–90, 203–4
 critique of morality, 2–3, 9,
  63, 192, 199–205
 harms of morality, 3–4,
  26–27, 63–5, 130–1, 203
 the moral-conceptual world,
  7, 22, 74, 99–101
 noble morality, 44, 57, 59–63,
  79–80
 slave morality, 44, 57–8, 59–63
 value of morality, 17, 24
Mullin, Amy, 78n

narrative, 54–6, 79–80, 198,
  200
nature, 32, 85, 89, 92–3, 132
 human nature, 31, 34, 98,
  105, 107, 112
naturalism, 23–4, 72–6, 88–90
Neuhouser, Frederick, 58n
Nietzsche, Friedrich
 The Antichrist, 203n
 The Birth of Tragedy, 21
 Beyond Good and Evil, 1n,
  17n, 21, 53, 81n, 107n,
  127, 145n, 150n, 182n,
  188n
 Daybreak, 21, 47n
 Ecce Homo, 30, 78n, 133n, 135

The Gay Science, 21, 32n, 73,
  133, 145n, 176, 197
 Human, All-too-human, 21, 78n
 Thus Spoke Zarathustra, 140,
  145, 146n, 191
 Untimely Meditations, 87
nihilism, 53, 58, 131, 138, 162,
  172, 175–6
nobles, 35, 38–40, 45, 59,
  61, 79
nothingness, 144–5, 148, 178,
  193–4; *see also* nihilism

Owen, David, 2n, 84n, 209

pathos of distance, 38, 162
Patton, Paul, 23n
perspectivism, 178–82
philosophers, 17–18, 150–8
Pippin, Robert, 14n, 66n, 211
Plato, 153
Poellner, Peter, 211
political realism, 121–3
power, 39, 91, 117–8, 123,
  139, 152, 156, 161,
  165–6, 170
practices, 3–4, 8, 18, 21, 56,
  71–3, 94–6, 97–9, 113–22,
  124, 126, 131, 163, 189,
  191, 193, 200, 202
Prange, Martine, 147n
prejudices, 19–24, 204–5
priests, 41–4 138, 158–68, 179
promising, 85–8, 90–2, 98–9
psychology, 3, 5, 33, 72, 76,
  160–8, 188–9
punishment, 96, 102–3, 112,
  115–21, 124–7, 189, 204

purposes and goals, 3–4, 56,
62, 85–6, 89, 116–7, 120,
124, 128, 138, 139–40,
142–6, 159–60, 165, 167,
169, 170, 176, 193

reaction, 46, 48–9
reasons, 8–9, 50, 60, 106, 123,
166–7
Rée, Paul, 17, 24
Reginster, Bernard, 210
responsibility, 91–3, 101, 119,
174, 202
ressentiment, 35, 44–5, 52–3,
138, 163–4, 179
revenge, 35, 44–6, 50, 76,
102–3, 138
imaginary revenge, 35, 44–8,
50, 68
revaluation of values, 64–5
Richardson, John, 211
Ridley, Aaron, 66n, 84n, 209,
211

Schacht, Richard, 23n
Schopenhauer, Arthur, 17, 138,
150–3, 161
science, 13, 30, 138, 140, 141,
171–5, 194, 196
Searle, John, 89n
Sedgwick, Peter, 211
self-knowledge and self-
understanding, 3–4, 10,
11–15, 28, 49, 58, 65, 101,
119, 137, 139, 141, 155,
161, 164, 167, 186–90,
201, 203

self-transformation, 3–4, 71,
83, 88–90, 96, 134, 144,
157, 167
seriousness, 14, 27, 95, 98, 114,
146, 158–9
sickness, 26, 59, 104, 108, 138,
162, 166
silences, 43, 77, 82, 128, 136
slave revolt in morality, 35,
44–5, 53, 56–7
Snelson, Avery, 41n
social relations, 39, 41–2, 50,
57, 60–2, 71, 83, 91, 93,
94, 99, 104, 106, 114–15,
124, 162, 201–2
soul, 27–8, 38–9, 43, 104–5,
157, 166–8, 190
sovereign individual, 84–5,
89–93, 202
Spencer, Herbert, 36
spirituality and spiritualisation,
12, 44, 46, 52, 99–100,
119, 127, 134, 154, 157,
173, 195
Stern, David, 18
Stern, Tom, 156n
suffering, 20, 45, 53, 94, 98,
100–1, 108, 138–9, 159,
163–8, 176, 189

tartuffery, 25, 187–9
Taylor, Charles, 90n
Thatcher, David, 30n
time, 14, 81, 86–7, 131, 168
tragedy, 28, 149, 194
truth, 13, 32, 140, 173–5, 182,
184–5

faith in truth, 172–3
the value of truth, 173, 182–6
the will to truth, 137, 173, 176–7, 182–3, 185

values, 35, 59–60, 140, 142, 157, 159
assessment of values, 56–65
value judgments, 22–3, 37, 38, 45, 75
value of values, 22, 24–7, 63
voices, 28, 43, 51, 77–8, 128, 130

Wagner, Richard, 138, 147–50
Warren, Mark, 210
White, Alan, 210
will, 13, 67, 92–3, 138, 144, 169, 170, 178, 183
will to power, 107, 126, 162, 165
Williams, Bernard, 47n, 66n, 120n, 183n
Wittgenstein, Ludwig, 155
women, 142–3
  wisdom as a woman, 145

Zamosc, Gabriel, 58n

EU representative:
Easy Access System Europe
Mustamäe tee 50, 10621 Tallinn, Estonia
Gpsr.requests@easproject.com

www.ingramcontent.com/pod-product-compliance
Lightning Source LLC
Chambersburg PA
CBHW070347240426
43671CB00013BA/2431